Stephen Anderton's
Garden Answers

Stephen Anderton's

Garden Answers

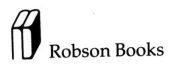 Robson Books

First published in Great Britain in 1997 by Robson
Books Ltd, Bolsover House, 5–6 Clipstone Street,
London W1P 8LE

British Library Cataloguing in Publication Data
A catalogue record for this title is available from the
British Library

ISBN 1 86105 117 4

Illustrations by Simon Dorrell

Typeset in North Wales by Derek Doyle & Associates,
Mold, Flintshire.
Printed in Great Britain by Creative Print & Design Ltd.,
Ebbw Vale

Contents

Stephen Anderton's

Garden Answers

1

Herbaceous Plants

Q Last autumn we moved to an old house with a garden full of plants we do not know. We were told by the previous owners that there are many lilies in the back garden, and the leaves are clearly visible now, in winter. We would like to simplify the garden and remove the lilies. When and how should it be done? – L.R., Lincolnshire

A Most lilies disappear below ground in autumn, just as the madonna lily (*Lilium candidum*), is coming up. If your leaves really are lilies, then they will be the madonna lily, which produces a rosette of leaves that stay through the winter before pushing up into a flowering stem. The time to divide or move this species is in late summer, before the new rosette forms. Wait until August to clear the bed, if you can bear it. If the work must proceed, lift your lilies very carefully with an undisturbed rootball, and replant elsewhere at once. Spring is the correct time to move all other lilies, at the first signs of growth.

Q My clump of agapanthus is growing too large for its situation. Should it be lifted and divided, or left alone; and is it advisable to cut the leaves right down in autumn? – K.S., Middlesex

A By all means dig out and remove some parts of the clump next spring, but for better flowering leave the remainder undisturbed. As a rule of thumb, those agapanthus with broader leaves, which try to retain their foliage into winter, are the less hardy kinds. Protect them well with bracken or old fern fronds, and cut off the leaves only when the frosts have yellowed them. The tougher forms, mostly those with narrow leaves, turn yellow and shed their leaves with the first hint of frost. In cold gardens the crowns can be covered before the worst of the winter with sand or bracken, but in sheltered places this is barely necessary.

Q How can I eliminate acanthus from my herbaceous borders? Digging seems to make it worse. I am not sure which species I have. Is there a non-invasive one? – G.A., Avon

A Much as I love the long hooded spikes of mauve and green, and its splendid foliage, in the wrong place acanthus can be a problem. White, succulent roots spread out from the crown for several feet, throwing up a new crown here and there, especially when cut or damaged. For this reason it is always worth buying a plant of a good known form. When you discover, after a couple of years, that your specimen has a poor leaf, is shy of flowering and a martyr to mildew, it is too late to get it out easily.

Digging is the first resort, as deep and wide as you can manage, removing roots even of pencil thickness and less. People say it drinks the weedkiller glyphosate and asks for more with no ill effect. If so, give it more; for glyphosate is known to require several treatments on stubborn weeds. It may be helpful to ring the changes and try a brushwood killer like SBK on it. But whatever you use, do make sure you use a wetting agent (such as detergent) in the spray, so that it stands at least some chance of adhering to the leaves. Acanthus leaves are notoriously difficult to spray, because water runs off so readily from their glossy leaves. This lack of contact may be the truth behind the ineffective glyphosate theory.

A small amount of salt put in crowns popping up in gravel will polish them off.

No species of acanthus is easy to eliminate when established, although some are smaller and less vigorous.

Q I have a huge clump of a large blue hosta, which I am told is *Hosta sieboldiana* var. *elegans*. I would like to divide the clump and have tried lifting it but it seems firm as a rock. How should I go about it?

A Take a deep breath and a strong spade. Forget about the text-book method of division, by prising a clump apart with two forks back to back: there isn't a fork strong enough to do this.

An old hosta clump (10–20 years old?) is like a great pie waiting to be divided. Using the spade in an upright position, slice through on a radius to the edge of the clump. It will be as hard as new white cabbage, and just as crunchy. Then do it again to free a wedge of the clump: 45 degrees is generous. I use the word 'free', but you will still need a strong fork or the spade to lever out your wedge, and the roots will extend as far again as the radius of the clump.

The wedge can be planted just as it is in a new hole. You may feel that the wedge should have roots all round, instead of being sliced through on two sides. But this will not worry it. And, more to the point, the parent plant will never know it has happened. There is certainly no need to disturb the whole clump and put your back out in order to get a division.

Old hosta clumps become mounded in the centre, as new shoots clamber up on top of the old. Much of the depth you slice through in making a division is expendable old root. If you were really to go to town with a big old clump, and divide as far as possible, pulling it into small pieces, each with a pair of buds, and disposing of all that depth of old root, you would probably finish with 60 or 70 plants. What an awful thought (unless you are a nurseryman)! They might not look such chunky clumps again for a year or two, but you would have a whole lot of hostas, if you could use them.

Q Five years ago I was given an offset of a pampas grass, and it has grown well but produced no fluffy flowers. A neighbour said it has to be 'charred' in order to make it progress. If so, how is this done, and will it ever flower? – J.B., London SE9

A Given full light and time your pampas grass (*Cortaderia sell-oana*) will flower. Very small divisions can take a few years to build up to flowering, especially in dry, poor soils, so feed and water yours hard to push it on.

'Charring' refers to the short-cut method of tidying up the plant in winter by setting fire briefly to the old foliage. The aim is not to cook the plant but just to remove as much as possible of the dead tangle of sharp-edged leaves. The result should be *flambé*, not *brûlé*. The time to do this, if it appeals to you, is in January or February, and it is entertaining rather than necessary. The plumes of my pampas grass were still looking wonderfully fresh and effective even in late March this year, and I would not have set fire to them for the world. But after harder winters firing can save an unpleasant session fully clad in goggles and heavy gloves while you chop back the viciously sharp-edged old foliage. On balance I go for the goggles, finding the association of charred black stump with spring bulbs a little too daring for my taste.

Dividing nerines

Q I have several clumps of *Nerine bowdenii* in my garden, and in each one a large bulb has come to the surface and is almost on top of the soil. What is the reason for this, and should I take any action? – M.R., Hampshire

A Nerines are South African bulbs, flowering in various glowing shades of pink in autumn. They should be planted with the nose of the bulb out of the soil for good drainage and to receieve maximum summer heat. In this position, in the south at least, they are quite hardy enough, although in the far north they may require protection away from the coast. Leave yours well alone. You will find that more bulbs will come to the surface as time goes by, until you have a mound of bulbs sitting there. If they start to flower any less well, that is the time to divide them, in April or August.

Q I should like to propagate from a 4-year-old *Euphorbia poly-chroma* – (syn. *E. epithymoides*), which is now 30in across. Should I lift and divide it, and if so when, or should I take cuttings? I do not want to risk spoiling a beautiful plant. – K.C., Devon

A When *Euphorbia polychroma* is in flower in May it looks more like a domed yellow bush than a herbaceous plant, and I can see why you do not wish to spoil its shape. However, you can propagate from it without affecting the shape of the canopy. Whatever number of shoots is left, they will always fill out to form a rounded specimen every spring. Cuttings of herbaceous euphorbias are not particularly easy, and the milky sap can produce an allergic reaction in more sensitive skins. I prefer to slice away with an old knife small pieces of the crown, of say 3-4 shoots, when they are only an inch long in spring, taking with them some smaller roots. Plant them straight into the ground. There is no need to dig up the whole crown unless you want to divide it into very many pieces. In any case, the shoots around the edge of the crown always make the best new plants. The centre is older and woodier, and less useful for propagation. Leave it undisturbed.

Q I have an excellent carpet of lesser periwinkle (*Vinca minor*) under a 30-year-old birch, but of late it has ceased to flower well. When should I cut it back, or should I trim and feed it? – A.H., Surrey

A No doubt climatic drought and birch-root drought are giving your periwinkle a hard time. Shear it off to ground level now, and plaster it with a 4in layer of old compost. It will soon sprout again, although you may lose this year's blue stars. The tangled stems of periwinkle are never easy to weed, and if your compost is likely to bring with it a crop of weed seeds, I would consider the easier option of a heavy dose of artificial balanced fertiliser, such as Growmore, followed by a weed-free, proprietary mulch.

Q I was given some corms of *Geranium tuberosum* recently. I have potted them up, and they are growing well. But I cannot find anything about them in my gardening books. Are they indoor or outdoor plants? – R.S.J., West Sussex

A This is certainly an outdoor species. It flowers a rosy purple in spring, at about a foot high, and the leaves are finely dissected. It comes from the Mediterranean and eastwards as far as Iran, so it expects a hot summer. Its way of coping with that is to become dormant in summer. The flowers appear very early with the leaves in spring, and then it disappears completely until next year. In a summer garden in Britain you need to grow something alongside it which can cover up the gap, or tuck it in amongst small shrubs.

For this year, I would enjoy your plants in their pot; keep them dry for the summer, and plant them out in the garden in autumn.

The tubers spread quite quickly, but the species is not invasive like *G. orientalibeticum*, a Chinese species which runs in strings of little tubers like chick peas; charming on the surface, while the hordes multiply in darkness underground. Do grow it, but with caution.

Q I have been given a plant of a white-variegated honesty which I admired. It had some variegation when I planted it, but now the leaves are just green. Is the problem my soil? – A.W., Northamptonshire

A Variegated honesty (*Lunaria annua*, a biennial despite its specific name) does come true from seed, to a very high percentage. Even in variegated progeny, the variegation often takes a long time to make itself apparent. Sometimes the variegation hardly shows at all in the first seedling year, but makes itself obvious in the second flowering year. Your plant is probably just enjoying its new life in some good soil. The variegation should show up again in due course. Try begging some seed this year, and grow a group of them to increase the chance of success.

Q My wife grows hellebores with great success, but when they are cut for the house they droop almost at once. She has tried boiling the ends of the stalks but this does not seem to help. She has now taken to floating the flowers in a bowl of water, but would like to be able to use them as cut flowers in a vase. Can you suggest anything? – S.H.N.V.T., Somerset

A The hellebores typified by the lenten rose (*H. orientalis*) have such a long stalk for the time of year that the temptation to use them as cut flowers, like daffodils, is irresistible. But they do droop. The trick is to pick them only after they have set seed and begun to be papery. Put a pin several times right through that part of the stem which will be under water, or, if the stem is very thick, lightly score it with a pin over the same part. Stand them up to their necks in cold water for an hour before arranging.

Q Can I sow seeds of the biennial sweet rocket (*Hesperis matronalis*) outdoors? I no longer have a cold frame or propagator. – M.S.M., Yorkshire

A What a wonderfully scented plant this is. It flowers in June, rather like a 36in honesty (it belongs to the same cabbage family), and similarly comes in a range of colours from white to mauve. There are double forms, too, of both colours. The doubles are sterile and are propagated from cuttings, but the singles seed themselves enthusiastically enough outdoors. Drive up the A1M motorway just south of Wetherby in June, and you will see them by the thousand on the embankments, in all colours between pure white and mauve. They, along with massed cowslips, are the saving pleasure of the northern section of this motorway.

You can sow sweet rocket seed in a row outdoors in May/June and transfer the young plants to their final positions in September, or sow them in position where you intend them to grow.

When they have flowered, either save some seed and start again, or trust to luck that seedlings will reappear. If you are really keen on them, it would pay you to sow seed for the first two years running, so that you set up a succession of flowering years for these biennials, without a seedling-year gap.

Reluctant Peonies

Several readers (including T.D. from Renfewshire, J.H. from Lancashire, and S.K. from Oxford) have written to enquire about problems with peonies which make either small brown buds which fail to open or full-sized buds which become slimy and mouldy and never open. Brown dry buds on peonies, only half the usual size, are a symptom of underfeeding. Give a small handful of sulphate of potash to each plant, and wallop on some good cow manure. They like the rich life.

Full-size slimy but aborted buds are the result of moulds attacking the bud case before it opens. Some varieties are especially prone, and more so in cold or wet years. Exhibition growers solve it by fixing a bag over the buds to keep them dry. In a garden a change of variety may look better.

Q Where can I buy seed of *Echium pininiana*? – J.R.C-B., Brighton

A Does this grow in Brighton? It might well. It is a huge (up to 12ft high) member of the borage family (those with that particular allergy beware), and makes great leggy rosettes of coarse foliage a yard across, from which rise tall spikes of blue flowers. Once flowered (after about 3 years), it dies, and you must rely on seedlings to replace it. It is one of the great to-die-for architectural plants, and is sold as plants by Architectural Plants, Cooks Farm, Nuthurst, Horsham, W. Sussex RH11 6LH, or as seed from Chiltern Seeds, Bortree Stile, Ulverston, Cumbria LA12 7PB. The plant is only just hardy, but succeeds well in coastal gardens of the south. See it looking desperately exotic at Portmeirion, North Wales, St Mawes Castle, Cornwall, and Ventnor Botanic Garden, Isle of Wight.

Q Where can I get hold of the orange form of the Welsh poppy which you write about? My books admit only yellow. I have inherited orange poppies in my garden, but I think they are not the Welsh one. – J.J., London NW3

A The orange form of *Meconopsis cambrica* is known as var. *aurantiaca*. There is also a gauche double form called *flore-pleno*. Both can be bought from Chiltern Seeds, Bortree Stile, Ulverston, Cumbria LA12 7PB. There are various true poppies with orange flowers, notably the large hairy Oriental poppy, *Papaver orientale*, the smaller Icelandic or Arctic poppy, *P. nudicaule*, and the 20in *P. heldreichii*, with pale green hairy rosettes of leaves and flowers of a lovely milky apricot. The last is a gem of a plant.

Q Can you tell me where I can obtain bulbs or seed of *Asphodelus microcarpus*, which I have seen in Crete (and read of as growing in Elysium)? I understand it is not listed in *The Plant Finder*. – E.C., Oxfordshire

A This asphodel is a fleshy-rooted perennial in the lily family, with long, branched wands of pinkish-white flowers. It grows in rocky, dry places as you know. It is in *The Plant Finder*, cross-referenced to *Asphodelus aestivus*, by which name it is now known. It is sold by Cally Gardens at Gatehouse-of-Fleet, Dumfriesshire, and by Perhill Nursery, Great Witley, Worcestershire. Two lessons here: we all need our own copy of *The Plant Finder*; but if you get stuck there (it can cross-reference only so many name changes), consider the name may have changed, and look for an alternative in Mark Griffiths's *Index of Garden Plants* (Macmillan, 1994). For serious plant hunters *The European Plant Finder* is available on CD-ROM.

Why does asphodel sound so romantic, and where was your reference to it in Elysium? I have always wanted to grow amaranth, just because of those lines of Walter de la Mare's in 'All That's Past':

> We wake and whisper a while,
> But, the day gone by,
> Silence and sleep like fields
> Of amaranth lie.

Q I have plants of mossy saxifrage on a rockery in full sun. However, after several years of looking attractive, they are starting to become brown and hollow at the centre. Is there anything I can do to fill the centre with new growth, or must I throw them out and start again? – P.R., Kent

A As with human balding, you will not fill the centre again once it has started to become threadbare. Many low cushion plants do this in old age, especially in the soft growing conditions of a garden, as opposed to an alpine scree or grazed turf. Instead of throwing the plants away, pull them into pieces just before growth commences, with a little root attached, and bury the pieces in refreshed, well drained soil, up to where you would choose the neck to be. Make sure you do not allow leaves to lie on cushion plants (or heads) in winter, since damp close conditions can lead to bald patches.

Early Wilting

Q After the dry cold spring, many of my perennials wilted on the first warm days. Does this matter, and what should be done to help the plants? – B.R.S., Norfolk

A This is a sad but not infrequent occurrence. Perennials which are early into leaf and flower, like pulmonarias and *Brunnera macrophylla*, can wilt pathetically when a sudden hot day takes them by surprise. They are simply not used to transpiring at that rate. It helps to give them water if they are genuinely dry. But more often it is just that the plant cannot transpire fast enough, and watering is irrelevant. I even had daffodils wilting in spring 1996. The damage is usually only to flowers, whose life is dramatically shortened by serious wilting, but leaves soon recover.

Q Where do I buy, and how do I grow, the opium poppies and oriental poppies you wrote about? – S.W., Surrey

A Opium poppies are easy 2–4ft annuals. Sow the seed directly where they are to flower and just watch. You cannot miss the seedlings as they are glaucous grey right from the start. Only be careful to reduce the number of seedheads left to self-sow, or you will quickly reach a glorious epidemic. Oriental poppies are long-lived perennials, with deep roots which are difficult to remove, so plant them in the right place first time. The leaves are mid-green, hairy, and the whole plant dies away after flowering, so it needs to have a neighbouring plant to fill its space in later summer. Alternatively you can grow it in the foot of a coarse hedge. Oriental poppies are available from garden centres, and the more unusual or new varieties from specialist nurseries. Seeds of the annual opium poppy, in double and fancy forms, are available from Chiltern Seeds, Bortree Stile, Ulverston, Cumbria LA12 7PB.

Q In early June I sowed a packet of winter-flowering pansies. They were subsequently planted out in a reserve bed in July, since when they have bloomed prolifically. Initially I tried to disbud them but soon gave up the battle. I am concerned that they will fail to flower again in late winter/early spring as they should. Ought I to shear the heads off? – J.L.S., York

A When you buy a 'winter' pansy what you are getting is a variety bred to keep flowering at low temperatures, i.e. late into autumn and again early in spring. So there is no need to worry that your plants will not have another flowering next spring. Enjoy the autumn flowers now, but do not let them flower so well that they are exhausted by mid-winter. Keep up some dead-heading to divert their energies from seed production, and go over them thoroughly at the end of the autumn flowering. (Some varieties seem reluctant ever to stop flowering in a mild winter, so just keep dead-heading.)

Q Where can I buy the poppy 'Constance Finnis'? – B.K., Wiltshire

A This is a variety of the Icelandic poppy, *Papaver nudicaule*, a short-lived perennial with good flowers for cutting. It seems to be almost the sole preserve of eastern nurseries. Try mail order from Monksilver Nursery, Oakington Road, Cottenham, Cambs CB4 4TW (enclose six first class stamps for catalogue), or Hopleys Plants Ltd, High Street, Much Hadham, Herts SG10 6BU.

This particular strain of Icelandic poppy came from New Zealand, sent as seed after the Second World War to Commander Steriker Finnis, father of the plantswoman Valerie Finnis. The commander's wife, Constance, grew the poppies for 27 years in her Reigate garden. When she died in 1971 the poppy appeared to be lost until, some time later, Valerie Finnis traced it to friends living in Ireland. She then named the strain 'Constance Finnis' as a tribute to her mother.

Q All my gardening 'bibles' say I should cut down my blue hardy geraniums after flowering, leaves and flower stalks, to encourage a second flush of flowering. So why is it I never have a single further flower, let alone a flush? – D.B., Sussex

A My guess is that you have the wrong 'blue geranium'. Many species will flower again, – *Geranium pratense, clarkei, sylvaticum, himalayense* and others. Even without cutting back they will often throw a few later flowers. But *Geranium* x *magnificum*, one of the commonest blue geraniums, with coarse, hairy leaves, only ever flowers once in early summer. I have never persuaded it to do otherwise. Could this be yours?

Q I have been struggling to find acanthus plants in central London for my father, who lives in Clapham. Please tell me where I could find them locally? – P.H., Sussex

A In plastic pots and peaty compost, acanthus does very badly through summer, and so you rarely see it in garden centres after the spring, which is the best time to plant it. Try Clifton Nurseries, at Little Venice, London W9 on 0171 289 6851, or buy it mail-order from most good nurseries. If you are after plenty of flower, look for *Acanthus spinosus* rather than *A. mollis*.

Finding your favourites

Q Garden centres provide only a limited range of dahlia tubers and no list. Can you recommend a couple of specialist dahlia growers who have a proper list? – R.C.A., Wiltshire

A I am tempted to say that things are improving at garden centres on the dahlia front. As the plant becomes fashionable again the range of cultivars for sale in prepacks grows, too, although they are mostly in the dwarf, bedding end of the range. You can even buy black and scarlet 'Bishop of Llandaff' off the peg now. For a real dahlia nursery, try Halls of Heddon, Heddon-on-the-Wall, Newcastle-upon-Tyne NE15 0JS, tel. 01661-852445, or Oscroft's Dahlias, Sprotborough Road, Doncaster, DN5 8BE, tel. 01302-785026, or Aylett Nurseries, North Orbital Road, London Colney, St Albans, Herts, AL2 1DH, tel. 01727-822255.

When looking for suppliers of a particular kind of plant, a useful source of information is *The Gardener's Yearbook*, published by Macmillan for The Royal Horticultural Society at £14.99. It includes a section listing suppliers of many specialised areas, from dahlias and delphiniums, air plants and alpines, to topiary and wild flowers. A really useful book, and a mine of information on all matters to do with gardening.

Q *Begonia evansiana* **is supposed to be hardy outdoors, but I lost mine last winter. What am I doing wrong?** – H.S., Derbyshire

A Reluctantly hardy might be a better description. It needs a warm sheltered corner, moist in summer and dry in winter. But when it does well it is a lovely plant, with 18in stems and large green leaves (red beneath), and loose, pink, typically begonia flowers in late summer and autumn. The best place is tight under a west wall, where it will be dry in winter and can be given extra water in summer. It looks wonderful with pale pink kaffir lilies (*Schizostylis*) in September. It cannot be planted more than 2in deep or it rots, but you may find that a mounded covering of sand will save it from the cold. Alternatively – and more certainly – the plant produces bulblets in the leaf axils in autumn. You can save a few of these and grow new plants the next year. The orange cascading *Begonia sutherlandii* can be propagated the same way.

Q **Several years ago I purchased a few crowns of the pink lily-of-the-valley, which I planted in a large pot. They bloomed perfectly for a year or two, but this year I have had only one flower. Should I divide and plant in the garden in a damp shady position?** – M.C.H., Kent

A There is nothing like the perfume of a potful of lily-of-the-valley in a conservatory in spring, and the pink form, *Convallaria majalis* var. *rosea*, is charming, although I prefer the purity of the plain white.

Lily-of-the-valley has a white creeping rootstock, with 'pips' every so often which throw up the leaves and flowers. While it will stand congestion and drought, it can be starved to a standstill. I suspect your plants have used up their nutrition long ago, and perhaps also have been rather wetter in the pot than they prefer, especially during their summer rest after flowering. Here and there in the woods of the Yorkshire dales they grow in steep limestone scree, under the dappled canopy of trees, cool but excellently drained.

I would pull the potful into two halves now, and plant out both halves in a cool shady part of the garden, dividing them next spring, and putting the fattest pips back into a fresh pot of soil.

If you like the pink form, look out for the very glamorous variegated forms 'Albostriata', 'Hardwick Hall' and 'Vic Pawlowski's Gold'.

Q I have germinated *Alstroemeria ligtu* hybrid seeds for the last two years, and planted the seedlings into beds when 3in high. They all died. How high should they be at planting out? My last two to germinate this year are 4–5in high and still in a pot. I don't want to lose them. – M.R., Hertfordshire

A Plant your potful now, but do not expect to see much from them this year. These lovely Peruvian lilies are tenacious when established but not quite so easy to get started.

Prick on seedlings into 3–4in pots, and when well established in the pot, plant them out into their final position in good time – late May or early June. The chances are they will make no more leaf that year, and they will certainly yellow off and die down in midsummer, just as established plants do. Don't worry; the root should still be growing. It is white, succulent and runs horizontally, often at considerable depth. Next year you should have a few shoots from your plant. Mark the position generously, as they may appear a few inches from last year's shoot, and be careful not to hoe them off. In subsequent years they will build up to strong clumps, but never of the same colonising vigour as the plain orange *Alstroemeria aurantiaca*, which may please you.

Try the species *A. psittacina* for a parroty blend of pinks and greens. A few planted in a greenhouse border cut most beautifully.

Q With each year my clump of alstroemeria gets larger and the flowers get fewer. It stands in a sunny position in a lightish alkaline soil and receives regular feeding. Is there any way of encouraging bloom, or should I simply dig it out and start again? – C.R.K.P., Gloucestershire

A Old clumps of *Alstroemeria aurantiaca*, the orange Peruvian lily, usually flower best around the edges. At the centre, root congestion is such that life becomes very mean. The fat white roots build up into a solid mass of live and dead matter, making water penetration difficult. It is also a very persistent root and difficult to dig out. Deep pieces of root always spring up again without replanting. I once saw an old patch of alstroemeria rotovated in an attempt to kill it, and the following season it flowered better then ever.

I would first of all dig around the patch, removing root back to a suitably sized area and before it spreads into other plants. It is a great smotherer of other plants. Then I would dig the remaining patch over for a spade's depth only, getting rid of 75 per cent of the root to the bonfire, and give it a heavy mulch of old compost or manure. Then leave it to show willing. Less rampant varieties, like the *A. ligtu* hybrids, can be given a much gentler treatment.

Success with irises

$\boxed{Q}$ This year my well established plants of *Iris unguicularis* (*I. stylosa* as was) have not flowered. Should I be doing anything to them to make them flower again next year? They are planted under a large sequoia tree, and against a south-facing garden wall and the house wall. – E.MacG., Shropshire

$\boxed{A}$ This is the winter-flowering iris featured on Christmas cards, which picks so well for a vase. It comes from north Africa, and what it likes above all else is a good summer baking to make it flower. Hence the need to give it a south-facing position where it can get all the heat available. At the foot of a south wall there is also the bonus of reflected heat. Even so, a poor summer can lead to poor flowering. It is said to like lime rubble, but I have grown it happily enough on acid sand. Certainly soil that is too rich will rapidly produce all leaf and no flower. There should be no question of feeding this iris with nitrogen.

Slugs can occasionally eat the buds as they emerge in the bottom of the clump, so look hard next year. This iris is especially vulnerable because it has virtually no stalk. What you pick as a 9in 'stalk' is in fact the tube – the trumpet, if you like – of the flower, and in fertilisation the pollen passes right down to an ovary at ground level. The seed capsules also appear at ground level, which is why selected forms can so easily be overwhelmed by seedlings germinating in amongst the clump.

In the cooler north, *Iris lazica* is sometimes a better bet. It is similar to *I. unguicularis*, but has a shorter 'stalk' and a broader leaf. It has to be said that *I. unguicularis* has an appallingly scruffy leaf which no one would tolerate were not its winter flowers so welcome. *I. lazica* does not pick as well, but it will flower from October to March in a normal winter.

Q How can I make my bearded irises flower? They make plenty of leaf but little flower. I came to my garden five years ago, and it was unworked clay, but I have done my best to improve it. I know irises do not like rich soil, but there must be something missing. I have given them a little lime. I know how to plant them, with the rhizome on the surface of the soil facing south in full sun. They are my favourite flower. What can I do? – B.O'R., Hampshire

A Bearded irises – the tall June-flowering ones, coming in many colours – ought to be easy to grow. All they need is sun and some decent soil. But what is 'rich' soil? Make no mistake, irises are greedy, and although they do not like a lot of nitrogen (which makes soft, leafy growth and no flower), they do like lots of humus, potash and iron.

On clay soil, I would double dig first, then work into the top spit all the old coarse compost, leafmould, and grit I could get hold of. And dress it with sulphate of potash (4oz per square yard) and sulphate of iron (2oz per square yard). If the result of all your additions is that the soil is mounded up, then so much the better; it will improve the drainage, which can be a problem for irises on clay. Lime is not vital, and too much can be harmful.

As your irises are established, you might try treating them with potash in winter and iron in spring before you decide to dig them all up and start again.

If you do start again, keep only the best, fattest, unflowered rhizomes for replanting. Bearded irises are like a ginger-beer plant – it is always hard to get rid of as much as you ought. Give the small ones away, burn them, but don't plant them, if you want immediate flowering.

As with so many flowers which have been seriously hybridised, many of the modern varieties are harder to please. Many modern irises are American and bred for much hotter summers. They do not always perform well in Britain. It may pay you to go back to some of the wonderful old varieties to be sure of flower.

The British Iris Society has a sales scheme for members, which you may care to investigate. The Royal Horticultural Society holds names and addresses of contacts for all the specialist societies in its offices at 80 Vincent Square, London SW1P 2PE. Or you could look them up in the RHS's *Gardener's Yearbook*, available from bookshops.

Q I was given a plant of *Osteospermum* 'Whirligig' in July which established well in the garden but got round to flowering only in October as the frosts arrived. I have taken cuttings for next year, but how should I ensure the flowers come earlier next year? – B.D., Middlesex

A This is a most attractive osteospermum, with daisy flowers whose individual rays are crimped in the middle. It is unfortunately a short-day plant, and it flowers more willingly in the spring and autumn. In high summer it rests. There are other osteospermums which do this too; notably the vibrantly coloured 'Nairobi Purple'. Both are delightful flowers, but plant them where they are required to perform only at the end of the season, or they will frustrate you.

You do right to take cuttings. This variety is far from hardy, whereas *Osteospermum jucundum* and 'Lady Leitrim' withstand all but the worst winters out of doors.

Q Two years ago I bought a pot-grown *Crambe cordifolia*. It has grown well for two seasons but so far has not flowered. Please can you explain this? – M.E.H., W. Sussex

A To see a well-grown clump of crambe in full summer sail is quite a sight. When it flowers a hollow trunk shoots up from coarse kale-like foliage to branch and burst into a thousand white stars. One plant is good, but three together are fabulous. The trunks deserve staking for they will rise to 7ft with a dome of flowers half as much across. Miserable gypsophila, eat your heart out!

Crambe grows from a huge, almost woody rootstock, similar to rhubarb, but more inclined to become hollow. The crown slowly increases, making side shoots which in turn reach flowering size and shoot their stars. It is not an easy plant to pot up. If you lift a crown, you will have to slice off a bud with some of the fat arm-like roots attached, and then wonder how to fit it into a pot. The chances are that the main flowering-sized buds will be in the middle of the clump, and almost unpottable without including the whole clump or without cutting off all the roots. Meanwhile, all the bits of root you leave behind sprout new crambe plants. Not surprisingly, therefore, crambe is most often grown from seed in the nursery trade, and by that means tidy young plants can be offered using modest volumes of compost. But you the buyer have to wait for the crown to reach flowering size, which I guess is 3–4 years. A word of caution: do not feed it too much nitrogen, or it makes the crown soft and it sometimes then rots or goes hollow. Give it rough, well-drained soil. The flowers have a spicy, cabbagy smell, of which I am surprisingly fond. The dying leaves in late summer have a distinctly cabbagy smell, and of that I am not at all fond.

2

Bulbs

Q This year I want to go to town with tulips, and plant some of the blacks and pinks together. Can you recommend some varieties please? – R.MacD., Surrey

A 'Queen of Night' is probably the best almost-black tulip. Try it with pinks like 'Queen of Bartigons' or 'Clara Butt', together with the perennial wallflower 'Bowles' Mauve'. 'Blue Surprise' has dark, bloomy stems which blend well with black tulips. 'Douglas Bader' is pink with similar stems, but it might be just a little early to mix with 'Queen of Night' or 'Black Swan'. 'Black Parrot' is a splendid tulip, with the frilled and feathered petals of the typical parrot. All grow to about 24in, but 'Douglas Bader' is a little shorter.

Q My present garden has a border of colchicums in it, which I would like to spread to other parts of the garden. Are they easy to divide, and when should it be done? – R.G.J., Lancashire

A The time to divide them is in August, before they run up to flowering in September and October. The bulbs increase just as readily as daffodils, and are just as easy to split up and plant, but remember that they are poisonous. It is advisable to replant them singly because they clump up so quickly. The fry – the smallest of the offsets – you may care to plant in rough grass somewhere; give them a couple of years and you will have another strong display. Ordinary purple *Colchicum autumnale* is a lovely plant, but try the white *Colchicum speciosum* 'Album', 'Lilac Wonder', or the double lilac 'Waterlily'.

Q I grow crocuses naturalised in grass. On June 9th I cut the grass down and found some light brown seed pods containing seeds varying from light brown to white. If left longer would they germinate in the soil? Should I now collect the seed and sow it in pots? How can I tell when the seed is ripe, and when should I mow to allow time for ripening? – E.G.W., Sussex

A Most crocuses will set seed every year, although a few, such as the yellow Dutch crocus, are sterile. If they like your soil crocuses will increase and even hybridise with each other, and the named forms of *Crocus chrysanthus* are notoriously promiscuous.

July or August is a better time to mow crocus grass, depending upon how hot the summer has been. By then the seeds will all be properly brown, and ripe. Mowing scatters them very effectively, and apart from losses to seed-eating birds and other animals, many will undoubtedly germinate. Seeding does not significantly weaken the corms.

There is no need to collect seed and rear new corms in pots, but if you wish to do so, sow the seed in a sandy, gritty, soil-based compost the following spring. Crocuses hate wet, peaty compost.

Q What are 'snowflakes'? We saw some white flowers very like large snowdrops in a garden recently and were told this is what they were. Are they easy to grow, and where can we get them? – P.C., Yorkshire

A The botanical name for the spring snowflake is *Leucojum vernum*, and you can get them from most bulb suppliers. They are just as easy as snowdrops, except that they do not do as well in turf. They prefer to be under shrubs or amongst other broad-leafed perennials such as hostas or acanthus. They grow to about 9in, and have a larger, more bell-shaped flower than snowdrops, sometimes with two to a stem. The foliage is bright green and does not have that glaucous (blue-grey) cast of snowdrops. The bulbs will increase very readily, and can be split up every few years. They have no objection to being split now, 'in the green', as you would snowdrops.

The summer snowflake, *Leucojum aestivum*, is bigger in all its parts, and follows on at the end of the daffodil season in April and May, which is not exactly summer. This too is easy, and in a heavy, moist soil it will make big clumps in rough grass, just like a daffodil. Divide old clumps in spring or autumn. The variety 'Gravetye Giant' is exceptionally strong, and is reputed to make 3ft in rich, damp soils, but 2ft is more usual.

There is a 3in autumn-flowering snowflake too, *Leucojum autumnale*, but this is far less vigorous and suitable only for an alpine bed or scree garden.

Q In November I moved to a new house and garden. I am pleased to see snowdrops coming up everywhere, but there seem to be crocuses up too, although showing no sign of flower. All the spring bulbs seem early this year, but will the crocus be harmed from coming into leaf so soon? – P.R.K., Yorkshire

A Despite the earliness of the season, crocuses do not usually accompany the first signs of snowdrops. Even *Crocus*

tommasinianus, probably the first to flower, usually gives snow-drops a head-start. I suspect your crocus leaves will turn out to be an autumn-flowering species such as *Crocus nudiflorus* or *speciosus*. For these species there is nothing unusual in being in leaf in December, and if you grow them in turf you need to remember to stop walking over them at the end of November, or you will experience that awful crunching feeling underfoot as you break the young shoots.

Autumn crocuses leaf early and disappear early, too, in May. The flowers appear without the leaves, in September – October, and are better grown in turf 2–3in long, which can support their leafless necks.

Q I have modern hybrid daffodils growing in semi-shade under trees and shrubs in the lee of a hedge. Despite seasons which have been variously dry and wet, the daffodils flower less and less, and make much leaf. Some have disappeared altogether. Wild daffodils seem to survive woodland conditions with only nature's help. What can I do to help mine? – B.B., Sussex

A Daffodils are perfectly happy in light woodland. They do all their growing and feeding early in the season while light is plentiful and before the full leaf canopy has developed overhead. But they are hungry plants. And the more hybridised they are, the less they thrive in such difficult conditions. They have usually been bred to produce large, sophisticated blooms in luxurious, uncompetitive border conditions or nursery rows. Without the optimum light and food, they cannot live up to expectations.

Your daffodils probably need dividing and feeding. The surface roots of trees and shrubs may be denying the bulbs adequate nutrition. Old daffodil clumps can also starve themselves by their very congestion.

It is of course a huge task to dig up and replant a 90ft border of daffodils planted among shrubs, and I would encourage you to experiment with a small patch only. Lift the most unsuccessful clumps and take a hard look at the bulbs. Are they congested and battling for space? Are they strongest at the edge of the clump where they can get more food and moisture? Replant them individually or in twos and threes, give them a good start with some bonemeal, and see what happens.

Never be afraid to dig up a plant which is visibly failing. Often the failure can be explained by a problem at the root, which careful inspection will bring to light. Finally, there are two kinds of narcissus fly which can kill the bulbs, but the only way you will be sure of their presence is by digging up some of the suspect bulbs to look for the grubs.

Too many muscari

Q Some years ago we took over a garden in which somebody had planted grape hyacinths. The things are spreading like a plague; they thrive on weedkillers like Roundup and Tumbleweed, and when they spread into gravel paths they shrug off the attentions of PathClear and even sodium chlorate. Any ideas? – M.D.B., Somerset

A A pretty blue, but insidious, aren't they? Muscari grow from a small white bulb, producing lots of bulblets every year as well as seedlings. They spread like mad, by fork and hoe and mouse and mole. Think hard before introducing them into an area of close gardening, however pretty they may look as an edging in a cottage-garden border. Growing them on a grassy bank solves the problem. Removal from a border is certainly difficult because, like celandines, their bulblets are so numerous as to be almost undiggable. Attempts at serious digging usually contrive to let some bulbs drop even lower in the soil, making them harder still to eradicate. Heavy shade stops them flowering but will not kill them except over many, many years. However, you might smother them into insignificance with a heavy herbaceous ground cover. Where the bulbs are in empty soil, you might try removing and sterilising the soil. What a job! Where they are amongst the roots of shrubs, persevere with the Roundup (glyphosate) but be sure to bruise the leaves first and to add washing-up liquid to the spray to make sure it does not run off the shiny leaves. There are many things which glyphosate takes several applications to kill, and bulbs are one of them. In gravel, sodium chlorate will work, even if the bulbs have sufficient energy reserves to produce several death throes.

Q I have a bank of wild cyclamen, and they are moving downhill. Please tell me at what time I should, or could, remove the corms uphill to put some flowers back at the top of the slope. The corms vary from 2–3in across to small seedlings, and I would prefer to move the larger ones. – H.C.M., Kent

A The little hardy cyclamen seed themselves very readily, and will naturally migrate downwards over their generations. They are well suited to poor soil or thin grass under the shade of trees. You can certainly move some back to the top of the slope. The smaller ones move most successfully – when, say, half an inch across – but larger ones can be moved too, with more care to minimise root disturbance. In ideal conditions, cyclamen can grow several times larger than your largest corm, so 2–3in is not too late to move them. The time to move them is just as the leaves begin to grow, in late summer. Move them with a little plug of soil if you can: they have little enough root to anchor themselves in the new position until they are established. I would also collect seedheads – they are easy to spot on those corkscrew stems – and scatter seed at the top of the slope.

When planting cyclamen in a garden for the first time, it is best to start off by planting a corm growing and flowering in a pot. This way you are certain of an established living plant and with luck some seedlings to follow. Dry corms are always more uncertain, and often frustratingly unsuccessful. Large corms 2–3in across are the most likely to have been stripped from the wild populations, and should be avoided on principle. Cyclamen colours vary a good deal, and a live plant tells you just what you are getting. The marbling of the leaves on *Cyclamen hederifolium* is also variable, and a live plant lets you choose an attractive form as a basis for your population. Some are green, some lightly marbled, and others completely silvered. Plant them very shallowly, just showing their tops on the surface, and with excellent drainage below.

Q We live on top of a hill and our garden is very exposed. We have an area of grass and trees in which I would like to grow a carpet of crocus. Is there a crocus which is wind resistant? – M.E.W., Avon

A Crocuses only give of their best in good weather, when the sun warms them and opens the flowers. But no individual flowers last for more than a few days, and if they are battered by wind or rain the show can be dismal. In windy places it is better to grow not the large Dutch hybrid crocuses but the earlier, shorter species such as *Crocus tommasinianus*, *C. aureus*, *C. chrysanthus* and their hybrids. *C. tommasinianus* is pale mauve and seeds well even in grass. It is followed by yellow aureus and the chrysanthus hybrids which can be a whole mixture of creams and bronzes and yellows. Look out for 'Snow Bunting', 'Cream Beauty', 'Blue Pearl' and 'Zwanenburg Bronze'. To give the crocus flowers some support, leave the grass a couple of inches long over winter, so the flower tubes are not broken by wind before they have a chance to open. Is this area of grass and trees rabbit free? Rabbits love crocus leaves.

Q Some of my daffodils and tulips have changed colour from yellow to cream when planted from pots out into the garden. Can you explain this? – H.M.P., Staffordshire

A Several possibilites here. If you pick daffodils and tulips in early bud, before the colour has developed, they are slightly paler in the vase than they would be outdoors, as the light stimulates the pigments. They also fade away more slowly, and one is inclined to remember that pale lingering stage, which outdoors is spoiled by wind and weather. But also, some varieties of tulip are unstable, and can change over the years. The apricots can tend to turn pink or creamy. Check that the plants concerned are otherwise healthy. Paleness may be a symptom of virus infection, root damage, or damage by weedkillers.

Q My local shop, not a garden centre, is selling 'wild tulip bulbs from Holland'. Is it likely these have been dug up from the wild, or will they be a cultivated wild-type tulip? – R.G., Gloucestershire

A Who knows? Probably not your shopkeeper. If you want to be reasonably sure of buying bulbs not taken from wild stocks, write to Flora and Fauna International, Great Eastern House, Tenison Road, Cambridge CB1 2DT for a copy of the *Good Bulb Guide* (£1.50 +A5 sae). This lists stockists who have agreed not to trade in wild collected bulbs. Flora and Fauna International has also set up an Indigenous Propagation Project to get Turkish villagers to produce their local species of bulbs commercially and to sell them abroad. For £12 p.a. you can join the FFI and receive the *Good Bulb Guide* and two newsletters for free. The FFI estimates that 23 million bulbs are still collected from the wild every year.

Q I have an area 4 by 5 yards covered in aconites and snowdrops. An old pear tree stood here until the great storms. Is there anything I can do to maintain interest during the summer without weakening and losing the aconites? I wondered about annuals, or *Geranium* 'Buxton's Blue'. Or should I sow grass and mow after the bulbs have died down? – A.P.R., Kent

A It is very telling that in the handful of years since those storms, the grass has not naturally taken over from the aconites now that the shade of the pear tree is gone. The area must still be impoverished and root-riddled from the pear. If you want to keep the aconites and small bulbs, I would do nothing to hasten the process of recolonisation by grass. Time itself will allow the ground to recover and become fertile again. But in the interim, why not plant a few dwarf narcissi and bluebells to follow the early bulbs, late-summer-flowering *Cyclamen hederifolium*, and *Crocus speciosus* for the autumn, with a few groups of colchicums too? *Geranium* 'Buxton's Blue' would give you some autumn colour, but for summer why not arrange a few clumps of hardy agapanthus or acanthus to give some height and substance to an otherwise large and perhaps bald area?

3

Climbers

Q L.E.F. of London NW11 writes: Two years ago I planted a *Wisteria floribunda* 'Macrobotrys'. Last year it was covered in flower buds which grew into 5in long drooping racemes, only to be suddenly denuded of flowers, leaving 5in green stalks. What is attacking the flowers, and what can I do about it?

A This is perhaps the most spectacular of all the wisterias, and the scented, lilac-and-purple flowers on a well-grown specimen can reach as much as a yard long. It is correctly known now as *Wisteria* 'Multijuga'. Your problem is the classic problem of wisterias: small birds eating the flower buds. Often they go for them just as the 'snout' of flowers emerges from the bud, and long before they begin to expand. (Mice will occasionally run up a small specimen on a wall to nibble buds, but usually they nip off the whole stalk.)

The answer is to weave a good deal of thin black cotton amongst the stems of the wisteria, to stop the birds landing and feasting on the flowers. It is reasonably discreet, if time consuming and fiddly, and it usually does the job, although very determined birds will sometimes do their best to thwart you if there are no easier pickings to be had nearby. Perhaps your neighbour should grow more fruit trees for them to spoil instead! In fruit-growing areas it is the orchards themselves which bring in large numbers of bud-eating finches, and they can make the growing of flowering cherries and wisterias simply not worth the effort. In a city you should fare better. The best wisteria I know grows two minutes' walk from Harrods; it flowers solidly from basement to second storey and perfumes the whole street.

Q We have a healthy, 8-year-old wisteria on a very sheltered north wall, but it has failed to produce any flowers. Can you tell us how to rectify this? – G.J., Nottinghamshire

A Most wisterias require as much sun as possible, although forms of *Wisteria floribunda* will manage with a little less. Replant this one on a south or south-west wall, or buy another.

Wisteria can sometimes be frustratingly slow to begin flowering, even when planted on the correct aspect. Eight years is unreasonable, but half that is not unusual. On the other hand, I have heard of people waiting 28 years for flower! The commonest reasons are too much nitrogen and too little sun. So long as a wisteria appears to be growing away happily, there is no need to feed it. It will grow and flower well when planted in the tightest of positions, with its roots constricted by walls and paving. Correct pruning also helps it settle down to flowering.

A word of warning: seed-grown wisterias can sometimes take a decade or two to begin flowering, so always choose a named, grafted variety.

Clematis problems

Q What started as a large-flowered, light-purple clematis has over the past ten years become a monster. It produces masses of foliage and reaches 10–12ft, but flowers have got fewer and fewer and smaller and smaller. It is growing in the corner of a shady courtyard with its head in the sun. Should I get rid of it and start again? – P.F., Shropshire

A Is it really as sunny there in that corner as it was ten years ago? Clematis must have sun to flower. It is one thing for a plant to like having cool, shaded roots, and quite another having to wait until August for the stems to reach a bit of direct sun. If this one is growing strongly I certainly would not get rid of it. Cash in on all that established root instead. Cut it down to knee high in March and feed it heavily, with a great mulch of cow manure or rich compost to kick it into action. Don't worry about over-feeding it; with clematis that is extremely hard to do. I would even give it regular high-potash liquid feed next year too, until it shows willing. Regular watering makes a huge difference to clematis, especially when the roots are in the rain-shadow of a wall.

Q I have a *Clematis alpina* 'Frances Rivis' growing up a trellis-covered rustic pole into an old apple tree. It looks lovely in spring when it flowers, but in winter the pole stands out and it looks dull. Would a companion planting of the evergreen *Clematis cirrhosa* var. *balearica* solve the problem, or some other evergreen climber? – M.S., Hampshire

A Had you considered that an evergreen climber might draw even more attention to the pole? Winter-flowering *C. cirrhosa* var. *balearica* is I think a good compromise. It is not a particularly vigorous plant, and should make a happy partner for *C. alpina*. It gets called the fern-leaved clematis, but the degree to which the leaves are feathery does vary a great deal. Good forms become bronzed in the winter cold. The flowers are small creamy bells, with, in some forms, a red or chocolaty spotting inside.

Q Any ideas what's wrong with this eight-year-old *Clematis viticella* 'Alba Luxurians'? Many of the flowers are all green. – R.H.W., Warwickshire

A This is a lovely small-flowered clematis, scrambling up to 8 or 9 ft. It is quite usual for its flowers to be all green, especially early in the season. Later you will find them more their usual selves – white with green tips. The reason for this is that, genetically, it is rather a confused plant; it has trouble telling what is supposed to be sepal and what is supposed to be leaf, and it gets it wrong. Other clematis, too, have varying flowers through the season, the doubles in particular. 'Vyvyan Pennell' is a large purplish blue, which produces thoroughly double flowers in its early summer flush, from last year's wood, and then in late summer it can produce a flush of singles as well from the new wood. You must prune accordingly, not cutting down to a couple of feet as you do some of the large-flowered clematis, but just tidying up and taking out the dead in February. This allows the old wood to produce the double flowers. Harder pruning produces a singles-only plant, and you will wonder if you have been sold the wrong plant.

Q We planted a *Clematis* 'Lasurstern' some years ago which quickly died on us, although our other clematis do reasonably well. Some forms of *C. viticella,* planted to hide the bare lower stems of a *C. montana,* also died, although this particular bed is mostly builder's rubble. The garden generally is on a chalky clay soil. Where did we go wrong? – V.W., Sussex

A Clematis do best in a rich, open-textured soil. *C. montana* (30 ft) is tough enough to survive almost anywhere, but to ask the delicate *C. viticella* (6–8 ft) to grow under a *montana* in builder's rubble is like asking a mouse to tie an elephant's shoe laces on the move: death is almost guaranteed. But don't be put off.

What you need to do is make a proper pit when planting something as greedy as a clematis on poor or heavy clay soil. Make a hole at least 2 ft deep and wide – more if you can – and fill it up with 20 per cent decent topsoil and 80 per cent old garden compost, adding a couple of handsfull of bonemeal for good measure. The plant is going to live there for many a year, and the more you can do to get it off to a rich start the better. Mulch with manure every year, and never let it go short of water in summer.

Q **I should like to move an established *Clematis* 'Perle d'Azur' to a place where it can climb into a tree of the yellow *Robinia pseudoacacia* 'Frisia'. The robinia is surrounded by delphiniums, Canterbury bells and blue hardy geraniums, and the combination of yellow and blue is stunning. Will the clematis survive being moved, and how can I support it without harming the robinia? – P.S., Cambridgeshire**

A It is possible to move old clematis, lifting them in October with a large rootball at least a foot across, and the stems cut down to 18in. But it is usually better to spend a fiver on a new one, not least because all clematis should go into deeply dug holes which have been well enriched with old manure or compost. Under a tree, cowmuck is much more valuable in the hole than an old rootball.

The dusky blue flowers of 'Perle d'Azur will look fine in the feathery, brilliant yellow leaves of your robinia, and it can be allowed to scramble around as much of the tree as it has appetite for. It will do no harm there. But below ground robinias are shallow rooted and will rob the clematis of food and water. So plant it at least 4 ft from the trunk in a good new hole, and give it a firmly-fixed cane-and-netting ladder to get it up into the tree. When you make the hole, beware of severing larger robinia roots, since the tree has a tendency to sucker, which is aggravated by damage.

Q I cannot get my *Clematis* 'Nelly Moser' to flower in summer, although it does well in autumn. One year I cut it down hard and got no flowers at all. How should I prune it? – M.E., Yorkshire

A 'Nelly Moser' is one of those large-flowered hybrid clematis which should flower twice a year – once in early summer and again in late summer or autumn. To get that first crop of flowers you must not prune it down to 18 in as you might the common purple *C.* 'Jackmanii'. Instead, just cut out the dead stems and shorten the rest to one or two pairs of buds. (The same goes for 'Lasurstern', 'Mrs.Cholmondley', and 'Miss Bateman'.) If you do cut it right down, you will miss the early crop of flowers, but should get a better autumn crop. If the late crop is poor, then probably the plant is starved. So prune it lightly (as above) this winter, and give it a banquet of ordure.

Q We have a reasonably sunny London courtyard garden which I am replanting much more simply, with just a few shrubs and bamboos. I would like to make the best use of climbers, as the walls go up to between 12 and 15ft. Can you recommend some suitable climbers with a good perfume? – G.B., London SW7.

A Top of my list would be the evergreen *Clematis armandii* and *C. finetiana*, which would enjoy a warm London garden. *C. finetiana* is fabulously perfumed; *C. armandii* is less so, but it has such architectural foliage for a climber that it would be perfect in your sheltered courtyard. Summer jasmine has wonderful perfume. Grow the larger flowered form, *Jasminum officinale* 'Affine'. Honeysuckles smell, of course, but are prone to mildew in hot dry conditions so beware. Have you space for wisteria? On the shady side you could grow *Hydrangea petiolaris*, which smells of coconut and Nice biscuits.

Q I have a climbing *Hydrangea petiolaris* on the side wall of my garage. It is over 20 years old and it grows out over 3ft deep, encroaching over the path to the front door. Is it possible to prune it back so that it will lie flatter against the wall, but still produce flowers? If so, how and when should it be pruned? – P.S., Leicestershire

A Certainly you can prune it. Take it back with a saw in February or March to the vertical stems attached to the wall (it grows by attaching itself to walls or tree trunks by aerial roots). Feed it well. New shoots will clothe the structure again over the year, and flowering should start again the next year. Like ivy, this climber has two kinds of growth, the non-flowering kind with aerial roots, from which grow the other, flowering, root-less side shoots. By thinning back the side shoots a little every year, it is possible to keep the plant flowering within a foot of the wall. Don't you enjoy the coconut smell of the flowers?

Q Do you know of any climbers which would make an attractive substitute to barbed wire? Something thorny and especially fast-growing for a fairly exposed site? – M.McM., Yorkshire

A In another climate I would suggest bougainvillea, in which even cats can lose their way and be trapped. In this country we have no really vicious climbers. The best you might do is a thorny rose. I take it you want to keep people or animals out or behind a wall? Try *Rosa multiflora*, which is thoroughly rampant and smells good too. It has loose clusters of single white flowers. For a more formal flower, 'Cerise Bouquet' is a fine rose, long flowering, and with thorns which would stop a grisly bear. So would 'Zigeunerknabe', a very vigorous Bourbon rose with crimson flowers.

North wall climbers

Q My small suburban semi is pebbledashed in grey and faces north. I want to plant an evergreen flowering climber to cover up the front wall, but the only ones I can find in books are *Berberidopsis corallina* and *Pileostegia viburnoides*. Would either of them be a good idea, and where could I get one? They are not in the local garden centres. – M.O., Oxfordshire

A If only there were more evergreen flowering climbers for our climate! Berberidopsis is on the tender side and too unreliable for such an important purpose. Pileostegia, which belongs to the hydrangea family, would succeed, but it is slow and you would need to be patient. It has good evergreen leaves, and is self-clinging by means of aerial roots. It appreciates shelter. In time it will build up into generous billows of foliage on the wall, rather as the deciduous climbing *Hydrangea petiolaris* does. On a pebbledashed wall aerial roots, as found in pileostegia and ivy, can find their way into surface cracks and will encourage penetration by rain-water, so be sure the surface is in good order before using these plants on such a wall. Deciduous alternatives might include climbing roses suitable for a north wall, or the Virginia creeper look-alike, *Parthenocissus tricuspidata* 'Veitchii', also known as Boston ivy, which clings by harmless suckers rather than aerial roots.

Q I have a beautiful passion flower, *Passiflora caerulea*, which covers the walls of my patio. But every year it suffers from mould, which a friend says is due to lack of water. How do I treat this without spraying, and can I eat the golden fruits? – J.W., Sussex

A Aphids sometimes attack the shoots of passion flowers, causing mould on the lower leaves from excreted honeydew, so check that first. Plants with insufficient water and in very dry air sometimes die back at the tips, giving the impression of a fungal wilt. But if your plant is fruiting well it cannot be too short of water. Try watering more generously and hosing the plant over now and then, when the sun is not directly on it. You can eat the fruit of blue passion flower, the only one we can really grow well outdoors, and also its white-flowered variety 'Constance Elliott', but they are insipid. There are more than twenty edible species, but only a handful are grown commercially for fruit, including bright-pink-flowered *Passiflora mollissima* with banana-shaped fruits. Of those species suitable for a cold greenhouse in Britain, the following have good fruit: *P. actinia*, *P. edulis* (the common granadilla), *P. mixta*, and *P. mollissima*. (For more information on this genus, look at John Vanderplank's book *Passion Flowers*, recently revised and reprinted by Cassell at £30; ISBN 0-304-34216-5.)

Q I have a *Rosa banksiae lutea* on the west side of the house. It is three years old and has grown well but only flowers here and there. Have I cut it back too much and at the wrong time? When should I prune it? – J.P., Kent

A This extraordinarily vigorous rambling rose first flowered here in 1824. It is the hardiest of all the forms of *Rosa banksiae*, if the least scented, and will grow to 30 ft. The double yellow flowers appear in spring at the same time as those of *Clematis montana*. To flower well it needs summer heat and lots of it, to ripen the wood sufficiently to induce flower production and to get the growth through winter cold. In southern England a good summer is just about hot enough to do the trick. A rose as rampant as this is difficult to prune as you would a normal rambler. If there is space, it can just be allowed to let rip, sorting it out every now and then after a bad winter cuts it back.

Q I have grown *Campsis radicans* from seed. It grows well enough, and sprouts again from the base after a bad winter, but it never flowers. What to do? – D.S., Perthshire

A A fabulous orange- or red-trumpeted climber, with leaves like wisteria and, when happy, similarly long gangling shoots. It flowers on the end of the current season's growth and needs a long, properly hot Mediterranean summer to have much of a chance. In Provence or the Haute Loire, it will thrive, but not in Perthshire. Waste no more time on it – unless the challenge is more important than the flowers.

Q I am growing a Chilean potato-tree, *Solanum crispum* 'Glasnevin', as a wall shrub. It has grown and flowered well since the spring, but it is leggy and nearly 20ft tall. How should I prune it? Also on the wall I have a 15ft summer jasmine, *Jasminum officinale*, but this too will need pruning. How should it be done? – A.D.H., Surrey

A This solanum is a climbing, scrambling shrub with blue, potato-like flowers, and it is 95 per cent hardy. Because it is naturally so vigorous, it is not easy to train into a neat or formal shape. It is better to plant it where it can ramble with relatively little pruning; perhaps with the removal of weak or damaged growth in spring, and a little thinning. In order for this to be successful, it needs to be encouraged in the first few years of life to make plenty of low shoots to cover the wall sideways, before it is allowed to sprawl. Some prefer to grow it into a small tree or into the lower branches of a large one.

Summer jasmine is another scrambler, all too willing to make great tangles of shoots up to 20 ft high. It is best grown where this habit can be accommodated. If you want to thin it, remember it flowers on the sides and ends of last year's wood, so pruning is best done in summer after the main flush of flower. Ancient tangles can be severed *en masse* in spring, and subsequent new growths kept under more control.

Q I have a rather stark, octagonal dovecote in my garden, and would like to train climbers up to about 20ft on the south, east, and north-east sides, which are all predominantly shaded. We may not be able to prune them regularly in years to come. Can you suggest some low- or no-maintenance possibilities? – S.T., Herefordshire

A Anything which climbs to 20ft is vigorous, and there are no real no-maintenance possibilities. Vigorous climbers will always need drastic cutting back after a few years, and make the maintenance of the structure itself difficult.

If maintenance is the prime concern, consider planting tall slender shrubs, or small fastigiate (columnar) trees, which could screen the dovecote rather than be trained against it. *Azara microphylla* or *A. serrata* would do, or a fastigiate yew or rowan. You might not manage narrowness to 20 ft from shrubs, but they would be much easier than climbers.

If climbers it must be, why not grow things which will climb up a series of strong strings attached up high, and which could simply be cut free at the top and dropped every year or two? This would save you any regular high pruning or tying in. Hops would do well, and need cutting down every year in autumn: two minutes' work up a tall ladder. *Clematis montana* would work, cutting it down perhaps every third year after flowering, and re-stringing. You might also try the semi-evergreen *Akebia quinata*, which is a reliable self-twiner up to considerable heights, or the Dutchman's pipe, *Aristolochia macrophylla* (syn. *A. durior*). The string would have to be plastic, perhaps, to last reliably for three years.

4

Shrubs

Q I have inherited a border of primarily yellow plants, and have decided to add blue and white flowering plants for next season. However, underneath a 10ft yellow Moroccan broom is a bright pink hydrangea. Can I use a proprietary blueing agent to change the hydrangea's colour? Would this affect the broom, and when should I use it? Or should I replace the hydrangea with a blue form? – S.W., London SW19

A Hydrangeas are bluest on acid soils where there are plenty of iron and aluminium salts available to the plants. In limy soils these salts are not available and the colours become pink or red. By all means use a blueing agent according to the manufacturer's instructions. It is unlikely to affect the broom in any detrimental way. But if you are on a limy soil and you want to go in for careful colour combinations, it may be better to change the hydrangea for a plant which is more naturally at home on that soil. If the shrub is growing healthily, try the colour change first before you dig it out. Winter is the time to get the bluing agent on. The blues of hydrangeas vary a great deal and the result may suit or jar with your colour scheme. I used to grow the variety 'Westfalen' on acid sand. It is supposed to be one of the best red hydrangeas, but there it was – a stunning midnight purple!

Q I pruned my hydrangeas in late autumn after leaf-fall, but there were no flowers the following summer. The next year I left them unpruned, and the following year there were scores of flowers. By then they had grown too large, so I tried pruning them in spring before they began to shoot. Result: no flowers. Do they have to be unpruned and straggly to flower? – J. de V-T., Kent

A Pruning the common mop-head or lace-cap hydrangeas is easy once you grasp the principal. The flower buds form at the end of the current season's growth, remaining dormant over winter, and producing blooms the next summer. If you cut those buds off in autumn or spring, there can be no flowers to follow.

To keep hydrangeas flowering well, prune them in spring, cutting out at ground level 10–20 per cent of the older and weaker wood, and taking back last season's flowering shoots by 6–12in to a strong pair of buds. (The old flower heads are left on over winter as frost protection to the flower buds.) In this way you will keep an uncongested bush which will ripen its wood better and therefore flower better. Winter-damaged shoots can be shortened to a strong live bud.

It is a rare hydrangea which, in conditions it enjoys, will make a bush of less than 5ft each way. In places with warm, moist climates like County Kerry (Eire) they can make 8–10 ft. Too much pruning only reduces flowering, so it is better to plant where there is sufficient room for full development. No hydrangea is a pretty sight in winter, but if well fed and pruned it need not be straggly.

Q I have a *Hydrangea paniculata* 'Grandiflora' which, at 7ft in all directions, is getting rather too large. I would like to know when is the best time to prune, and how? – B.L.S., Lancashire

A Unlike the mop-head hydrangeas, this species happily produces flowers on the ends of the current season's growth, and should be pruned back to a framework of main branches in

March/April. Average flowering shoots are 18–24in long, so your framework needs to be low enough to allow for that summer extension every year. Simply prune hard into older wood next spring, at the height of the desired framework, and prune to the same level in subsequent springs.

Because this species does not need to bring buds through the winter in order to flower, it is more successful in cold gardens than the mop-head hydrangeas. With generous feeding and good cultivation, the white panicles of flowers can be a foot or more long, rather like a huge, August-flowering white lilac.

Q I have a healthy 10ft 'japonica' (*Chaenomeles japonica*) with dozens of stems, but the flowers are all at the top, and it is too large for its position. I have tried thinning the stems, but they are hard to get at. I am tempted to root it out, but in a London garden disposal is a problem. What do you suggest? – A.R., London W4

A It sounds as if you have the larger *Chaenomeles speciosa*, rather than *C. japonica*, which is a small shrub. Both these flowering quinces are similar in flower and fruit, and have been hybridised to form the *Chaenomeles* x *superba* varieties.

Chaenomeles are best either unpruned, as a bush mounded to the ground, or hard pruned on a wall. Here, they first need training to cover the wall with a fan of stems. Then, once flowering commences on short spur growths, they may be pruned hard every year to a few buds after flowering, and kept nipped back in summer too if you have the patience.

After very hard pruning they take time to settle down again and make short, flowering shoots, and major rejuvenative pruning can be a long business.

I would get rid of your bush, as they are not high-value shrubs and do not merit a lot of space in a small garden. You might replace it with a neater variety such as 'Simonii' or 'Crimson and Gold'. If you do remove it, get out all the root you can, as they have a nasty habit of suckering from pieces of old root.

$\boxed{Q}$ I have a 20-year-old Moroccan broom, *Cytisus battandieri*, which is growing in a narrow bed against a fence. Until recently it did well. Then last year I had to cut off two or three branches. Over the winter the leaves were rather small and the flowers have been stunted too. New shoots with normal sized leaves are now coming from the base. Is it dying and can I do anything about it? – D.P.A., London NW5

$\boxed{A}$ What an attractive plant this is when well grown, with its silky grey laburnum-like leaves and pineapple-scented heads of yellow flower. Because it is slightly tender it is commonly grown against a wall, but the best plants I have ever seen were free-standing, even in northern England. Grown this way, it makes a loose arching shrub 8–10ft tall and across. Seed-raised plants put into their final positions in the first year stand the wind in an open position far better than large, pot-grown transplants.

On a wall Moroccan broom is harder to keep in bounds. It always wants to flower at the top, and is not easily persuaded to fill the wall space evenly or low down. More importantly it is in the pea family, many of whose members are notoriously short lived and do not respond well to hard pruning. I suspect your broom is dying of old age. Twenty years is a good innings for one, and if it is sprouting from the base, then the cause of death of the main stem is unlikely to be root disease. I would cut out the old stem now, and hope that the new shoots will survive to fill the space.

$\boxed{Q}$ How can I control black aphis on a 15-year-old *Picea abies* 'Reflexa'? I have tried various systemic insecticides over the past two years but I am not winning. Currently I am using an ICI Bug Gun and spray directly onto the infestations which is very laborious. Last year I lost a 'Sky Rocket' juniper to this pest. – M.N., Worcestershire

A Two thing surprise me here. Firstly, a sensible regime of spraying is not working, so perhaps the pest is not what you think. There are adelgids which infest conifers, and which are genuinely difficult to destroy. Secondly, I wonder why your conifers are succumbing to insects when they should be so tough? Perhaps you are growing them in too hot, enclosed, and dry a position. They much prefer cool, moist conditions, and when softened by a pampered position they can often fall prey to insect attack.

Bamboo blues

Q We have several clumps of bamboos which are fairly well established. Last year they were covered by flood water for several days. This has killed many of the old stems, although a few weak stems are now struggling through. Should we cut off the old dead canes or leave them as protection for the emerging shoots? I have read that bamboos should be supplied with silica to encourage strong growth. Would this help? – A.A.N., Cornwall

A Cut out all the dead stems at once, to let in the light to the new shoots. You should find that they then grow more strongly. (You will also gain a stock of garden canes.) It may be that the new shoots, if they are long and have been hemmed in by dead canes, are too weak to support themselves, and you may need – for this year at least – to cut the dead canes down to a height which still gives the new shoots some support. If the new canes are not self-supporting by next year, cut them off to the ground, too, and make a completely fresh start.

Next spring give them all a heavy dressing of ordinary, rich old manure. That is quite sufficient. Bamboos which have been knocked back so hard do take a year or two to get going again, but if there are signs of life they will make it in the end.

Some of the smaller bamboos, such as the yellow variegated *Pleioblastus viride-striatus*, can be cut to ground level every spring to good effect.

Q Some of the cistus in my garden are looking very sorry for themselves now (March) after a cold wet winter. Should I cut them back? Some are five and six feet high, and as many years old.

A Cistus are Mediterranean plants, and it takes more heat than the English weather can produce in March to cheer them up and get them growing again. Wait until early May to cut back withered shoots. It is better not to cut into old wood if you can avoid it, as cistus do not break new shoots freely.

The best pruning for these plants is little and often during the growing season, by regular pinching of the tips, so that a dense, fully furnished bush is produced. Without this the taller species especially, such as *C. laurifolius* and *cyprius* become very gangly, and it is often plants with bare trunks which succumb to a bad winter. If a cistus looks brown all over, look for bark split on the main trunk. Older specimens are not worth the wait to see if they recover. Cutting them down to ground level is no use; in any case, five or six years is a good life for a cistus. Heave them out and get a young one in, or try something new.

Q We bought a Ghent azalea last year. It was leggy, with tufts of leaves only at the ends of the 2ft stems, but it was the colour and fragrance we wanted. The hope was that it would bush out afterwards, but it has not. Can it be encouraged to do so?

Apart from this it seems strong and happy: but we are not. –
B.M., Suffolk

A The Ghent azaleas are a group of deciduous rhododendrons
bred first in the period 1830–50. They are known for their
wonderful perfume and honeysuckle-like flowers, but they do tend
to be on the leggy and twiggy side. Many of them grow up to 6–8ft.

If you pinch out the leaders in the next couple of years you will
encourage bushiness, and if it is really growing fast you might
reduce one or two of the present stems by half in spring, to force
some lower growth. But do not expect to have an especially
rounded bush from the Ghents; they will push upwards.

There are some stunning colours amongst them. 'Coccinea
Speciosa' is an outrageous orange-red, and can be seen upstaging
most other azaleas at the Savill Garden, Windsor. 'Gloria Mundi' is
orange with a yellow flare. 'Daviesii' is more restrained all round –
white flowers with a yellow flare; very fragrant, and of bushier habit.

Q The garden of the house I moved into this year has a splendidly
plumy, lemon-scented verbena (*Aloysia triphylla*) which is 8ft
high and 10ft wide. I was dismayed to receive the informed advice
that it should be cut down to 12in next April. Instinct tells me this
is too drastic. Could you please advise? – S.C., London SW18

A The central London microclimate is a wonder! Lemon
verbena is often grown as a conservatory plant for its very
lemony leaves and scarlet flowers. Older books list it as *Lippia citri-
odora*. In a sheltered position it will survive the winter outdoors,
but usually by spring it is a mess, or dead to ground level, and this
is the time to cut it off to 12in. Your plant sounds as if it has had a
run of damage-free winters, and so long as it continues to look
good it can be left alone. Presumably outdoors your bush is free of
the whitefly which make such a meal of it indoors.

Climatically, inner London obeys no rules. All that surplus heat does remarkable things. I have seen avocados thriving outdoors close to a gas flue, and the cup and saucer vine *Cobaea scandens* surviving into a second year with the kind of grey, leathery stems Tarzan would not hesitate to swing on.

Sucker problems

Q For several years I have had to deal with suckers of *Elaeagnus commutata*, but now they have spread into the lawn and I am at a loss to know how to get rid of them. Have you any advice short of removing the shrub altogether? The same thing is happening with my *Rosa spinosissima*. – R.H., Hampshire

A The deciduous *Elaeagnus commutata* gives a wonderful flash of silver-white foliage in a garden, but suckering *is* a problem, especially with the passing years. The only effective way of removing them from lawns is to dig out the running roots under the turf, and then regularly cut round the roots of the shrub in its border to contain it. The trouble is, the more you cut round it the more suckers there will be in the border. Having first severed the parent plant from the lawn suckers you might also care to try using a chemical brushwood killer on the lawn suckers.

This elaeagnus is better suited to informal or wild gardens, where it can colonise as it wishes and where suckers appearing in rough grass can be mown off with little visual detriment. Nor is it an especially shapely bush. You might like to try silver-grey *Salix elaeagnos* as an alternative, or the broad leaved *Phlomis* 'Edward Bowles'.

Q We have a *Philadelphus* 'Virginal' which is now 6 years old. It grew quickly, was pruned back, and is now once again close on

10ft high. It is in full sun, but it never flowers. What should I do, beyond pruning it hard back again? Do I perhaps need two plants, given its name? – J.LeM., Fife

A There is nothing so dreary as a philadelphus when not in flower, unless it be a lilac or a forsythia. But in flower, the perfume from philadelphus is luscious, generous, and altogether a necessity for a summer garden. The variety 'Virginal' has double flowers of the purest white.

But it is a great tease. There is nothing demure about it. It likes to make a round-headed matron of a bush 12ft in all directions, and given this space it settles down to flower well enough. If you prune it hard, great wands of new growth shoot up, all promise but no flower.

It has no place in a small garden. I would replace it with one of the small-flowered singles, such as 'Avalanche' or 'Erecta', which flower with abandon on a medium sized bush, loading the air with perfume. The larger-flowered 'Beauclerk' and 'Belle Etoile' have an attractive maroon blotch at the base of the petals, but they never flower quite so freely.

Q This year my pink potentilla bush is flowering very poorly and even some of the buds are turning brown without opening. My soil is light and we get little rain here, so I water well but also feed with tomato food to encourage flower production. Have you any ideas? – A.S., Suffolk

A The shrubby *Potentilla fruticosa* comes in various colours, from the common yellows to orange, white, pink and brick red. It is best in a cool, heavy, loam soil with a rainfall above 30 – 35in per year, where it will flower generously over a long season. For all your watering I think it is disliking the dry hot weather and hot roots. If you were in Wales or the Yorkshire Dales it would be another matter, but in dry, east-coast Suffolk potentillas will never do as well. Even in cool Northumberland I decided to give the heave-ho to a group of white potentillas, which in recent drought years have been thoroughly miserable. Where rainfall is below 27in per year I do not think they are worth growing. *Cistus* x *skanbergii* would be a much better bet for you.

Propagating kerrias

Q When my wife and I moved to this house, we inherited a *Kerria japonica*. It is such a pretty flower that I would like to put it in other parts of the garden. Can I take cuttings, and if so when? – E.S., Buckinghamshire

A This is indeed a pretty shrub, and tough as they come. Most common is the double form, 'Pleniflora', but to my eye the flowers share, along with double daffodils and the double Welsh poppy, more than a passing resemblance to sucked oranges. I much prefer the type form with single orange flowers, 1–2in across, like single orange roses on bright green twigs. 'Golden Guinea' is an improved form with flowers up to 2in across.

Propagation could not be simpler. It spreads by suckers, and these can be detached and replanted between November and March. Cut the offsets down to 6in for better, bushier establishment, rather like raspberries. You can also take cuttings of newly ripened wood in late summer, stuck in a pot of compost with a polythene bag over the top, and a little rooting hormone on the bottom of the cuttings. Even the smallest bits will root easily.

If you like kerria, try growing *Rhodotypos scandens* (syn. *kerrioides*), which is very similar but white-flowered. It propagates just as readily, and has the same arching habit. It grows very well in New York, where the climate is bitterly cold in winter.

Q I have a Mexican orange blossom (*Choisya ternata*)in my new garden. It is covered in fragrant white flowers. When and how should I prune it, and will it grow beyond its present 4ft tall? – L.F.L., London

A What a good plant this is. Usually – but not always – I manage to resist pulling off a leaflet when I pass a choisya, because the spicy aroma of the crushed foliage is so wonderful.

Grown in full sun and shelter, a choisya should need little pruning, until perhaps one day the odd stem will die back, or snow break the crown. In shade the growth is always weaker. Sometimes a little pruning is necessary in spring, to cut out winter-damaged shoots. Cuts made into old wood break freely.

If you prefer you can prune back the shrub by 9in all over, after the April-May flowering, which tends to make an autumn flush of flower more certain, especially in a hot year.

In warm, sheltered gardens choisya may reach as much as 6–7ft, but 5ft is more usual. The yellow variety 'Sundance' is smaller and more compact.

Q I have recently bought two purple cordylines, *C. australis* 'Purple Tower' and 'Torbay Red'. They are both planted in the ground, and I realise they are tender, but I would like to keep them outside during the winter. What is the best treatment to ensure their survival? – W.D., Norfolk

A Norfolk is a cold county, but nevertheless you might get away with your cordylines outside. The more sheltered the position, the longer the life. Cordylines – New Zealand cabbage trees – make great rosettes of long strappy leaves which stand the seaside weather well if it is not too cold. In the south west and in central London they do especially well. Most cordylines are grey leaved, but the purple ones are fast becoming popular.

Wet and cold combined will be your enemy, more than cold itself. If your plants have wall shelter, you might erect a temporary frame over them of polythene or bubble film, to keep off the worst weather and icy winds. Free-standing frames are harder to support, and of course less warm. Put the frame on only when the weather becomes properly cold with a few degrees of night frost, but leave the sides open when the temperature is above freezing: the last thing you want to do is to make a little hot-house, producing soft growth. In bitter weather, stuff the frame with screwed up newspaper.

Cordylines grow fast and can branch, and after a year or two such protection may no longer be practical. Let your plants take their chance then; it is surprising what will survive once it is established, and the first few years are always the greatest risk.

Q Two years ago I planted out a potted *Fatsia japonica* in my north-facing paved garden. It has thrived and grown enormously, but the leaves have gradually changed from shiny mid-green to a very yellowy green. I feed it regularly through the summer with Phostrogen in (limy) tapwater. How can I make it green again? – G.B., Kent

A This house-plant is just as happy outdoors, where it can really make an imposing evergreen, with fingered leaves a foot or more across. It is lime-tolerant, but I would not expect it to thrive in heavily chalky soil. The leaves to worry about are, of course, the new ones; the plant always drops some of its old leaves in summer, and they turn to yellow and brown first.

It sounds as if your plant has either met something inimical such as builder's rubble in the soil, or it is starved. If it was pot-bound when it was planted out, it may never have rooted out into the surrounding soil, and may be hungry and drought-stressed despite your feeding, and simply unable to support its top growth properly. Scrape away some soil to see what is going on below.

A choice of mallows

Q I have plants of the pink tree mallow *Lavatera arborea* and its paler form 'Barnsley'. Both have reached 6–7ft tall, and are growing well. I would prefer a more compact, bushy shape. When do I prune to achieve this? – G.W., Dorset

A Tree mallows should be pruned in spring when growth commences and the cold weather is over. They can be taken as low as 12in, but they will still make 6–8ft of growth by the autumn. If you wish to restrict the height, take out the top foot of the leaders of the main vertical stems just as they are coming up to first flowering in midsummer. The sideshoots will then develop more thickly and a little shorter. Shortening back more leaders later only removes more flowers.

The forms 'Burgundy Pink', 'Candy Floss' and 'Ice Cool' are naturally lower growing, and will flower at about 4ft. So will the semi-double 'Pink Frills'.

Another alternative is to use the herbaceous mallow, *Malva alcea* 'Fastigiata', which makes a pink fan 5–6ft high and flowers over the same long period from July to October. Both the shrubby and herbaceous mallow give only a few years of life before they get tired and shabby. They should be started again, from cuttings and seed respectively.

Q Four years ago I planted three camellias out in the garden. They had flowered well in tubs in my conservatory, but were too large to keep indoors. Two went in a shady place without much direct sunshine, but not deep shade. One went in a sunny place. Those in shade have not flowered as well as the one in full sun. Am I mistaken in thinking these are shade-tolerant shrubs? – N.J.D., Stirling, Scotland

A A certain amount of shade can be useful in combating a camellia's dislikes. These are (1) hot, dry roots, (2) early morning sun during frost caused by an east-facing position, and (3) cold winds. Dry roots can cause bud drop, and sun on frozen buds can burst them. Icy winds do damage to both buds and shoots. If you can offer a position without those problems, then camellias will take full sun very happily. I have seen them flower splendidly in the garden squares of Chelsea, well mulched and watered, in full sun.

In the south, dappled shade also keeps a degree or two of frost off the opening flowers. But southern dappled shade is still warm enough in summer to ripen the wood and induce flower bud production. In the north, shady positions can mean few or no flowers, especially after a poor summer. A sunny woodland glade, or its climatic equivalent, is the place to grow camellias. The soil must of course be acidic, as for rhododendrons.

Q I have five *Camellia williamsii* in various parts of my garden, they are about 2–3 years old. Only one has flowered this year, and the top leaves of the others are turning brownish. What can I do for them? – H.S., London NW11

A Camellias require warmth, shelter, and moist roots. If you let them dry out in summer, any buds that have formed may drop there and then.

The *C. williamsii* hybrids were originally made by J.C. Williams of Caerhays in Cornwall by crossing *C. japonica* with *C. saluenensis*. They remain some of the toughest camellias in cultivation, and the hybrid 'Donation' must surely be the most widely sold camellia.

Even so, browning of the young new leaves at the top of the bushes is most likely to be frost damage. The new growth is very succulent and tender, and even temperatures very close to freezing can spoil and distort it. Low temperatures, coupled with strong winds, are bad news for camellias once they have started into growth.

Snip out the damaged shoots and leaves in a few weeks, when the extent of the damage is clear, and hope for better luck next year.

Transplants

Q Would it be possible to transplant successfully a *Garrya elliptica* planted too close to a *Viburnum farreri* (syn. *V. fragrans*) three years ago? Both are now 4ft high. – S.S., Essex

A It would be easier to transplant the viburnum. This autumn- and spring-flowering shrub has matted, fibrous roots which will happily withstand a great deal of disturbance. But if the garrya must go, then it can be dug out carefully with a large rootball next March, giving priority to garrya over viburnum where the roots overlap. You may well need to stake it for a few months so that rocking does not stop new roots getting a grip on the surrounding soil. It may well shed all its old leaves before it recovers.

Might it be possible to retain both shrubs where they are, but to keep the garrya hard-pruned to a framework? Is there a fence behind, on which it could be trained? Garryas are lovely in winter with their long green tassels of flower, but the rest of the year they are a very drab evergreen. A supporting role at the back of a border is often the best way of using this shrub.

I grow the male-flowered variety 'James Roof', which is usually recommended for its length of catkin (14in is quoted, but 8in is nearer the mark). Last year I was given a (rarely seen) female bush, which has catkins only 3–4in long, but the tassels of maroon berries were an unexpected bonus and more than compensation for the shorter catkins. Larger gardens should plant them both.

Q Five years ago I planted a tiny broom (I am not sure which). It flowers beautifully every year, and is now 6ft tall. But it is

seriously top-heavy, and the lower branches are beginning to die off. Is this the normal habit, and should I prune it down in the autumn? – K.B., Herefordshire

A The common yellow broom, *Cytisus scoparius*, and its cultivars grow like rockets, and need to be planted small for later stability. But they (and indeed most brooms) hate heavy pruning at any time of year. They should either be regarded as a short-term shrub to be pulled out after 4–5 years and replaced with seedlings (or a cutting, if it is a named variety). Or you can prune them every year after flowering, cutting back the new growth by two thirds all over the bush. It looks like butchery for a few days, but very soon further growth softens the outline once again. In doing this you remove many of the seed pods and thereby strengthen the plant for better flowering next year. Never cut into a stem of more than pencil thickness if it can be avoided, since regrowth from larger wounds is uncommon.

It is probably too late to turn your broom into a shapely bush again. Have it out now, and plant another, taking a few cuttings first if you are fond of the variety.

Q How do I prune my rose 'New Dawn', which seems to be a rambler type but has a second blooming? – R.E.M., Kent

A 'New Dawn' is a climber not a rambler, and should be pruned in late winter, keeping strong growth in hand, and removing dead or diseased wood. True ramblers, with smaller flowers in clusters, should be pruned in the weeks after flowering, taking out old or diseased wood back to strong new shoots near ground level. A few ramblers are repeat flowering such as 'Albéric Barbier', and should be pruned in winter. Some are extremely vigorous, like 'Wedding Day', and hard pruning to keep them small reduces flowering. The old favourite 'Felicité et Perpétue' flowers best when left unpruned but it soon become a very unruly tangle. Its double, creamy flowers look good growing through *Acer negundo* 'Variegatum', a small, structurally hopeless tree but which offers daintily splashed yellow foliage. It is a marriage in which the rose wears the trousers.

Q I ordered a winter-flowering *Viburnum bodnantense* 'Dawn' in spring and planted it out on arrival, cutting away the elastic netting on the rootball but keeping it otherwise intact. (There were no instructions about this.) By last week it was flourishing, with strong, healthy red-tinted leaves. Unfortunately an overnight rainstorm caused the leaves to collapse and hang down like seaweed. I have given it temporary cloche protection from further heavy rain, but after three days see no improvement. Will it recover, and when is normal leaf drop? – K.J., Herefordshire

A First, you were quite right to cut open the elastic net over the roots, and to spread out the roots on planting. The net is only there to keep roots moist and in close contact with the soil during transit. Net or hessian are both better cut away from the neck of the plant after it is placed in its hole. The net can simply be spread sideways in the bottom of the hole. There is no need to remove it from underneath the plant, as the disturbance could undo all the good it did during transit.

Viburnum bodnantense, like *V. farreri*, has quite orangy foliage in spring until it is fully expanded. It is leafless in winter. If the foliage is actually red, this may be a symptom of being overdosed with fertiliser at planting. Heavy rain may knock about new shoots, but not beyond recovery in a day or so. On the other hand, a heavy overdose of fertiliser may cause a plant to wilt very quickly, by creating a salt imbalance in the roots, allowing water to pass out through the cell membranes instead of only coming inwards. This is why house plants kept dry with restricted root systems should not be suddenly given heavy feeds; some will wilt within hours and some will die. I suspect your plant has taken a deep storm-induced drink of strong fertiliser. I would carefully replant it in unimproved soil, and wait.

Another possibility is that the plant was already in growth before transit, and spent too long in the post, causing weak, spindly, rain-vulnerable shoots, not strong enough to pull themselves up again. If so, time will put it right and the newer shoots grow upright.

Q I have had a bush of *Chimonanthus fragrans* for 20 years, with hardly a flower. Last year in desperation I cut half the bush hard back, and after that the old wood produced masses of flowers. What is going on? – D.P., Warwickshire

A Winter sweet is one of the most deliciously scented shrubs in the garden, although the flowers themselves are not showy and come on leafless winter twigs. New plants take a few years for the growth to slow down and the production of flowering wood to begin. The flower buds are produced in the heat of the preceding summer, and poor summers or cold climates lead to few or sometimes no flowers the following winter.

Pruning is best kept to a minimum, though who could (or should) resist cutting some sprigs for the house? Older branches may be cut out if they become weak, and new shoots from below allowed to fill the gap. Harder pruning is required only on wall-trained specimens.

Twenty years of little flowering suggests a hotter, sunnier, more sheltered position is required. It may be that your plant flowered not because you pruned it, but because something else altered nearby to give it more light and sun?

Sun and soil for rhododendrons

Q Three years ago I moved to a house with three rhododendrons and an azalea in the garden. They are taking it in turns not to flower, or to flower poorly. Could the soil be too acidic? Do they need lime? – J.W., Warwickshire

A It is a rare garden soil indeed that would be too acidic for rhododendrons, and I would never go near them with lime. Check first that they are receiving enough light. Dappled or midday-only shade is fine, but for azaleas and most hybrid rhododendrons full sun is better than too little light.

Rhododendrons can develop a biennial flowering habit following a year of very heavy flowering. They feel they have earned a rest after all that breeding. Dead-heading after flowering will help, if the plants are small enough for this to be practical. But the degree of flowering is partly governed by the weather. In a year following a drought, rhododendrons will often concentrate on making only leaf growth for a year to build up their strength again, and will flower little the following season.

Poor root growth often leads to poor growth and flowering. Rhododendrons are remarkably stubborn about dying and will often hang on miserably for years. It may be your plants are just being long-suffering about an unsuitably heavy soil. They need an open, peat-like, woodland soil, and will never do any good in lime or clay. So if they are not too large, dig them up (they should have a wide, fibrous root system like a large Alka Seltzer), improve the soil with coarse compost, leaf mould, peat, even grit, and replant. If the soil is limy, then you would do better to settle for growing something else altogether.

Be sure they are not planted too deep. They hate that, especially on heavier soils. It is the perfect recipe for an inexplicable, lingering death. They say that in parts of Scotland, where it is nearly as wet on land as at sea, that you do not so much plant rhododendrons as drop them down where you want them to grow!

Q I have a plant of the cork-screw hazel, *Corylus avellana* 'Contorta', growing very well in a large container. It is three years old, but last year it threw a very strong, straight stem from the base. Should I cut it off, and will that get rid of it permanently? – S.L., Nottinghamshire

A The other nick-name of this plant is 'Harry Lauder's walking stick', on account of the way the stems twist in spirals. It is caused by an irregularity in growth rate, which makes one side develop faster than the other, forcing the shoot to curve.

It is usually propagated by grafting, and your shoot from the base will be a sucker of ordinary hazel. It needs to be removed or it will overwhelm the existing plant. Rather than cut it off leaving a small stump to regrow, pull the sucker away from the stem as you would a rose sucker. This ought to solve the problem; but once a plant has started to sucker, it often recurs. The important thing is to take suckers off while they are small, and not to let them draw strength from the grafted plant. Rub them off with a thumb while they are still soft. The same problem occurs on plants of *Viburnum juddii* and *V.* x *carlcephalum*, which are grafted onto *V. lantana*: rub off suckers while they are small.

Apart from that, your corkscrew hazel should need little pruning. The willow *Salix babylonica pekinensis* 'Tortuosa' also corkscrews, – presumably in an attempt to flee the botanists who changed its simple name *Salix matsudana* 'Tortuosa' to the present correct mouthful. This plant, like all willows, is easy to strike from cuttings, and can be hard pruned without fear of suckering. It tends to be rather a congested shrub or small tree, showing off its corkscrews less well than the hazel. Abbey Dore Court garden, in Herefordshire, has a good specimen in its car-park; it has been heavily thinned out to produce a fascinating 'giant bonsai' of twisting, elegant stems. Perhaps it deserves this treatment more often.

Q A myrtle bush purchased three years ago has been tended, fed and cosseted, but as yet has produced no flowers. Do you think it is a hopeless case? – G.S., Merseyside

A Far from it. The common European myrtle, *Myrtus communis*, comes from the hot countries of the Mediterranean. While it will survive outdoors close to the sea around much of the coast of Britain because temperatures are mollified by the sea, even so it prefers some good summer heat. In Merseyside I would not expect great results every year since the average temperature and hours of sunshine will be rather low for it. I hope you have it against a south, sheltered wall. Now it is established I would let it grow as hot and mean as Merseyside can offer. It may be that you are over-cosseting it, and producing nothing but soft, non-flowering wood.

Q Five years ago I planted a pair of lilac trees in my garden, but one has died and another is dying gradually, I suspect from waterlogging of the soil in winter. We are on London clay, to make matters worse. Near neighbours succeed with lilacs. I would dearly love to make them grow here too. – W.F., London NW3

A Lilacs are tough as old boots. I have seen them layer themselves into a shady wall top, and grow there after the rest of the bush had been cut down. Equally, lilacs are happy on heavy clay soil, and do better there than on lean sandy soils. But waterlogging will kill them, as it will most woody plants. It does sound as if the roots are being killed by spending the winter up to the neck in water. Dead roots can also be a way in for fungal diseases during the drier part of the year.

There is no future in transplanting your lilac now. But if it is looking any better by autumn, replant it; if not, buy afresh. Plant the new lilacs on a wide, 9in high mound of soil, grit and garden compost, where the crown of the bush (the point at which root meets trunk) is lifted out of the winter wet. This helps most shrubs on permanently wet soils.

Lilacs, for all their ravishing perfume, barely deserve this cosseting; they should be so easy. Perhaps some serious drainage of the waterlogged area is called for.

Q I bought a witch hazel (*Hamamelis*) from my local garden centre 10 years ago and planted it in plenty of light. But it refuses to grow any taller than 4ft, and I understand that normally this shrub will grow to 8–10 ft. Can you explain this lack of growth? I mulch it with compost occasionally and give it Sequestrene. It looks healthy and flowers every year – exceptionally well this year. – C.A.S., Norfolk

A I can understand your frustration; it is wonderful to be able to cut a few twigs of witch hazel to bring indoors for its perfume. Most witch hazels are produced commercially by grafting, which means that the top of the plant you buy is from an older, flowering specimen, and therefore your plant will be flowering in the nursery when you buy it and inclined to continue after you plant it. This is why they are expensive. But this also means the plant does not have the vigour a seedling would have for concentrating on making plenty of wood before settling down to flower. Witch hazels are known in gardens for their rather horizontal habit, with long drooping side branches from a short trunk. But in the first few years it is better if they put their energies into growing rather than flowering. So a newly planted witch hazel should be fed hard, and really kept moving, not letting it settle down to family life until it has put some enthusiastic growth into some (reasonably) upright stems. Thereafter it can concentrate on flowering.

If the graft itself is not fully successful, the plant can linger on for years, hardly growing and flowering in desperation, until perhaps one day the union snaps.

Witch hazels dislike badly drained heavy soils, and are better on a free-draining neutral to acid soil. If yours has really grown so little, I would dig it up, make a really big hole for it, enriched with old compost, and replant it on a slight mound.

Remember, too, that witch hazels are long lived and relatively slow growing. A 10ft specimen can be anywhere between 20 and 50 years old. Equally, this almost total lack of growth is not uncommon and need not be tolerated.

Q I am looking for a conifer which will not grow taller than 3ft at maturity, and which will be slender rather than squat. Does such a thing exist? – A.F., Hertfordshire

A What is maturity? Ten years? Fifty? How many years have you got? Dwarf conifers have a nasty habit, as you suggest, of becoming great shed-sized blobs after 50 years or more. To find a really slow grower, it is best to look at the yellow cultivars which are naturally weaker through having less chlorophyll. You might try *Thuja orientalis* 'Aurea Nana', which is narrowly pyramidal, and gets to about 3ft in ten years. The same speed might be found in the form of golden upright yew, *Taxus baccata* 'Standishii', and this at least, if it grows too fast or large, can be clipped. It is parallel-sided rather than pyramidal. You can of course keep a conifer miniaturised by 'bonsai' means, nipping its foliage and pruning its roots every year; but what effort!

Q Our problem plant is Adam's needle, *Yucca gloriosa*, which blooms too late in the year, at Christmas. Can you suggest a

way of curing this? It is otherwise a very healthy plant. –
J.N., Lincolnshire

A With leaves as sharp as a yucca's around, Adam would soon
know if he were naked or not, never mind which tree
produced the groceries. Who can blame him for wanting to stitch
himself up a loincloth? And yuccas are fabulous in bloom. But that
6ft white candle is always late. In a cold garden it pays to plant it
against a south wall to speed nature along, or to plant the smaller
but earlier *Yucca filmentosa*.

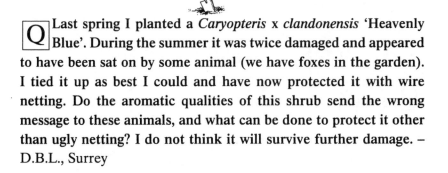

Yucca Salad

B.F.T. has written from Spain to inform me that the fleshy white
petals of *Yucca gloriosa*, which grows so widely in Spain, are edible.
'As far as I know, they are not eaten in Spain. I was introduced to
this delicacy a couple of years ago in Costa Rica, where their
market value is quite high. My husband and I enjoy the petals in
salads, but they can also be lightly cooked and served in a white
sauce.' No mention of taste; I must experiment next year.

Q Last spring I planted a *Caryopteris* x *clandonensis* 'Heavenly
Blue'. During the summer it was twice damaged and appeared
to have been sat on by some animal (we have foxes in the garden).
I tied it up as best I could and have now protected it with wire
netting. Do the aromatic qualities of this shrub send the wrong
message to these animals, and what can be done to protect it other
than ugly netting? I do not think it will survive further damage. –
D.B.L., Surrey

A Caryopteris produces its blue flowers on the end of the
current season's growth in late summer, so you need to prune
down your plant to 3in in March anyway. This will strengthen it and

produce vigorous new shoots. Damage to last year's growth does not matter. I am not aware of regular animal damage to this shrub; try pushing in sharp pea sticks over and around it for the early part of the season, to deter them. No animal likes one in the eye or anywhere else. In a year or two the bush should be strong enough to recover from such mishaps on its own.

Q I have a three-year-old ceanothus growing vigorously on an east wall, but it has failed to bloom. What is wrong? – G.W., Yorkshire

A Ceanothus need all the sun they can get. Californian lilac is the common name, and in their natural habitat they enjoy Californian heat. In the south you might just get away with ceanothus on an east wall, but in the north of England a south wall is more certain. Ceanothus do not enjoy disturbance, so either take cuttings this summer to be planted elsewhere, or move your plant in March, carefully, with a big rootball of soil attached. A south wall also helps give winter protection to ceanothus, and May flowering species like the rich blue *C. impressus* gain protection from late frosts on a wall.

Q Would you please suggest suitable growing conditions for a recently purchased *Stranvaesia davidiana* 'Palette'. I am told it will not tolerate lime and is difficult to grow. My soil is good but limy. I do want to see those pinky cream variegated leaves and spring white flowers – exquisite. – Anon, Avon

A The evergreen *Stranvaesia davidiana*, (or *Photinia davidiana* as it is now more correctly called) is not difficult to grow, and it will tolerate lime, as you might expect from a member of the rose family. Its greatest attractions are its red berries right through the winter, and the way its leaves turn red before they fall. To ensure good variegation in the form 'Palette' it would be sensible to give it plenty of light, but perhaps not a full blasting south-facing position, to avoid the chance of scorching. Once established this is a vigorous shrub or small tree, if it does not always show that vigour and ease of cultivation in a pot. Be careful where you plant it: pretty leaves or not, the flowers stink in the manner of the nastiest of the sorbus species. Keep it well away from the house or terrace.

Dividing ruscus

Q Two years ago I transplanted some clumps of butcher's broom, *Ruscus aculeatus*, from the south of France. It has taken reasonably well with a moderate amount of new growth, but has not flowered. I now wish to transplant it to another part of the garden, preferably shady. What is the best way of doing this; can I break up the clumps, and when is the best time to do this? – T.L.C., Avon

A Butcher's broom is an oddity, a woody evergreen member of the lily family. The 2–3ft stems last for about three years and make thickets of spiny foliage. The 'leaves' are not in fact leaves, but cladodes, upon which flowers appear in the middle of the 'leaf'. Like most of the lily family it does not like careless disturbance. I find the best time to divide it is in spring. It can be divided into small pieces, but they take a lot longer to re-establish. It does need shade, and will survive in horrible, dry-rooty shade. Establishing it there is another matter. Decent soil in shade is far more rewarding. Once established it can be left indefinitely without disturbance, simply cutting out dead stems and feeding every few years to keep it strong. Female plants bear berries upon the 'leaf' and need a male plant to fertilise them. There is a hermaphroditic form which, unless you have lots of space, is the only one worth planting.

Q My soil is sandy and, despite adding plenty of compost and watering during drought, roses do not do well. My favourite rose is 'Sutter's Gold', a deep gold flushed with pink. I have this variety but have lost others. I would like to find a stockist so I can buy more of it. Can you help? – E.W.B., Fyfe

A 'Sutter's Gold' is an upright-growing hybrid tea rose, and this group does not do well on sand. You might have more success on sand with rugosa roses, or hybrid musks, or Scotch briar roses (varieties of *R. pimpinellifolia*). You can buy 'Sutter's Gold' from the big rose specialists such as David Austin or Peter Beales.

Q We have an elderly hebe about 7ft tall. It throws up suckers, and in the last year has colonised a flower bed of ours and one of a neighbour's. How do we stop it suckering? We will sacrifice the main shrub if necessary. – M.N., Yorkshire

A This, I see from your sample, is no hebe. Hebes do *not* sucker. This is *Spiraea douglasii*, which has pinkish plumes of flower – and suckers like mad. The flowers are quite hebe-ish, but are all upright. The leaves are deciduous, whereas most hebes are evergreen in our climate. You must either dig the lot out or restrict it, by regular digging around, to a limited area. You can cut the whole colony down every spring with a brushcutter if you wish. It will still flower. I would in any case cut down the main shrub after flowering, unless you particularly need height, as the young growth is more attractive than the old.

Q Three years ago I planted a *Leycesteria formosa*, brought back from Cornwall. It is now a lovely shrub about 5ft tall, but I would like to move it. When is the best time? – J.A.J., Yorkshire

A By all means move the shrub. Any time between November and March will do. Leycesteria makes stout hollow stems from ground level, sea green for the first year or two, each stem lasting only a few years. If it is too gangly and unmanageable you could cut down your plant entirely to move it. It will spring back up to 3–5ft next year, with clean new stems. Some people like to cut the plant down every year in spring, like a red-stemmed dogwood, for the quality of the stems, and so the plant carries less dead wood. Alternatively, you could save some berries and grow some new plants. You will probably find seedlings in the garden anyway, now you have the plant established. The drooping clusters of red-bracted flowers make purplish black berries which pheasants are supposed to like. I cannot think why; they smell quite disgusting when crushed.

Q My *Hydrangea sargentiana* is now no bigger than when it was planted four years go. It is in part sun/part shade. The leaves on its 15in stem are small. Should I move it? – S.C.L., Cambridgeshire

A The aspect is right. And this is a very hardy hydrangea, although new growths are sometimes caught by late frosts. Are you growing it in clay, or, worse still, heavily alkaline clay? I would certainly dig it up as soon as the leaves drop and replant it in new open-textured soil well enriched with old compost. Next year you should start to get those enormous hairy leaves, and some proper growth. Look out for rotten, stinking roots which may be due to nematodes (microscopic worms) having eaten into the roots. Such plants are better burnt and replacements planted elsewhere, or the soil changed.

Q I have a variegated dogwood, *Cornus alba* 'Elegantissima', in a hot, dry place, so I let the hose run on it twice a week. This year it flowered hard, and I have cut out much of the flowered wood. I am afraid I have spoiled it. What should I do? I don't mind being drastic. Have I leached the soil with so much watering? – A.S., Suffolk

A The value of this dogwood lies in its white variegated leaves and red winter stems. The flowers are not much to look at, and are lost against such striking foliage. Rest assured, you have not spoiled it; it is an immensely tough plant. But it is also hungry, and it does like a soil which is both moist and cool. So in spring cut it all right down to 2–3in. Plaster it around with a thick mulch of rich compost or manure. You could even give it artificial fertiliser as well if it is slow to respond. By next autumn it should have made a thicket of 3–4ft high red stems, which you can cut right down again the following spring. This is a hard life for any plant, having its top cut off all the time. Like a lawn, you must feed it regularly to keep it strong. Poor, dry soils simply cannot provide all the plant needs.

Colour reversion

Q Having reduced by two-thirds a very robust *Lavatera* 'Barnsley', I read with horror that they revert to the common pink when pruned severely. Is this always the case? I had planned to move it this winter, and wonder if it is now worth doing?

A Lavateras are the most generous of flowering shrubs, but they must be pruned or they get straggly and shabby. With or without pruning they are not long lived shrubs, and 5–6 years is a long life for a lavatera. Snow, or cold, or a wet winter usually finish them off. The common *Lavatera olbia* is insistently purplish pink, and 'Barnsley' (now thought to be a hybrid) was one of the first of the many softer coloured variations now for sale. Yes, it does tend to revert, with or without heavy pruning, although the problem is sometimes more common after heavy pruning. So wait and see, and take some cuttings next summer of a true branch, to keep you going. As a general rule, it is better to leave the hard pruning of sappy, short-lived shrubs until later in the spring, apart from a little reduction to stop wind rock.

Q Where can I find the rose 'Madame Speaker'? Our local garden centre has not heard of it. Another said sales were restricted as it is a new rose. – C.E., Hertfordshire

A There are two main avenues of enquiry if anyone is having trouble finding a rose variety. One is The Royal National Rose Society at Chiswell Green Lane, St.Albans, Herts AL2 3NR; tel. 01727 850461. The other is a booklet called *Find That Rose*, produced annually by the British Rose Growers Association. It is available from the RNRS at St Albans for £2.50 including p&p.

Q I have a 4ft oleander growing outside here in Jersey. It is 10 years old, but does not open many flowers. It gets sun from morning until noon. Should I move it to a sunnier border, or leave it and take cuttings? If so, how and when? – J.M., Jersey

A You are correct to look for a sunnier position. Oleanders need all the heat and sun they can get. If you wish to move it, do so in late February or early March, with a big rootball of soil attached. Cuttings are made in June or July, under plastic, from 3–4in half-ripe shoots, inserted in a shady corner.

Q I planted a stag's horn sumach in a corner of my garden for autumn colour, but since it suckered badly and did not colour particularly well I had it cut down. My neighbour now has a line of its suckers making trees under his side of the fence, and more suckers keep creeping back to me. My neighbour is happy to have his sumach trees, but how do I deal with the suckers on my side? – M.D., Kent

A *Rhus typhina* will sometimes but not always produce excellent fiery autumn colour. The female is said to be better than the male for colour. It makes a small tree or large shrub, and usually meets its end by getting too large for its shallow roots and falling over. It suckers – and how! The more you damage its roots by gardening under it, the more suckers are produced from the damaged roots. Either cut down the suckers in your garden and treat the fresh stumps with Root Out, or try to cut back and remove the invading root as far as the fence. I doubt very much if Root Out, applied to suckers here, would be powerful enough to damage the neighbour's young trees. It would be interesting to know what case law says about damage to and ownership of a plant coming from your neighbour's garden, but which began life in yours.

Q My flourishing 10-year-old castor oil plant, *Fatsia japonica*, has splendidly transformed a dark, depressing corner where nothing would grow. Every November it is covered in white flowers, but never gets the black berries such as I see in other gardens. Why is this? – G.S., Surrey

A Fatsia is so good grown out of doors in a shady, sheltered place, it makes you wonder why ever we use it as a house plant. There are so few evergreens with broad foliage which are hardy outdoors in Britain, and this is an important one. Like its cousin, ivy, it is a late-flowering plant – so late in fact that in some situations the flowers never open. And when they do there are only groggy old bluebottles left around to pollinate. The flowers are bisexual and so two plants of opposite sexes are not required. In the warmth of central London fatsia does particularly well. I suspect your plant is in just too chilly a spot to open properly and be fertilised. Can you contrive to give a little more sun to its head, while leaving the main part of the bush in shade? Are you sure that birds or other creatures are not taking the fruit?

Q Three years ago I planted out a container-grown witch hazel, *Hamamelis mollis*, when it was a healthy, large-leaved shrub 4ft high. Since then it has gradually ceased to flower. The leaves are now small, and growth is negligible. What can I do to save it? – M.F., West Midlands

A A good witch hazel is invaluable for its sweet-scented, spidery winter flowers. To succeed it needs a soil which is neutral or acidic, but not limy. It also needs an open-textured soil, and hates heavy clay soils. In limy clay soils it does just as you say, almost shrinking rather than growing. If you are on limy soil, re-containerise it and dose it with Sequestrene. If your soil is simply too heavy, replant it in a well-prepared new hole, with lots of grit and old compost.

Q I have two six-year-old *Daphne bholua* 'Jaqueline Postill' bushes, one in front of the cottage in a bed with little competition, and another in front of a tall eucryphia tree. Both plants have reached 6–7ft. The one at the house is always smothered in flowers, starting from Christmas, but the other is now almost barren. Would it stand moving to somewhere with less competition? – F.A.B., Devon

A *Daphne bholua* is an erect shrub, with powerfully perfumed flowers making up for a gawky habit. It is largely deciduous, but the seedling of the form 'Gurkha' named 'Jaqueline Postill' is evergreen. It likes a rich moist soil, with plenty of humus in it, just the sort of thing which your eucryphia will have filled with its fibrous roots, for it shares similar tastes. Neither party would enjoy having its roots separated, the daphne especially since the genus as a whole resents disturbance. Better to collect seed (a fleshy berry) and grow some new plants. Sow it fresh, and rub off the fleshy coat first. They can take some time to germinate.

Tender sages

Q My variegated sage seems to have been killed back to the roots by winter cold. Is it likely to sprout again? – H.J., Tayside

A The more variegated the sage, the less tough it is. The pink and yellow form 'Icterina' I find quite tender. Yours may well have been killed outright. Sage bushes of any colour (there are many named varieties), once badly damaged by cold, are better replaced by cuttings taken from regrowth the following year. Be patient with your variegated sage. If you can coax just one shoot from it before it gives up the ghost, it is so easy from cuttings that you should manage to root it.

Q I am moving to Cornwall and looking forward to being able to try growing the more tender plants I have seen on holidays abroad. However, none of my gardening books seem to cover tender shrubs properly. Can you recommend a book on tender plants, or do I have to glean bits and pieces from more general books? – H.F., Lancashire

A Get hold of a copy of *The Milder Garden* by Jane Taylor (Dent 1990). You will find it concentrates on the tender things we cannot grow without going again through all the tougher ones we can. You might also look at *Plants for Dry Gardens* by the same author (Frances Lincoln 1993). Cornwall may not be dry, but Jane Taylor has gardened in the West Country and is an enthusiastic plantswoman.

Q In March I cut down and transplanted a large purple hazel, *Corylus maxima* 'Purpurea'. The prunings were put in a vase and opened green, while the new shoots on the bush opened purple as usual. Why did the prunings change colour? – N.C., Oxfordshire

A Think of the the purple pigment found in some plants as self-protection against the sun, like dark skins in humans. The plant responds to sunlight by producing these purple pigments. Look at the lowest shaded branches of a purple plum or purple elder, or the leaves at the centre of the tree's canopy, and you will see they are greener than those in the full light. Your indoor shoots had insufficient sun to produce the pigmentation. If you want good colour from such plants, they require a position in full sun.

Q Can you please recommend some perfumed rhododendrons? There are many rhododendrons in my new garden, but none that has any perfume. – A.L., Tayside

A Grow *Rhododendron fortunei* if you have a sheltered spot. It will take your breath away in May. It is the parent of the Loderi hybrids such as 'King George' and 'Venus', which share its powerful perfume. At the end of the rhododendron season in July and August there is *Rhododendron serotinum, R. auriculatum,* and its offspring 'Polar Bear', with huge white trumpets. Don't forget the deciduous rhododendrons (azaleas) such as the common yellow *Rhododendron luteum,* and the Occidentale hybrids. You could do no better than to visit Glendoick Gardens, the rhododendron specialist near you at Glencarse, and see what they have to offer. Most garden centres do not stock the perfumed rhododendrons.

Q I have a weeping 'Kilmarnock' willow on a 28in stem in a mixed border. How do I maintain its attractive umbrella effect, have plenty of 'pussies', and not have branches reaching the ground? – G.H.P., Hampshire

A This form of *Salix caprea* is grown for its stiff, weeping habit, and must be grafted on to a stem of the ordinary, upright *Salix caprea* if it is to have any height at all. It is a male clone and has golden pussy willow catkins. (The silver-catkined forms are known as Weeping Sally.)

To keep it well-flowered and healthy requires regular cutting, to maintain a regular fresh fountain of weeping stems. This is done by thinning the canopy and shortening back some growths to the top so that they weep again. The flowers are produced best on the branches which receieve the most light, so it is important not to to take off all the outer branches in the thinnning process, even though you may wish to keep the plant small. The longer branches may be shortened back in autumn so that they do not sweep the ground.

This is a curiously formal plant, and not everyone's favourite. It is widely available as a waist-high standard, but it might be interesting to use it on a 6 or 7ft stem even more formally, as curtains to a pergola or weeping over the top of a wall. Curiosities like this (or monsters, if you prefer) cry out to be used for all they are worth.

Moving evergreens

Q **The leaves on my bay tree have become scorched during the cold winds of spring. Will it recover? If so, when could I move it to a more sheltered spot? – A.D., Manchester**

A The time to move evergreens is just before the season begins or just before it ends, in March or September. At this time, plants have just enough time to re-establish roots before new growth starts or winter cold slows root growth sufficiently to stop re-establishment. The time not to move evergreens is during summer growth or real winter dormancy. The extremes of transpiration in both cases damage the plant before new roots have established to supply water again. If your bay is only scorched at the edges, it should recover. However, if it is badly damaged by the cold, it may be better to leave it to recover undisturbed, and to move it in the autumn, when it has had a chance to show willing. Move it with as large a rootball of soil as you can manage. Evergreens dislike being moved bare-rooted.

Q **My husband and I have made a heather and conifer garden, in which we have collected a number of conifers which change colour in winter. We bought them in winter colour, so we know they are capable of turning from green to yellow or red, depending on variety. However they are failing to colour properly in our garden, staying totally green or with only a tinge of colour, despite growing**

healthily. *Juniperus communis* 'Depressa Aurea' and *Thuja orientalis* 'Southport' are especially disappointing. Can you shed any light on the problem? – J.E.L., Lincolnshire

A The winter bronzing of some conifers can come as a shock to people who buy them in their summer green. In most cases it is an attractive addition, once you are used to the idea. Colouring does not depend on the soil but rather on light and temperature. Mild winters produce poorer results, and shade adds to the problem. Perhaps this winter you will be luckier. Colour is often enhanced at the time of purchase because, when a plant is in a pot or container, its roots as well as top are more susceptible to the cold.

Q Recently builders damaged my camellia which grows in an angle of the house, breaking branches, and plastering it in cement dust and wet mortar. I removed as much mortar as possible and hosed clean the foliage. Will it survive the lime and can I prune it back to shape, or should I start again? – P.M.S., Surrey

A Established camellias will survive a good deal of physical damage, and shoot out to make an attractive bush again, so no problem there. You did right to pick off the mortar and to hose off the cement dust which is caustic as well as alkaline. I hope you did it quickly and thoroughly. Unless the roots were thick with cement dust, you should have no problem with lime at the roots. To be sure, scrape off half an inch of topsoil (above the roots only) and replace it. If you see any yellowing of the leaves this time next year, dose the plant with chelated iron (Sequestrene). Press for some financial reparation from the builder. What would you pay for a mature camellia in a tub? £70–£200?

5

Hedges

Q I have a 3ft tall yew hedge some 60 years old. One side of it is dying, I suspect because it is close to a building and is deprived of sun. I think it is too late to change the cut and propose to cut it down and start again from the bottom. The trunks are thick and healthy, but I am not sure exactly how low to cut them, or when. I shall feed with dried blood and compost unless you can think of anything better. – C.R., Suffolk

A I would be reluctant to cut down strong healthy trunks of that age. There is no real need to go so far. Instead, cut off all the back of the hedge, right to the top, to leave bare vertical trunks only on that side. The cutting will be invisible from the front, but it will let enough light in to regenerate a new back. Your feeding recipe is ideal, except that you should also water copiously. Could it be that drought, in the rain shadow of a wall, is a major part of the hedge's problem?

Q I have a large yew hedge. Would you please tell me if the clippings can be used in a medicinal way and whom to approach about collecting them? – E.W., Dorset

A Yew clippings can indeed be used in cancer research. There are several companies in the business of collecting now. The remarkable thing is that there is even a small payment for the clippings, based on weight. They are interested in relatively small amounts, despite the logistics of collecting them from you. A couple of large bin liners full is worth their while. It pays to get in touch first with whichever firm you intend to sell to, as there are certain things you need to know in advance, not least their price per kilogram. Clippings must be kept cool before collection. Small amounts can be spread out in a shady place, but large heaps will heat up quickly like compost, and some firms supply their own special sacks before you cut, complete with a fan to push air into the centre of the sack. Clipping and collection are best co-ordinated to follow each other as quickly as possible. Some firms offer different prices according to the quality of the clippings, ranging from clean, feathery clippings to twiggier stuff with a small amount of grass or soil in it. Most are not interested in clippings any woodier than pencil thickness, which unfortunately means that major prunings of yew are not usable, unless you cut off the the twiggy pieces first. At 50p per kilogram for large quantities, maybe some country estates should think about putting down a few acres to yew; but how long will it be before the chemical extracted can be made synthetically? Certainly anyone with large existing volumes of yew to clip should see they are put to good use, if only to offset the cost of clipping.

For collection, try contacting the following: Friendship Estates, Old House Farm, Stubbs Walden, Doncaster DN6 9BU; tel. 01302 700220. Limehurst Ltd, PO Box 118, Chichester, W.Sussex PO20 6ZA; tel. 01243 545455. Yew Clippings Ltd, Milton Mill, West Milton, Bridport, Dorset DT6 3SN; tel. 01308 485693

Repairing beech hedges

Q Two beech hedges in our garden have been uncut for 20 years and have become trees. How can I turn them back into hedges without damaging or killing them? – L.D., Gwynedd

A Neglected beech hedges do not reshape as successfully as yew, but it is possible. Damage, in the form of large wounds, is inevitable, but it should not be fatal unless you want a short 6ft hedge. In winter, cut out the tops to 18in below the desired height, and cut back side branches on the sunnier side only so far as will leave some twigs left to sprout. Cut back the other side 1–2 years later. If there are no low side branches left, then cutting to a clear trunk is unlikely to produce new ones, and you should settle for trees rather than a hedge. Beech will not spring up again if cut to the ground.

Q Six years ago I planted a beech hedge 120ft long. A few of the plants have almost refused to grow, while the rest have grown well. As the problem plants are scattered I do not think this is a soil problem. Should I replace the stunted plants, or cut them back in the hope they reform their ways? – K.M., County Durham

A Life in a hedge is very competitive, and it sometimes happens that the odd plant gets left behind in the race and becomes a runt. This is why good initial preparation and manuring of the trench is important. Beech aphids can also debilitate young trees to the point where some become runts. I would watch for fly and leave well alone. If you planted at 18in centres, you could after six years quite happily lose the odd plant and never notice. The adjoining plants will merge to cover the gap. (This happens in old hedges all the time.) Feed and water your runts, and make sure they are aphid-free. If they do not make it, pull them out.

Q We have a 7ft high green privet hedge, essential as the boundary between the garden and a public footpath. The soil is light and free draining, and the hedge is regularly mulched and composted. We cut it three times a year, but it is becoming bare at the base. Can you recommend any way to stimulate bottom growth please? – J.G.E., Clwyd

A All hedges have a tendency to become bare at the base, and the faster growing the subject, the greater the problem. It is always worse on the shadier side. One option would be to cut the hedge right down and regrow it, making sure it is well-furnished low down before you let it push too far vertically. In your case, privacy will not allow that. But you could plant other things into the bottom of the hedge to thicken it. For all your feeding and mulching it will be an impoverished site amongst those privet roots, and I would choose something very tough and evergreen, like Oregon grape (*Mahonia aquifolium*). It has holly-like leaves, yellow flowers and grape-blue berries in late summer, and can be easily kept in line with a pair of secateurs. It is often at its happiest in a hedge bottom.

All hedges stay thicker at the base if the sides of the hedge slope inwards to the top of the hedge, because this allows the light to reach the lower branches. Vertical-sided hedges will stay fully clothed (just), but hedges which are fatter at the top than the bottom will always become bald in time.

Q We have a deep, south-facing flower border which is backed by a privet hedge. The privet roots make the soil in the back of the border particularly dry. Is there anything which can be done to reduce the roots, and will cutting them damage the hedge? – P.T., Devon

A Borders in front of hedges always suffer from the competition for light and nutrition. If the border is deep enough, it pays to have an unplanted space at the back, in which the hedge can have surface roots and where you can tread to clip it. Which is the more valuable to you – hedge or border? I would be prepared to chop at the privet roots (it's tough enough) and plant into the back of the border, adding lots of compost to the soil as you replant, and expecting to have to repeat the operation every couple of years – the privet roots will come running for the compost like sharks for a pound of offal. When placing a hedge near ornamental plantings, it pays to line the trench with corrugated iron or some similar material, which will rot away over the years, but which in the interim will force the main feeder roots downwards.

Q We have several clumps of bamboo which have spread over a lawn and into a privet hedge. With great labour we have dug up the lawn, removed the runners, and applied glyphosate to the leaves of the bamboo in the hedge, but all to no avail. We do not wish to dig up the hedge. What do you advise? – K.C.B., West Glamorgan

A Why not consider developing a bamboo screen rather than a privet hedge? There would be no clipping to do, and bamboos can make just as dense a boundary. Cut away the privet over the next few years to give the bamboo the upper hand, if it appears to require assistance. And feed it well.

If you want to retain the privet, cut down all the bamboo stems to weaken it, and then when regrowth occurs do not wait for it to be tall enough to have sprayable leaves, but cut the tops off the shoots at a few inches (and eat them if you fancy it). Then into each hollow stem pour a little of the diluted chemical for maximum results. Give it no quarter for a year of two, if you expect to win.

Q I have a *Lonicera nitida* hedge in good condition which has been invaded by a fast growing ivy. Will the ivy just make a denser hedge (which I would welcome), or will it eventually strangle the honeysuckle and cause it to die off? – G.H., Berkshire

A Left to its own devices, ivy will eventually eat any hedge for breakfast. In the short term you may have a thicker hedge, and the contrast between the large palmate ivy leaves and the tiny rounded leaves of the honeysuckle will be attractive. But you are inviting a conflict in which you will have to keep the peace for ever. Either settle for a mixed hedge in which you must perpetually be keeping the ivy within certain bounds, or get the ivy out now while it is easy. Once it has become established in a hedge – on the trunks and on the ground underneath – it will be an almost impossible task to clear it off permanently.

Fast growers

Q I recently planted four Leyland cypresses (x *Cupressocyparis leylandii*), in the golden form 'Castlewellan', to form a hedge in my front garden. Ideally I want a hedge of about 6ft. Since planting, the press has been full of horror stories about these cypresses growing to 60ft and above. How tall can I expect my 'Castlewellans' to grow, and what is the best way of maintaining them at the desired height? Should I abandon them and plant afresh? – S.S., Surrey

A Leyland cypresses are very useful if rather graceless plants. They do grow like rockets and they can indeed make huge trees. Luckily they do not seed, or we should be smothered in them and shouting 'Bring back the sycamore!' Often, however, their root system is insufficient to support such rampant top growth, and they are inclined to blow over in exposed positions.

For hedging purposes their great merit is that they are fast. Plant them a yard apart and you can have a reasonably dense, 6ft hedge in three years. The rub is that to keep such a vigorous tree to only 6ft requires a lot of clipping. Three times a year is not too often. If you clip less (and you could clip just once a year) then you will have an extremely woolly-looking hedge for most of the season. More importantly you would be cutting into older wood, leaving some stumps half an inch across or more. The result is a hedge with a face of poor density, and which before too many years have elapsed will look very woody and chopped.

If speed is paramount, then keep your leylandii hedge, and expect to replace it in under 10 years. If a dense hedge and easy, long-term maintenance are more important, then replace the leylandii this winter with yew, planted 2ft apart. Initially they will cost much more (perhaps £3–£5 each) but the result will be infinitely superior. Contrary to popular wisdom, yew is not especially slow. In good rich soil and full light it will put on a foot a year, which is plenty for a 6ft hedge.

Q Please could you recommend a hedge that is not toxic to horses and is not eaten by them? – R.E.E., Hampshire

A Horses will eat anything, good or bad for them. The only way to establish a hedge where there are horses is to fence it off. You must either fence tall (which is expensive in materials) or fence well away from the young plants (which is expensive of space, and begs the question of how you keep the grass down amongst the trees). Horses can and will reach 5–6ft over a fence to reach the shoots of young trees. Of old, established hedges stock-proof against horses, perhaps the best is a mixture of thorn, holly, and field maple, none of which is toxic. They will graze it back to the woodier growth, and make a mess of it, but it will survive. Thick, tall hedges survive best, where the animals cannot reach across the top.

Spiny Hedge Clippings

H.M.F. writes from Dyfed to say that he shares my liking for plastic-bodied Fort wheelbarrows. 'The best barrow I have ever used', to be precise. However, after two punctures in one week, "I had the tyre replaced by a heavy-duty trailer tyre at the local ATS depot." Not a bad idea if you have a garden full of thorn and berberis hedges, whose clippings spell disaster for wheelbarrow tyres unless you are ridiculously tidy with the clippings.

Q Could you please suggest first aid for my ageing escallonia hedge? It has withstood years of sea-side gales but this year was attacked by a neighbouring farmer's bullocks, which had developed a craving for escallonia. A new wire fence has been erected, but the hedge has gaps and broken branches. – G.McC., Devon

A Escallonia will regenerate perfectly well from drastic pruning. I would cut the whole of your hedge down to a few inches, and give it a dressing of artificial fertiliser (Growmore will do), topped off with a mulch of old compost to keep it moist. Or if you think the hedge is particularly old and starved, use a higher nitrogen fertiliser such as fish, blood and bone meal, or dried blood. If the summer is dry, try to keep it watered to ensure you get a fast response. When you take the hedge down, you may find the odd lower branch which has layered itself down and rooted. These might be transplanted into the gaps if the cattle have actually killed any plants outright. It is more likely that all the old plants will regenerate, and the ones the cattle cut back first will probably shoot first, having been encouraged the sooner. It is no bad idea to cut back periodically flowering hedges such as escallonia, to keep them flowering more generously, so perhaps in the long run the cattle may have done you a favour. Did they manage to put any manure on for you?

Q Would a hedge of the evergreen holm oak, *Quercus ilex*, thrive as a windbreak on a hill in north-west England overlooking the Irish Sea? If not, what are the alternatives? – A.H., Yorkshire

A It would survive, but it might not look particularly glamorous. It can be very shabby in the north. Holly would provide the best alternative and be hardier. Both are slow to establish, and there would be nothing to choose for speed. If you want to avoid having to prune a prickly hedge, you could use a smooth-leaved holly such as 'J.C. Van Tol'.

Q I would like to plant a camellia hedge. How far apart should I plant, and will any variety do? – H.O., Cornwall

A Choose upright varieties such as 'E.G. Waterhouse', 'Tiptoe', 'Freestyle', 'Anticipation' and 'Brigadoon'. Plants should be set 30–36in apart in acid soil enriched with plenty of organic matter. Pruning is done preferably with secateurs after flowering has finished, nipping here and there to maintain a dense, even wall of greenery in which the top growth does not overshadow the lower branches, discouraging flowering. Camellia habits vary a good deal, and attractive though a mixed hedge might sound, a much more even hedge will be produced from the planting of one variety only.

6

Screening

Q Ten years ago I planted a Leyland cypress in my garden to hide a telegraph pole with many wires coming to it. I planted it close to the pole which it soon obscured, but two months ago the tree had to come down as its roots were becoming a potential danger to my neighbour's footings. What can I do to disguise the eyesore? I would prefer year round cover. – M.H., Suffolk

A The fastest option for complete cover is undoubtedly to plant another Leyland cypress, and to have it out again when its size becomes a problem. (You may have a more understanding neighbour by then!) Line the planting hole on the neighbour's side with corrugated iron a few feet from the trunk, to force the roots downwards. Alternatively plant a broader but less dense tree, such as a birch, closer to your house; this will hide the pole and wires in summer, and give a good screen of twiggery in winter.

Q On our boundary to the road we have an old holly hedge which has diseased leaves and gaps in it. I have attempted to cut out dead and spindly growth. What would you suggest to improve it? – M.L., West Midlands

A The leaves you sent show symptoms of holly-leaf miner, an insect which lays its eggs in the leaf in May and June. The grubs then make a narrow channel into the leaf, and later expand the tunnel into a cavern which shows as a discoloured area on the leaf, of red, yellow and black.

It sounds most disfiguring, but in reality most hollies carry some leaf miner and their overall health is none the worse for that. On important clipped specimen hollies it might be worth treating the problem by spraying with lindane during the egg-laying period. But in a hedge which is struggling anyway, your energies would be better spent simply reinvigorating the hedge.

Old hollies with dead or dying wood can linger on forever. Cutting part way back does not usually induce good new growth. It is better to cut old hollies right down to the ground, to within a couple of inches of the soil, and then they will throw up a forest of strong new shoots, making 2ft or more a year. So I would give your hedge a heavy dressing of old manure this winter, and cut it right down in February. Gaps can be replanted with new, pot-grown hollies. Once growth reappears on the old plants, feed again with blood, fish and bone. Where there is competition for moisture from tree roots, water the hedge liberally in the first two summers, in order to encourage vigorous growth.

Q I have a 6ft wooden fence 8 yards long which faces south-east. What would cover it with colour all year and require little attention? Something edible perhaps? – R.J.P., Essex

A The honest answer is: nothing. No one climber will give colour all year, and fruit into the bargain. You will have to use a combination of talents to achieve your end.

First, I would plant a large-leaved ivy for the length of the fence, at 8 ft. intervals. Perhaps the yellow-variegated *Hedera colchica* 'Sulphur Heart' or in a warm town garden the white-variegated

H. canariensis 'Gloire de Marengo'. With a little help these would weave through the fence and in a few years give you a wall of attractive greenery throughout the year.

On to this you can now put other flowering climbers. Any of the large-flowered, hybrid clematis would do, or the small-flowered species such as *Clematis alpina* and *C. macropetala*. On a plain green ivy the perennial scarlet nasturtium, *Tropaeolum speciosum*, would look wonderful, and it winds itself in without any help whatsoever. So does the less reliably perennial, Chilean glory vine, *Eccremocarpus scaber*, with tube-like flowers of orange, brick red or yellow. You could add hops, or any of the perennial peas, and there are climbing annuals such as morning glories and black-eyed Susan. And of course, for flower and fruit, runner beans.

Q An 80-yard stretch of our garden has a stream running along only 5ft from a stock-proof fence behind which is a field containing horses. We have been told to plant at least three feet away from the fence. Can you recommend any shrub or tree which horses will not eat or which will not harm them if they do eat it, which grows quickly, looks attractive, and will tolerate wet conditions in winter? – F.H., Wiltshire

A Horses will have a go at eating everything, and decide whether they like it afterwards. They will always browse the back of your trees and shrubs, and if they can reach it they will take out the leader first.

Two options: you can plant a line of sacrificial willows, alders and dogwoods on the far bank of the stream, and expect them to be eaten up on that side. Or you can plant groups of trees on your bank of the stream, where they can make better specimens unmolested. Leave some glimpses through to the stream. Along the streamside you could then play with some marginal gardening, using irises, marsh marigolds, loosestrife, and candelabra primulas.

As your trees develop they will arch over the stream to give you shade for other plants beneath. Eventually the lower branches will grow to within reach of the horses, and so long as you avoid poisonous yew and laburnum they will come to no harm. You might consider planting the Italian alder, *Alnus cordata*, for its glossy foliage and good cones, and the American river birch, *Betula nigra*, for its shaggy bark. All the poplars would thrive, as would the wingnut tree, *Pterocarya fraxinifolia*, which resembles a large walnut. Deciduous conifers such as swamp cypress (*Taxodium*) and dawn redwood (*Metasequoia*) both grow in wet soils, and have warm autumn colours.

Coastal problems

Q Friends on the coast east of Edinburgh have a space in their garden 15ft by 40ft where large conifers were taken out. The soil is very sandy and dry, and the space is overshadowed by the house and sparse, tall trees. They want to fill the space with leaf and flower to 15ft, and could afford to move in something established. Local trees are conifers, beech and sycamores, and they have been advised to plant sycamore and ash. What do you advise? – J.W., London SW1

A Cold east coasts require iron-clad planting, at least on the windward side, and there may be a deal of sense in the local advice to plant tough, straightforward species. I would go for tough plants which offer some colour and interest, and which will not get too huge, or can at least be cut down to regrow. Think of willows, sea-buckthorn, guelder rose, and ornamental varieties of elder. Once you have some cover established, that is the time to spend on more exotic ornamental plants, trying different things to see what succeeds by making gaps here and there in the initial planting. But, for now, install a few sacrificial tough species to create shelter.

Q We wish to plant two or three rhododendrons at the bottom of our garden to hide our highly prized but inelegant compost heap. Ideally we would like a clump 5–7ft high and 15ft across when fully grown. Our soil is clay and the shrubs would be in impoverished partial shade from a large ash tree. Early flowering to coincide with spring bulbs would be preferred. – P.R., Staffordshire

A The earliest rhododendrons are the species, which are not so easy to grow and would succeed less well in impoverished competitive root conditions. The easier hybrids flower from May through June. Is that early enough for you? You say the soil is clay. Not limy, I hope, or you might as well choose something else. Acid or neutral clay is acceptable if you build up a foot of good open-textured soil above the clay and plant into that. I would plant three 'Cunningham's White', an old variety with a pinkish bud, which starts off the hybrid season in early May. It is tough as old boots, and I have even seen it tolerate a little lime reasonably well. In old age it will be taller than 7ft, but you can always cut a few armsful for the house. You can cut away at the hardy hybrids without doing any harm at all, and I would definitely go for a variety which covers your compost heap quickly and can be cut later, rather than some difficult slow grower which struggles.

Q I have a 50-yard chainlink boundary adjoining a playing field and want to plant an evergreen, prickly hedge, or better still a prickly evergreen man-high shrubbery. What could I plant to provide foliage colour, and what flowering climbers could I add? – R.J.B., Avon

A Think hard before you plant a prickly hedge. They are foul to deal with, and the spines of fallen clippings so often lead to wheelbarrow punctures. Behind solid chainlink fencing you could simply plant an evergreen screen. Would a hedge of mixed hollies be a compromise? Choose carefully, since many fancy varieties – green and variegated – are spineless. Common holly is the most spiny. If you really want a fast, vicious, spiny hedge plant *Berberis stenophylla*, which has narrow leaves, arching growth and orange flowers. You could add a few tamer berberis to the front of a holly hedge – species like *B. verruculosa*, *B. julianae* and *B. darwinii*. Solid evergreen hedges tend to be shaded out and made patchy by vigorous climbers, and gentler climbers find the competition from the hedge difficult. Why not plant an instant screen of self-twining hops on the chainlink for the first few years? And plant some colourful shrubs in front of your prickly ones?

7

Trees

Q I have a 60ft 'tree of heaven' (*Ailanthus altissima*) which is swamping both my house and garden. I would like to cut it down but I have been advised that it should be reduced in stages before felling. Is this necessary, and over how many years should it be done? – H.McK., Hertfordshire

A Trees with legal protection, such as those in conservation areas or those with tree preservation orders on them, may sometimes be required to be removed gradually (assuming felling has been approved at all by the local authority), so that the impact on the local environment is less sudden. Occasionally the removal of a tree allows new winds to bear upon neighbouring trees for the first time, and it is sensible to introduce them to exposure gradually.

But the felling of a 60ft ailanthus piecemeal over several years is going to be expensive on tree surgery, and will cause you more damage to plants below. If it has got to go, then I would certainly get it over with in one go. In a restricted space this will mean dismantling the tree and carefully lowering the sections on ropes to avoid damage to plants and buildings. Perhaps this was what was meant by 'reduced in stages'?

A word of warning. If you fell a mature ailanthus, you are almost certain to get suckers from the base, and occasionally from distant roots. If you do not want this, get your tree surgeon to treat the root chemically so it cannot regrow. On the other hand, the sucker growth is rather wonderful. Thirty feet in five years is not unusual, and the long pinnate leaves can become anything up to 4ft long. This almost tropical-looking growth can be a desirable feature, and I have planted ailanthus in the past precisely to cut down for this purpose. Before they get too big, you can cut them down to grow again. The only loss is those attractive orangy-red fruit, the keys, which look so good on mature specimens in the inner London parks.

Q Please could you advise as to the ratio of roots to height of a blue Atlas cedar, *Cedrus atlantica* 'Glauca', of which we have a splendid specimen in our front garden? – V.G.M.S., W. Sussex

A Generally speaking, tree roots extend sideways 10–20 per cent further than the height of the tree at any stage in its development. It is sensible, therefore, to plant trees no closer to a house than 1.5 times their ultimate height. But there are better epitaphs for a gardener than 'sensible'. Who would wish to see felled in a hurry the towering cedar in the lee of some stately Jacobean pile, or the ancient walnut close by an equally ancient brick cottage? Let common sense prevail, but not too much. The place to be really careful is on clay soils. Willows and poplars are notorious for burrowing their roots deep into the heaviest soils, which then shrink and move as they are sucked dry, and move yet again as they reabsorb water. Small, modern houses are most at risk from such movement.

As good an indicator as any of a tree being too close to a house for comfort is the robbing of light from windows and the risk of branches dropping against the house. Such trees can be taken down with righteous relief, or tree and risk enjoyed simultaneously.

Q My neighbour has a 28-year-old monkey-puzzle tree in her garden. It has reached 24ft growing in nothing more than clay with flints. Is it likely to grow any taller? This year it shed a lot of yellow dust: would this have been pollen? It is carrying many cones. The tree is 14ft from the back wall of my house. Is it likely to do harm? It certainly does not seem to affect any plants between itself and my house. – J.A.S., Kent

A In thin dry soils and where humidity is low, monkey-puzzles do less well. Yours is growing at a good speed and seems happy enough to bear plenty of cones. This year has been good for cones after last year's hot summer, and, yes, the dust will have been pollen. The tree will get bigger. Probably much bigger than the house. Monkey-puzzles are wind-firm trees and unlikely to fall over on the house. But there may be movement problems on your clay soil. More to the point, you will soon have a house smothered in heavy dry shade, and loomed over by this cuckoo of a tree. Much as I love a monkey-puzzle, and much as I love them used in small gardens, it would be better for you if the tree was removed in the next few years. Heart-breaking, isn't it? Why not offer to buy your neighbour a new one 6ft tall for £150? It might be money well spent.

Preservation: the law

Q My garden is in an area covered by a tree preservation order. For legislative purposes, what constitutes a tree? It would seem prudent to avoid planting species controlled by law in case pruning, topiary or other training contravened the law. As a lover of trees, I find it inexplicable that legislation to enlarge and enhance the tree population should be so formulated as to provide a disincentive to the planting of trees. – P.R., Cornwall

A TPOs can apply to any species at all, so long as it is big enough. In conservation areas (not quite the same as a blanket TPO) a protected 'tree' is one which has a diameter of 75mm or more at a height of 1.5m, whether it be an oak or an elder. Permission must be sought to work on trees over that size. Check with your local authority just which legislation applies.

Q I wish to remove two 6ft conifers which are about 15 years old with trunks 6in thick. They are in a narrow bed between the garage and patio. How difficult will the roots be to remove? – M.P., Lincolnshire

A They will be difficult, but not too difficult. Whatever you do – and this goes for the removal of most 'small' trees – do not cut them off at ground level first. Cut off all the branches but leave 4–5ft of trunk standing, to give you leverage. Dig down to the main roots and cut as many as you can find with a spade, a saw or an axe. Then you can heave away on the trunk, and push it backwards and forwards until it becomes apparent where that last cursed root lies (there is always one). Once that is severed you can pull out the trunk.

Most of what is left can be chopped out with a spade. The soil will be very impoverished, and you should dig over the soil down to a couple of feet, and either replace it or incorporate plenty of manure or old compost, before replanting. Take out all the old root you can find.

Q I have three 25ft golden 'Castlewellan' Leyland cypresses, which I would like to reduce. If I cut them off at half their

height, will they sprout and green over again? Is there any other way of reducing the height without removing the tree? – P.W., County Durham

A You can cut them off at half height, and they will sprout, mostly from the top ring of side branches rather than the trunk, but you will be laying up problems for later. Cuts of that diameter (perhaps 6in) across the main trunk of a conifer usually lead to die back at some future date. The new shoots will need plenty of topping out themselves, to make them bush out and cover the hollow centre of the tree. Therefore it is advisable to cut the main trunks 2–3 ft lower than the final desired height.

It is always better with such strong-growing conifers to stop the leader long before they reach the desired height, when a cut of only half an inch diameter is needed. The tree will more readily bear many such small cuts every year than it will a major wound into old wood. The result looks better, too, especially from an upper window.

Remember that to some degree close-planted trees will starve each other into slower growth. So taking out a middle one to let more light in will only encourage the others to grow faster.

If you can bear to, why not remove the trees, replant, and top them out at the correct height? You will get them back to 12ft in 3–4 years.

Q When I had my drive resurfaced a year ago, I built a 20in high circular wall around the base of an oak tree close to the house, and filled it with 20in of earth as a raised flower bed. I now wonder if this will harm the tree, which I am anxious to keep. – R.B., Kent

A Remove it all at once. Most plants can be killed by building up the soil level around their stems. Effectively, they suffocate. Even a modest increase in level of 6in can kill a tree. It is a slow death which can take years, and is therefore often put down to any number of other, more immediately possible causes. It is for this reason that gardening textbooks advise planting new trees and shrubs at the same depth as they were planted in the nursery row or pot.

I am unsure if after a year of live burial your tree will survive. If the bark still looks sound, then perhaps it has a chance.

Q Can one restrict the eventual height and spread of a tree or shrub by planting it in a container sunk in a border? – L.F.L., Sussex

A The only container sunk in a border which is likely to restrict growth is one with its bottom intact. By this means you may starve it into submission, and for your trouble will have all the worries of instability, drought and waterlogging to contend with.

On the other hand there are advantages to bottomless containers made of materials which will rot or rust away over the years. They will force the main roots downwards before they can spread out, which can be useful in greedy plants like yew, when you want to garden close by. But it will have little effect upon the ultimate height of the tree. The technique is not suitable for plants which rely on fibrous surface root, like eucryphia, rhododendron and pieris. They may well become unstable.

Q We have recently moved to a house which we intend to pull down and rebuild. The garden is well stocked and we hope to save as much as possible from damage during rebuilding. However we are concerned about a large 12ft by 6ft bay tree. Could we move the whole thing? Could we take cuttings, and if so, how and when? – A.E.B., Merseyside

|A| At that size, bay (*Laurus nobilis*) is too large to move with any degree of success, and it would be better to start again either with a new plant or, if you have sentimental attachment to the old one, with a cutting. But the time to take cuttings, as semi-ripe wood in a shaded pot or cold frame, is late summer, by which time I assume building will be underway.

On the other hand, bay is often cut down by harder winters only to spring again with a number of smaller stems. Yours may have some. Look in the bottom of the bush, and see if there are any small stems at the base which have rooted into the surrounding soil or leaf litter, and might be severed now and replanted elsewhere.

Root problems

|Q| I have a 25ft silver birch on my lawn. I like everything about it except the way the roots run on the surface of the lawn, making it bumpy to mow and the grass poor underneath. Could I cut out the surface roots?

|A| Sorry; the answer is no. Birch is naturally a surface rooting tree, and you must expect some of the main roots to show. In the wild they grow on poor thin soils, where the only nutrition going is on the surface. Cut out these surface roots and you might find your tree falls over. But there are ways of getting round the problem. First, you could give the grass under the tree a regular top dressing of sieved compost in spring to stop the roots getting too prominent. It will also feed the grass. Not for nothing do those roots run on the surface: they are greedy for food and moisture. A top dressing will give the grass a much better chance.

Depending upon how low the branches sweep and how much shade there is under the tree in summer, you might usefully try overseeding in spring with a grass mixture specifically designed for shade. It would perform better than ordinary lawn grasses.

Controlling a cylinder mower as you drive over tree roots is no fun at all. You are as likely to bump into the trunk as you are to get a handlebar in the groin. A rotary mower on pneumatic wheels makes the operation slightly easier and safer, but if the roots are very proud of the soil, I would settle for a much longer regime of cutting, and not pretend it is part of the sweep of the lawn at all. You could keep it under control with a strimmer, down to perhaps 4–5in, or cut it once a month with a rotary mower set high.

Then there is opportunity to experiment with spring bulbs – snow-drops, scillas, aconites and crocuses. Birch shade is light in winter and will let in the warmth of the spring sunshine to pry open crocus flowers. The earliest of all the easy species is *Crocus tommasinianus*, a little pale purple fellow which will grow and seed in the rootiest of soils. You might try the autumn-flowering *C. speciosus* and *C. nudi-florus*, too, which will be in leaf from December to May.

Q I have a plague of trees of every kind in my garden. At my age of 76 cutting them down is hard work but digging them out intolerable. Is there a chemical I can use to kill the root? – P.D., London W12

A You need to buy ammonium sulphamate, sold by garden centres as RootOut. The newly cut stumps are drilled around the circumference, or frilled with a saw, and the crystals put into the holes, to be drawn down by the sap. Dry, old stumps do not take up the chemical efficiently. The stumps take 8–10 weeks to die, and surrounding planting is unaffected.

Q I have a small tree of the variegated maple *Acer negundo* 'Flamingo', which I have been pruning upwards for several years. This winter, snow broke many of its branches. How do I get it back on a leader? – S.G., Leicestershire

A This maple, known in the United States as the 'box elder', has leaves with three separate leaflets, quite unlike the typical Canadian maple leaf and our own sycamore. The form 'Flamingo' is an exotic mixture of cream and pink and green. I hate it, but that is my problem. However, dispassionately speaking, the box elder is never a strong tree in northern Britain. Elder is not a bad comparison. It struggles to make a strong leader, and late summer growth without a hot continental summer to ripen it can lead to frost damage. And snow damage. (The same is true of the silver maple, *Acer saccharinum..*) If your box elder is badly broken and has lost its leader, I would prune the whole thing back next winter, and treat it as a foliage plant, encouraging long new shoots every year. In that way you will get maximum impact from that remarkable foliage.

Magnolia raised from seed

Q My mature magnolia has set a considerable number of seeds this year. There has been just a single pod in other years, and the birds have eaten the seeds. I have saved some seed this year, but how do I germinate them? – W.E.G.M., Middlesex

A Mature magnolia seed pods are an extraordinary sight, knobbly as squeezed handfuls of putty, and when the individual compartments split open, the orangy-red seeds dangle out on threads to tempt the birds.

Mix your seed with a couple of handfuls of 50:50 sand and peat mixture, and put it in a clear polythene bag. Seal the bag and hang it somewhere frosty for the winter where the birds will not peck it open. In March move the bag to a warm place – a greenhouse or sunny window – and watch for signs of the seeds germinating. As soon as you see any tiny white roots appearing, carefully open the bag, spread out the contents, and prick out the germinating seeds into small pots or a modular tray. A compost which is not soil-based will suit them best at this stage.

Q People comment upon the unusual elder tree we have in our garden. It has burnished red leaves and pinkish-coral flowers. Do you know its name? – J.H., Somerset

A This is a form of the common elder *Sambucus nigra* known as 'Guincho Purple', and what an excellent plant it is. It is just as easy to grow and prune and propagate as the wild elder, just as free flowering and berrying, just as good for elderflower champagne or elderberry wine; but it is a top-rank foliage plant into the bargain. In hot sun the leaves are almost black, and the pigment runs into the flowers, too, suffusing the creamy heads with winey pink – very telling against the dark foliage. For a touch of glamour, grow through it a large-flowered white clematis like 'Marie Boisselot' or, if you are feeling reckless, the strong pink 'Comtesse de Bouchaud'. Plant the clematis well away from the elder trunk and train it across; the elder is much too greedy to allow the clematis to give of its best if planted at its foot.

Prune the elder hard enough to get good vigorous foliage, but not so ruthlessly that there is no old wood left to produce flowers.

Q Winter cold has destroyed the leading shoots on a 6ft walnut tree I have grown from seed. I understand this tree is rather tender. Will it come again? – E.G., Leeds

A Walnuts are late to grow in this country, and in the north especially it is not uncommon to find soft, unripened shoots late in the season, which may succumb to frost during the winter. This is not disastrous. Simply cut back the damaged shoots now to a firm bud. It is especially important not to let two leaders arise where one stood before, so that the tree retains its structural strength. As the season progresses, select the best shoot to be the new leader, and remove or shorten its immediate competitors. This is a particular problem in trees with pairs of opposite buds, such as maples and horse-chestnuts; it is common to find two equally strong leaders replacing a damaged shoot, and this will make a weak fork in the tree in later life.

Q I would like to grow mistletoe in my garden, but have only a newly planted apple tree to grow it on. Will it harm a young tree? – F.J., Sussex

A Mistletoe, (*Viscum album*) does not have to grow on apple trees. If you have a white poplar or a robinia these too can play host to mistletoe. Occasionally it even grows on oak.

Mistletoe is a hemiparasite; it lives off its host plant as well as making energy from the chlorophyll in its own leaves. It would be better to give your apple a few years start before giving it the burden of mistletoe.

To 'plant' mistletoe, simply press a white berry on to the youngish bark of the host, preferably at a fork. The substance of the berry sets like glue, and the seed should germinate within and penetrate the tree. Plant several to improve your chances of a successful take. Male and female plants are required to produce berries.

In nature the job of planting is done by birds (not least mistle thrushes) which deposit the half digested berry direct onto the branches.

Q I understand that a variety of willow is a natural source of aspirin. Could you tell me the variety, and can aspirin be obtained by chewing or brewing a leaf? – C.R.A., Yorkshire

A To a greater or lesser degree all willows (species of *Salix*) contain the source of aspirin, but not aspirin itself. The substance present is salicylate which, I am advised by a toxicologist friend, is an anti-inflammatory drug rather than an analgesic as true aspirin is. Be warned; there is also a lot more than salicylate in these leaves, and it is much safer to use a preparation from the pharmacist than chew in hope.

A choice of willows

Q We were impressed this spring by a display of crocuses in a public garden. They were in grass under a group of willows with coloured bark. Could you advise what varieties the willows may have been, as we would like to repeat the effect in our own garden? – J.B., Derbyshire

A There are many good colour forms to choose from. Try yellow-barked *Salix alba vitellina*, or the orange form 'Britzensis' (often sold as 'Chermesina'). For a greeny purple bark overlaid with white bloom, try *S. daphnoides* or *S. irrorata*. All these species can be pollarded every few years (cut back to a bare 4–6ft trunk), to maintain the bright colour of the younger bark.

For contrast you might plant the black catkined *S. gracilistyla* 'Melanostachys'. It does not have the vigour of the others, but it is curiously attractive when in flower.

Willow catkins are of course of the 'pussy' variety – a fluffy bobble closely attached to the stem. But you could also plant hazel, with dangling catkins, a traditional and wonderfully satisfying companion to crocuses. Hazels are greedy, shallow-rooted bushes, which will keep your crocus corms helpfully on the dry side during summer.

Q Last year what I take to be laburnum seedlings sprang up under my laburnum tree. Is this likely, and will they make

good trees if I transplant them to another position in the garden? –
A.J.T., Lancashire

A Species laburnums (*Laburnum alpinum* and *L. anagyroides*) all set viable seed, whereas the hybrid 'Vossii' is grown for its long racemes of flower and the paucity of its seeds which, because they are moderately poisonous, can be a hazard to children.

Laburnum seedlings are best moved to their final position at the end of their first year's growth. You will find that what was moved as a 3in seedling may well have made a yard of growth by the end of its second year, and it will continue to grow away quickly if it is not further transplanted. It is not unusual to find the first flowers produced in the third or fourth year.

The quality of the flowers will be variable but none the worse for that. The shade of yellow will vary a little, and so will the length of the flowers. Seed is certainly an easy way of growing a few laburnums to dress a pergola, and whatever the variability of the flower, they will all blend together well enough. If you want a perfectly consistent and unvarying laburnum pergola, then the purchase of L. 'Vossii' will ensure success, as this can be propagated only by grafting.

Q Five years ago we planted a sweet-gum tree, *Liquidambar styraciflua*, hoping to enjoy its scarlet autumn colouring. The tree has put on growth and is obviously healthy, but so far, apart from a scattering of dark red and muddy brown leaves, its colouring has remained obstinately green each autumn. What are we doing wrong? – S.A.L.F., Kent

A Not often do you see a really good liquidambar. To give their best colour they need a position where they can get their roots down into water, a soil lacking in lime, and full sun. The promised crimson of their maple-like autumn leaves is seen far more commonly as you describe, a rather plummy brown and green, which may be intriguing but is far from spectacular. The clone 'Lane Roberts' is said to be reliably good for colour on the right soil.

Liquidambar is not the shapeliest of trees and has the loosely conical habit of an alder. There are better options for autumn colour on limy soils, such as Norway maple, field maple, crabs and rowans.

Q Last summer and this summer my eucalyptus trees have taken to shedding large quantities of leaves onto my lawn. Is there anything which can be done to prevent this? Can anything useful be done with the leaves? They do not seem suitable for composting. – R.T.W., Dorset

A Sorry, but that's what eucalyptus do. Like evergreen oaks and hollies, they shed such old leaves as they wish to discard in summer, having made new leaves in spring to keep up their energy supply from sunlight. Young trees shed little, but as time passes the quantities become large. A tree with large leaves like the (commonest) *Eucalyptus gunnii* will smother the grass under its crown with leaves if they are allowed to remain; it wants to be self-mulching. So it is best to remove them fairly regularly, even though their orange and straw colouring is attractive.

If you want a perfect lawn, then eucalyptus do not make the ideal plant, partly because they shed leaf in summer, and partly because they take all the moisture out of the soil surface and impoverish the grass.

Eucalyptus leaves are slow to break down, and would not help a compost heap, but they make an excellent surface mulch for beds and shrubberies. They do blow around, however, and are better put through a shredder to reduce them and make them less wind-resistant. Pine needles can be used in the same way.

Coppicing eucalyptus

Q Three years ago I planted a *Eucalyptus gunnii*. It is now 7ft tall and the trunk is 4in across at ground level. I would like to coppice it to make a fan of stems about 5ft tall. When and where should I cut it? – J.W., Tyne and Wear

A *Eucalyptus gunnii* is one of the hardiest species, and has that blue-grey, evergreen foliage for which the genus is renowned. It is a greedy and potentially huge tree, and needs space to develop. Alternatively it can be coppiced (cut periodically to ground level) and grown for its lush young shoots and foliage. It would then easily make shoots 5ft tall in a season, but I find the tree prefers cutting every other year. Trees 10 or more years old coppice less successfully than those started at 2–4 years.

The time to cut it down is in spring before the buds break and after the worst cold has gone – usually March or April. Saw it off at 3–4in above the soil. It is perfectly possible to cut it down later than that, but you risk inducing soft growth late into the season which may then be damaged by early autumn frosts. Sometimes a cold winter may do the job for you, killing the plant to ground level. Eucalyptus have a fat root known as a lignotuber, from which they can readily sprout, so long as the cold has not killed that too.

Q I have a conifer, *Thujopsis dolobrata,* I think, about 10 yards from the house. It is about 15 years old and as many feet tall. I am afraid it will get too big. Could I take out the leader and shape it, to keep it in hand? – J.A., Herefordshire

A What a useful conifer this is. It is relatively slow growing, and makes a large shrub or small tree, broader at the base than most cypress-like trees. The foliage is coarser and flatter than most 'cypresses' too, rich mid-green above and with attractive white resinous markings on the back.

At 10 yards from your house I would be inclined to let it grow. If it ever gets to be a particularly large specimen it will probably be someone else's problem by then. You could top it out and shape it if you wish. Nibble it all over with secateurs rather than taking the shears to it. Flower arrangers will be pleased to have the prunings. You may find that taking out the leader where it is 1–2in thick will slow it down quite enough for you not to need to touch the top again. On the other hand it will be spoiled as a specimen thereafter. The choice is yours.

Q Last October I planted two trees 8ft high, a variegated Norway maple, *Acer platanoides* 'Drummondii' and an Indian bean tree, *Catalpa bignonioides*. Every care was taken with the planting, and the trees have never been allowed to dry out. So far (June) neither has made any leaf at all, and I am concerned that they may never break. I have tried spraying with warm water, but with no success. What should I do? – H.H.V., Kent

A First, waste no more effort on spraying. There is more amiss than a moist atmosphere can correct. Trees planted in October have had all winter and spring to put out new roots, and ought to have been sufficiently established to shoot away vigorously. That they have not done so suggests they were sickly when planted, or have been drowned in wet soil over winter.

I do not like buying container grown trees in autumn, especially ones as large as 8ft. It means they have been in a pot all season, and have suffered all the possible (but not inevitable) problems of pot culture, such as hot roots, starvation, waterlogging or drying out. In October the leaves should be dropping off anyway, but if the cause is something other than the time of year, who's to tell? Beware of trees carrying dead leaves which refuse to fall; this means they have died on the tree, rather than being shed by the tree naturally.

If you do buy a container-grown deciduous tree in autumn, take the opportunity to open up the root system, get off all that stale peat compost, and plant it as you would a bare-rooted tree, spreading the roots out properly.

To tell if the wood of a tree or shrub is alive, peel a tiny sliver of bark with a thumb nail or penknife. If there is a moist green layer just underneath, then the wood is still alive and may recover. If all shows pale and dry, then the wood is dead. Test first close to the tips of the branches, and move downwards to see if any live wood remains lower down.

If a tree is not in leaf by July, then it is going to be further weakened by lack of energy from sunlight. It could be years before it is vigorous again, which defeats the object of buying a large specimen. So take your case back to the nursery or garden centre, and ask for a replacement.

Q I have a 5-year-old red thorn tree 6ft high (*Crataegus oxycantha* 'Paul's Scarlet'.) Last year it had no flowers. The trunk showed signs of canker. Could this be the cause? I have fed the tree generously with Tomorite, and this year it is well budded. – A.F.R., Kent

A It is more likely that the flower buds were eaten by bullfinches, which you say show an interest in the tree. Canker ought not to stop the tree flowering, and indeed stressed trees often flower all the harder.

Be careful with feeding. Thorns will survive in the poorest conditions and do not need a rich diet. If you feed them with a high-nitrogen fertiliser they may make a great deal of soft leafy growth which encourages canker, and no flowering wood. (Tomorite, being a high-potash fertiliser, would encourage flowering rather than leafy growth.)

Did you by any chance give the tree a big mulch of rich manure the year before it failed to flower? That could explain it. Flowering thorns and cherries often abandon all thought of flowering for a few years if they are planted into an extraordinarily rich new soil; the first flower buds, which were on the tree when you bought it, will open in the first spring, and then the tree will settle down to consume all that rich food and grow, grow, grow. This is serious body-building.

Poisonous parts

Q **Please tell me which parts of a yew tree are poisonous? We have a magnificent yew in our garden, and our neighbours are concerned about the berries which fall into their garden and which could be attractive to their children. It is a pity that the recent promulgation of lists of poisonous plants might make us fear our garden and countryside beauties. – C.S., Worcestershire**

A Three cheers for common sense! Poisonous plants are no cause for panic, but people must be aware of the risks and make children aware too. The alkaloids which make yew poisonous are present in all parts of the plant except the red fleshy coating around the seed. (There is an ornamental form with a yellow coating, too.) Look at the yew 'berry' and you will see it is a hard brown seed surrounded by a cup of red flesh, rather like a minute stuffed olive. The red flesh is not poisonous, and I have watched people eat this, pretending to have swallowed the poisonous seed inside too.

The seed has a hard coat which retains the inner poisons, and seed can pass through a small bird before doing any harm. On the other hand, mammals chewing the seed will be poisoned.

The effects of yew poisoning depend on the amount consumed, stomach activity, the degree of chewing and other factors. Death of humans, even sudden death in cattle, is possible (if very rare) as a result of eating leaves or seeds. So children must be warned. But who in their right mind would make a meal of yew prunings? Yew yields a promising anti-cancer drug.

Q My local electricity company is vainly trying to screen a new local substation in an exposed position swept by salt-laden gales. Can you suggest suppliers of suitable trees or shrubs which could be transplanted at heights of 3–4 metres? – T.B., Dyfed

A In exposed positions it is always better to plant small, even if it means waiting for things to mature. It is heart-breaking to see expensive semi-mature plants, which have been reared carefully under sheltered nursery conditions, suddenly asked to cope with extreme exposure. Physical and financial loss are great as a result, and valuable establishment time is lost.

I would suggest that for speed on the Dyfed coast you plant the fast-growing Monterey cypress, *Cupressus macrocarpa*, if evergreens are appropriate to the situation. They stand salt happily, and develop an attractive, wind-formed craggy profile.

Q We have been given a small tree of the yellow Scots pine. The label says it will go green in summer. Is this so? – C.J., Herefordshire

A Quite true, I am afraid. *Pinus sylvestris* 'Aurea' is a slow growing form of the Scots pine – slow presumably because it is naturally short of energy-making chlorophyll. In winter it is quite a gentle lemony yellow. But in spring, when the season warms up, it suddenly turns green, or at least so green as makes no difference. If it is any consolation, the change is always utterly reliable. It is propagated by grafting on to ordinary Scots pine stock. I am more fond of the plant than it deserves. For best effect, plant it somewhere it can hide in summer but catch the winter sun. Most yellow conifers, especially cypresses, require full summer sun to be bright yellow in winter. This pine, although requiring plenty of light for healthy growth, is less dependant for winter colour on preceeding summer sunshine.

Q Twenty-five years ago my wife and I planted a handkerchief tree (*Davidia*) and it has never produced any handkerchiefs. The tree is vigorous and healthy, and the soil is a mixture of chalk and greensand. What is wrong? – A.F., Surrey

A It takes on average about 15 years for a davidia grown from seed to start producing flowers. The flowers themselves are small and spherical but have two creamy, papery bracts which hang down beside them, in the manner not of a paper tissue but a linen handkerchief folded to a point and tucked into a jacket pocket. The whole structure of flower and bracts spins attractively on a long stalk. The tree prefers acid soil, but will stand some lime. It does need a cool, moist soil to do well, the more so in its early years. In hot, dry Surrey it may be lacking that rich, cool, moist soil and concentrating on self-preservation rather than the future of the species. I would water it as much as is practical and permissible, and mulch it really well, now and again every spring. You might also reduce the competition at the root, either from grass or shrubs. When this tree flowers it is wonderful. For the other 49 weeks a year it is singularly unrewarding, so don't break your heart over it.

Q We have alder trees on the banks of our stream which sprout many young shoots from the base of the trunk. Is there anything with which I can seal the cut ends after trimming to prevent re-growth? – T.H.S., Isle of Wight

A Restraining these epicormic growths on alders and limes is like putting your fingers over a hole in a leaky pipe; nothing seems to hold back the leak. No amount of sealing of the cuts will prevent further sprouts from coming from below and beside the previous sprouts. I find the best answer is to cut late and low. Leave it until bud burst, so the trees have to make new buds after the season has started. And cut as low and tight to the trunk as you possibly can. This removes all the dormant buds on the old sprouts, which are the fastest to regrow. Tight cutting allows you to rub off the new shoots mid season while they are still soft. On smaller trees I would be interested to try cauterising the edge of the cuts with a hot poker, to see if the peripheral dormant buds could be killed and the surrounding cambium persuaded to heal across the wound.

Q I have had a Japanese maple, *Acer japonicum* 'Aureum' for nine years, and for seven of them the leaves have turned brown at the edges in early summer and shrivelled. How can I prevent this? It is now 4ft high. Is it a dwarf, as I understood, or just slow growing? Should I move it to a position with more room to develop? – G.S., Surrey

A What a glamorous tree this is. Golden-yellow fan-shaped leaves and a fine balanced branch structure. To do well it needs dappled shade and soil which is never too dry. Wind and hot sun will shrivel the leaves. Too much shade makes the leaves lime green rather than yellow. It is not a dwarf tree really. It can make 25ft over the decades, and in maturity is a fine sight. So if you can offer suitable conditions by all means give it more space. Move it carefully in March with a big rootball.

Replanting a magnolia

Q I have a *Magnolia grandiflora* which I bought with a short leader and four side branches. Three years later the leader has hardly increased in height but the side branches are growing outwards hard and fast. What should I do to make a free-standing tree? – J.R., W. Sussex

A Shock it. Amaze it. Replant it next March or April in a really well prepared hole, with good rich, open-textured soil. If you are on clay, especially alkaline clay, really go to town on the soil and give it a luxurious fresh start. As the new growth starts, pinch out the tips of the side branches, and force the energy into the leader. But don't prune off the side branches; it can do with all the leaf it can get at present, to build up its strength. This evergreen magnolia, with wonderfully perfumed flowers, is at home in deep alluvial soils and a climate rather hotter than ours. In most of England it fares better against the heat of a wall rather than in the open. But see it in the Dordogne, free-standing like an evergeen oak, and covered in flowers the size of sideplates!

Q I have a Cantonese swamp cypress (*Glyptostrobus lineatus*) which I bought 15 years ago. It is only five feet high and struggles to hold its own, despite much care and attention. The *Magnolia delavayi* I bought at the same time is now tapping the bedroom window. How can I make the cypress grow? – J.G., London SE6

A This plant is a rarity but has a common problem. The Chinese swamp cypress, closely related to the American *Taxodium distichum*, is tender. It will struggle in Britain, especially in the dryer east. But there may be another more common problem. Rare conifers are too often propagated only from cuttings – cuttings from cuttings and sideshoots from sideshoots. They lose all seedling vigour in the process, and with it the inclination to make a good leader. The result is a shapeless shrub. The difference in seed-grown plants has to be seen to be believed.

Q Our 25ft tall *Acacia dealbata* was planted five years ago 10ft from the house for protection. How high will it grow? We read it grows to 80ft in Tasmania. Should we cut out the leader? – F.M., Dorset

A This is the florist's mimosa, with fluffy yellow flowers. It is tender, and rarely makes a large tree before a bad winter clobbers it here. I would not expect yours to get so much taller. By all means prune it to hold back growth. Do it in late spring, not winter, taking back the leaders and the main branches by 4–6ft, and repeating the operation every couple of years.

Q I have an upright Irish yew 9ft high. Would you recommend tying it loosely at intervals to protect it from damage and to keep the upright shape? We do not get a great deal of snow but it is quite windy. – V.H., Sussex

A Binding upright multi-stemmed conifers in this way is really only worthwhile against snow damage. It is the weight of heavy snows which bends down the stems and sprains them beyond recovery. Wind keeps them well excercised and strong, and unless there is a perpetual disfiguring sea-gale from one side, it is not a major problem. The worst conifers for snow damage are *Chamaecyparis lawsoniana* 'Ellwoodii' and 'Fletcheri', whose bundles of upright stems are indeed weak, especially when grown in too much shelter out of the wind. These are worth binding in snowy areas. The upright Irish yew, *Taxus baccata* 'Fastigiata' and its golden forms, are better at withstanding snow; but in areas where snowfall can be heavy it can still be worth protecting them. The yew eventually makes a very big tree, and so at some time you will have to sit back and let it take its chance. On young plants, loops of heavy string at 1–2ft intervals are sufficient protection, and are better taken off again in summer, to let the tree move properly and develop strong stems. Alternatively you can use large gauge plastic netting tied around the tree.

Q The *Eucryphia glutinosa* I planted in 1980 has actually flowered this year, to my delight. But it is getting rather tall and untidy. Should I prune it soon or in the early spring? – M.K., Sussex

A What is untidy? We get used to seeing, mostly in gardens, *Eucryphia* 'Nymansay' which is a columnar evergreen hybrid tree. *Eucryphia glutinosa* is deciduous and hardier, but not columnar. I used to have an old multi-stem tree of it 20ft tall and as much across, looking like an old thorn tree. By all means keep your tree tidy, but do not ask it to change its shape. Badly placed branches can be cut out in March/April, and a little encouragement to density given if you wish. Otherwise no pruning should be necessary.

Q Having got over a major operation in a hospital near Selly Oak, Birmingham, I have four acorns from Selly Oak which I wish to grow on here in South Wales. How best do I germinate them? And how best to fit four giant oaks into my modest garden? – S.C., Mid-Glamorgan

A They are so easy to germinate. I would suggest you simply plant them in a corner of the garden, but then mice or squirrels might take them. So put them in individual pots of ordinary compost, tall ones if you have them, or punctured cream cartons. Keep them cold over the winter, and put them somewhere warmer in spring. Once they have sprouted, plant them in their final positions, in the first spring if possible.

Will you keep all four? Why not plant four in potentially useful positions, and then see how they develop. One might die. One might be hoed off by a loving gardener. One might lose its leader in a gale. One might survive to remind you of a lucky escape from hospital. If all four survive, be bloody, bold and resolute, and long-term keep only those which you really need.

Getting the best from hollies

Q We have a well-established holly tree 8ft high which I would like to replant in another garden. When in the year is it best to move a holly tree? – G.S., Edinburgh

A There is no best time. It is too late to move an 8ft holly. Established hollies hate being disturbed. Even ones half that size which are established will, on being moved with a reasonably intact rootball, sulk or even drop their leaves. Even if they recover, they take years to get going vigorously again. I suggest you heave a sigh and buy another. You can at least buy container-grown hollies 6–7ft high, although the choice of varieties is limited. Expect to pay £60 or more. You will be buying that invaluable asset, time.

Q I have two hollies in my garden, planted four years ago, of the variety *Ilex meserveae* 'Blue Princess'. Although there is a good crop of berries, the leaves have become dull and are falling off green, in large numbers. Can you help please? – J.E.N., W. Yorkshire

A *Ilex meserveae* is a cross between our common holly and the Japanese species *Ilex rugosa*. All forms are known for their small, dark foliage, which has a purplish cast. 'Blue Prince' and 'Blue Angel' (male), and 'Blue Princess' (female) are the best-known forms. As with all hollies, a male must be planted nearby if the female is to bear berries.

It is not uncommon for hollies under stress to shed a very large proportion of their leaves. Most commonly it occurs as a result of drought stress, when a large specimen with a small rootball is newly planted and still trying to establish itself. Hollies are slow to grow and slow to react, and drought stress can lead to leaf-fall weeks and months after the stress has occurred.

In your case I suspect either drought stress earlier in the year, or root disease, or some form of root poisoning. Because hollies are so slow to react, I would not think of removing the trees until they have had a chance to produce new leaf next year. But you could scrape the soil back from the base of the stem now, and look for signs of root disease.

I. meserveae does like a very hot, continental summer to grow well, even though it should not be allowed to dry out at the root.

Q I have two large holly bushes grown from cuttings taken from a prolific berry-bearing tree. Every year they flower profusely but no berries follow. How do I get them pollinated? – E.B., Merseyside

A Your berry-bearing tree must have been a female, so what you need now is a good male to pollinate its cuttings. 'Silver Queen' is a handsome variegated male, as is 'Golden Queen'. Beware 'Golden King' – it is female. 'Hodginsii' is a green-leaved male, with wonderfully dark, broad foliage. All forms of the hedgehog holly, 'Ferox', which have spines on the leaf surface, are male.

Q I have a female holly 'Golden King' and would like to buy by mail-order two more variegated hollies, another female, and a male to pollinate them. Could you recommend suitable silver-variegated varieties? I do not want 'Silver Queen', which is yellow edged. – D.N.R., Yorkshire

A Silver-variegated males include 'Elegantissima', 'Silver Milkboy', 'Ferox Argentea' and, if correctly named, the creamy white 'Silver Queen'. Silver females include 'Handsworth New Silver' and the weeping 'Argentea Marginata Pendula'. Silver is always a word open to interpretation, and in hollies there is a great deal of variation in the actual patterning of the variegation too. If you have strong feelings about this, I recommend you look at the different varieties in a public or botanic garden before buying. In the garden centre trade there are a great many misnamed plants around. The Duchy of Cornwall does a good selection by mail order, from Penlyne Nursery, Cott Road, Lostwithiel, Cornwall PL22 08W. The specialist Highfield Hollies, at Highfield Farm, Hatch Lane, Liss, Hants GU33 7NH does mail order and sells over 50 varieties, some of them at specimen size. I would look hard in garden centres and buy something you like the look of.

8

Fruit and Fruit Trees

Q There are young apple trees in the lawn of my new house. Should I keep the soil bare under them, or can the grass remain up to the trunks? – E.B., Avon

A All trees benefit from the lack of grass competition, and especially productive fruit trees. However, large fruit trees can in maturity cope perfectly well with competition and still give a good crop. Smaller ones, especially those on dwarfing rootstocks such as M27 and M9, are better kept free of grass always, and the soil under them mulched to increase fertility and conserve moisture. Even large, vigorous fruit trees are better kept free of grass in the first few years, over an area of about one yard in diameter. Thereafter the grass may close in, although mowing is always easier if some bare soil is retained. There is also less risk of hitting the tree with a lawn-mower and splitting off a chunk of bark. So often trees damaged this way succumb to disease at the foot long before they reach their real old age. If you trust your mowing to the teenager next door during your holidays, then keep the grass well clear of the trunk.

Wye College in Kent undertook trials on sycamores some years ago, testing trees smothered in grass against others sprayed out in small circles or sprayed over their whole root area. The trees with no grass competition were four times the size of the smothered trees after just a few years.

Q I am looking for an old apple variety, 'Cornish Gillyflower', and the pears 'Catillac' and 'Winter Nelis'. Do you know who might stock them? – D.T., Essex

A The answer – as ever – is in *The Plant Finder*, a compendium of specialist nursery stock, which lists in the region of 800 apple varieties and their stockists. I will send you some addresses. 'Cornish Gillyflower' is certainly an old variety; it dates from 1813 and is said to flourish best in the warm, wet climate of Cornwall. Cold, dry Essex may not suit it. 'Catillac' is the great stewing pear, has plenty of flavour, and keeps well.

The Plant Finder can be bought from gardening bookshops, priced £12.99, and it makes a perfect Christmas present for a keen gardener. It lists fruit, vegetables, trees, shrubs, perennials, annuals, – the whole works – tells you who sells them, and whether or not they do mail order, catalogue cost etc. It is invaluable.

Q We have a two-year-old crab apple 'Profusion'. It produced flowers in May as usual but has failed to produce any fruits. What has gone wrong? – C.S., Hampshire

A What a good crab apple this is: wine-red flowers, red new shoots, and small blood-red fruits in the autumn. If a crop of flowers opened as normal but not a single fruit followed, the likelihood is that the flowers were spoiled by a touch of frost in May and that no fruit was set. Crabs are self-fertile and do not need a second tree to make them set fruit. However, better crops are often gained when two trees are present. Other easy and showy crabs include 'Golden Hornet' (yellow) and 'John Downie' (yellow blushed with red).

Q My son has a 'James Grieve' apple which I gave him 4 years ago. It bore some twelve apples this year, but it has got only two spindly side shoots. It has developed a kind of bulge all around the base, just above ground level. What can one do about this? – C.W.E., Hertfordshire

A It sounds as if the tree could do with some formative pruning, to encourage the development of a proper branch structure. Any book on fruit trees will help there. But why is it growing so weakly, and why the bulge at the base? I suspect that the bulge is the graft point, which is not properly joined and is making callus growth. If the graft is incomplete the growth above will be weak. It may be that the graft was not properly formed when the tree was purchased. Or it may be that the graft has partly broken open due to movement arising from inadequate staking. Grafts remain visible during the life of a fruit tree, but the transition from stock to scion should be smooth. Significant local bulging suggests there is a fault in the graft. If so, buy a new tree and start again.

Starting an orchard

Q I wish to turn an acre of pasture on Kent Weald clay soil into an orchard, for pleasure not profit, and more for my children's benefit than my own. What varieties would cope with this poor soil? – R.R., Surrey

A So much depends on the relative fertility of the soil and what size of trees you wish to produce. If you liked, on dwarfing rootstocks such as MM.106 you could have apple trees giving you a crop in 3–4 years, never mind a crop for your children. An orchard full of large apple trees is most picturesque, but your children might be thankful for smaller, equally productive trees, which are easier to manage and pick from. Are these trees to live in rough grass, in which case competition will call for a more vigorous rootstock? Think first about what maintenance you can offer, and with that in mind, choose apples on MM.106 stocks for smaller trees, or more widely spaced trees on MM.111 or M.2 stocks for large trees. Clay soil is not necessarily infertile, so take a hard look at how other things are growing round about before you assume it is so. Be prepared to keep the young tree roots free of competition from grass for a few years at least.

Q I have a 10-year-old 'Charles Ross' bush apple tree whose leaves are browning at the edges, increasingly with every year. There is some sign of canker, which I treat, but otherwise the tree is healthy and productive. – B.B., West Sussex

A This is probably due to a shortage of potash, which causes browning and scorching of the leaves from the edge inwards. Apply sulphate of potash to the roots in January at 1oz to the square yard. Also, mulch the tree with compost or give a dressing of a general compound fertiliser such as Growmore.

Q I have a large wall on which I would like to grow an espalier apple tree. Are there any particular dessert varieties which

lend themselves to this method of cultivation, and do they have any special requirements? – L.H., West Sussex

A First you must decide how your tree is to be pollinated. Two trees are required to set fruit, and they need to flower at the same season. Unless you can wed your espalier to an existing nearby tree, you must plant another wall tree or a free-standing tree nearby. 'Cox's Orange Pippin' and 'James Grieve' make a good pair for pollination purposes, and both are happy as espaliers. Equally, you might plant 'Lord Lambourne' with 'Egremont Russet'.

Like any fruit tree, they require good preparation of the soil first, with plenty of old manure or compost in the bottom of the hole. Espaliers require careful attention to their pruning, and it is wise to follow a book for a year or two until you get the hang of it. Go to a specialist fruit nurseryman who will advise on suitable varieties and rootstocks for your soil, and will be able to sell you a tree already pruned to form the beginnings of an espalier. A good source is the National Fruit Collection, at Brogdale, near Faversham in Kent.

Q I have a small vineyard from which I make wine for home consumption. This year I have had a problem with ladybirds hibernating in the grapes. Picking 'Madeleine Sylvaner' there have been a good ten ladybirds in every bunch. Picking 'Muller Thurgau' in October I expect to find the same. I cannot use insecticides, nor even flush them out with water, without affecting the grapes, which this year are superb. What do professional growers do about this? I cannot believe they are prepared to mash the whole lot up regardless. – R.P., Hertfordshire

A Talking to the growers, it seems that earwigs are more of a problem in this regard than ladybirds. Many are seen crawling out when the grapes are brought indoors, but the short answer appears to be that the creature who dwells or hibernates in a bunch of grapes is not long for this world. *In vino veritas!*

If the task is of a practical scale, try spreading out the picked bunches in a very warm, moist place for a few hours, perhaps with polythene over them, to see if you cannot stir the ladybirds into waking up again. Tempt them with a brightly lit cloth soaked in sugar solution, onto which they might crawl or fly. Depending upon whether your concern is for hygiene or poor dumb creatures, you will then still have the problem of rehousing them before winter. It may have been kinder to let them go down with the bunch.

Q I have a five-year-old 'Black Hamburgh' grape planted in my greenhouse, but the bunches and individual grapes are always small. I have fed well and watered weekly but to no effect. I prune back to the main rod each year, and growth is strong. – L.F., London E4

A There are two things to check here. First, are the flowers being pollinated properly? A little mechanical help may be of use here, in the warmth of midday. Second, how small is small? In England Mae West-sized grapes are produced only in greenhouses (and not always there) by thinning the berries with grape scissors in June before they begin properly to swell. Try this and see the difference. Also make sure that watering is generous; weekly sounds rather mean to me.

Q I am told that seeds from *Carpenteria californica* are used as capers for caper sauce. Is this true, and safe? I always thought nasturtium seeds were used for this purpose. – J.C.C., Northumberland

A True capers are pickled flower buds, not seeds. They come from a 4ft prickly Mediterranean shrub called *Capparis spinosa*. I have seen them growing wild in Malta, and the flowers are so attractive for their explosion of stamens that it seems wicked to pick the buds. Nasturtium seeds (in the cabbage family) are occasionally used as a poor substitute, and they do look surprisingly similar. Seeds of the caper spurge, *Euphorbia lathyrus*, also look similar but are definitely not to be eaten; most euphorbias can produce a nasty allergic reaction.

Whether carpenteria seeds can be eaten I do not know, but the hydrangea family, to which carpenteria belongs, is not known for its edibility. Garden hydrangeas, eaten in quantity, can cause cyanide poisoning. If in doubt, don't.

Berry problems

Q I have blackcurrants and gooseberries which have been neglected for two years. When would be the time to tackle them? – M.W., Shropshire

A If they are really out of hand you can cut currants down to 3–4in in February/March, and feed well, to get some strong new stems from the base. There will be no fruit until the following year. Gooseberries are better treated more gently. In winter, thin out the bushes a little, taking out some of the weakest branches to let light and air into the bush. Then reduce the lateral branches to two or three buds. Fruiting should continue without missing a year.

Q I grow currant and gooseberry bushes alongside each other, and this year I found what appeared to be five large, hairy blackcurrants growing on a red gooseberry bush! The flavour was

good, mostly currant but sweeter, and the fruits were later than either parent. Is this a recognised hybrid? I mean to grow on seeds from two of the berries, to see what I get. – D.G.P.C., Gwynedd

A This is not a new hybrid. (What is that remark about sex being a great 'leveller'?) In fact both Jostaberries and Worcesterberries are of this parentage. The Jostaberry is rather like a pale, huge blackcurrant, with good resistance to mildew. The Worcesterberry is more like a small, late-fruiting red gooseberry. A fruit-fiend friend of mine has just recently got hold, from Italy, of plants of the almost forgotten 'black apricot', a cross between an apricot and a plum. I shall be fascinated to see one.

Q Fourteen years ago I planted a 3–4 year old English greengage tree from a reliable nurseryman. It has grown well but manages only about four fruits per year. I have been told it needs another tree with which to cross-pollinate. Is this so? – D.A., Buckinghamshire

A I wonder which variety you bought? It sounds like 'Old Green Gage', which is indeed not self-compatible. It requires another tree to pollinate it, such as 'Marjorie's Seedling' or 'Shropshire Prune'. Assuming that the tree does actually flower well, and that those flowers are not always spoiled by frost, it makes sense to add another tree, as the fastest means to a crop.

Alternatively, if you have room for only one tree and time to start again, you could plant a self compatible greengage tree. 'Early Transparent Gage', 'Pershore Yellow Egg', and 'Ouillin's Golden Gage' are all self fertile.

Q I am building a 6ft south-facing stone wall in my garden. Could I grow a cherry against it and would it fruit satisfactorily? Could you suggest a suitable variety? – J.R.H., Lancashire

A Cherries, both sweet and acid (cooking) kinds, are vigorous trees, and a 6ft wall is small for them. However, you should succeed on a less vigorous rootstock such as Colt, with careful attention to pruning. 'Morello' is the classic, heavy cropping self-fertile acid cherry. Of sweet cherries, try the self-fertile 'Sunburst', a black-fruited variety. Both are available from Chris Bowers & Sons, Whispering Trees Nurseries, Wimbotsham, Norfolk PE34 8QB tel. 01366 388752

Q Could you please help me with the cultivation of the 'nashi', or Asian pear. I have grown a beautiful specimen from a seed and wish to know if it is self-fertile. – A.S.S., Gloucestershire

A The Asian pear, *Pyrus serotina*, flowers even earlier than our own edible pear, *P. communis*, and so it is not very easy to get a decent crop in Britain. The sexual and genetic preferences of a seedling pear are unpredictable, and yours may turn out to be partially self-fertile. European pears vary considerably in this regard, not least because of their early flowering habit when there are fewer insects; it is better to plant two to flower together. It would be sensible to do the same for your Asian pear, if you can spare the space. You could add one of the named varieties such as 'Siuko' or 'Nijisseiki'. The fruit, when it comes, is juicy but gritty, and the flavour is not remarkable.

Growing figs

Q We have a five-year-old 'Brown Turkey' fig planted as per instructions on a sheltered south-facing wall. Three years ago we started to train it diagonally. But we would like more growth low down the trunks and not just enormous piles of leaves at the top of the 6ft wall. How do we encourage it to be bushier? Should we prune it? – J.B., Surrey

A Did the instructions include giving the fig a restricted root run hemmed in by bricks or paving slabs? This does help to reduce growth rates and encourage shorter, flowering growth. Even with this treatment, 6ft is quite low for a fig and you may struggle to keep it down. Figs on walls do need regular pruning to keep them in hand and productive – pinching out tips, tying in, and thinning of shoots. You would do well to consult a book such as the RHS publication *Fruit*, by Harry Baker. Meanwhile, reduce a third of the stems to 2–3ft in February for the next three years, and pinch and tie in the resulting lower shoots. If you cut the whole bush down at once, there will a huge surge of soft growth, and it will be back at the top of the wall before you can say 'knife'.

Q We have a flourishing 12-year-old fig tree which always produces many figs. They grow to about two and a half inches then drop off, green and spongy. We hoped that this year's very hot weather would encourage them to ripen, but the same thing happened. How can we get then to mature and ripen properly? – N. McL., Hertfordshire

A Figs need a tight, restricted root-run to get them to fruit. But this does not mean they want a starvation diet. They like plenty of water and food, and without this – particularly in hot, dry weather – they will shed the immature figs. The answer is to mulch well, with good, rich compost or old cow manure, and to water copiously in hot weather when shedding is a problem.

Q We have an 11-year-old 'Brown Turkey' fig trained on a solid elm fence, and have never been able to pick a fruit from it. Pea-sized embryo fruits form on the new growth in summer, but by spring they have always hardened, gone brown, and dropped off.

Can you help? The garden is at 420ft above sea level and less than a quarter of a mile from the sea. The winter south-westerlies penetrate to all parts of the garden. – J.K-S., Devon

A More winter protection is required here to nurse the embryo figs through the winter. A wall rather than a fence would provide a warmer position. Try tying in a covering of fir branches, or bracken held in place with a fine-gauge plastic netting. It may also be worth planting shrubs at the back of the fence if you can, to reduce the wind chill. Figs do not mind salt-bearing winds, and will thrive at the seaside.

Mulberries

Q My hairdresser just told me his mulberry tree has once again dropped all its fruit. It is 13ft tall and seven years old, on a south wall. It looks healthy, but has never produced ripe fruit. What can be the reason for this total drop? – M.F., Essex

A Essex is dry. (In terms of total annual rainfall it is far closer to Egypt than Scotland.) The foot of a south wall is dry. And this is a very dry year. Lack of water is almost sure to be the problem. Tell him to get plenty of water on it when the fruits are ready to swell, and to mulch it with manure or compost next spring, to keep the moisture at the roots. As a hairdresser he'll know the value of putting on plenty of water.

Q I have four old mulberry trees which give wonderful shade but which also shed their fruit between June and August causing a sticky mess underfoot and spoiling grass and other plants. We do not want to cut them back too far as we would lose the shade, but is there a way of stopping them from fruiting? – T.J., Argelès-sur-Mer (France)

A What an enviable problem! I can think of no way to stop your trees fruiting. Burgeoning nature is implacable. But you might persuade someone to come and crop your mulberries if you do not like them. I would come like a shot, only I have this column to write. A heavy watering of the tree might get cropping over faster, once the fruits are ready to ripen. The traditional method of mulberry gathering was to put sheets under the trees to collect those fruits so ripe they dropped off by themselves. But when hand-picked dark red, if not yet quite black, the fruits are just as good for jam or wine making, so your picker could get busy and strip the tree sooner rather than later.

Q I have an old, very fertile mulberry tree which is almost 30ft high. A few years ago I felled a cherry which was shading it on one side, since when it has sprouted a dense growth of shoots from the main trunk, which is now totally hidden during the summer months. I would like to remove these shoots to reveal the beautiful bark, but I am unsure whether this is wise. – T.A., Cumbria

A The shoots sprouting from the trunk may be either the result of increased light to, and strength in, that side of the tree, after the cherry's removal, or the result of incipient senility of the whole branch structure. Either way, you can cut them off, perhaps saving the odd one to fill any gap in the canopy where the cherry tree had shaded it. But at 30ft your mulberry is both tall and old. At that size they have a nasty habit of keeling over or breaking up. Think about reducing it to stop it breaking up, if you want it to be one of those rugged, ancient specimens in another 50 years.

Q I inherited with my garden what I take to be 'Himalaya Giant' blackberries, which are very rampant. In November I got

heavily scratched disentangling the old growth from the new, and the plant makes far more new growth than I have space to tie in. Does the new growth contribute nutrients to the crop on the old growth,and how should I best train the stems? – J.R.P., Wiltshire

A 'Himalaya Giant' is certainly rampant. It thinks nothing of making shoots 20ft long in a season. Varieties as vigorous as this are best trained not in a fan but to the opposite side of the plant each year, to save the worst disentangling of old from new. Cut off the old canes as soon as they have fruited: they have done their job. Weave the new ones up and down on your wires, in a sideways S-pattern, and try not to stop the ends until late if possible, as this induces sideshoots. You may prefer to replant a smaller, more manageable variety such as 'Waldo'. There are thornless varieties such as 'Black Satin' or 'Thornfree', but their flavour is not as good. 'Loch Ness' is perhaps the best thornless variety for flavour, and sufficiently restrained in its growth to be fan-trained.

9

Exotica

Q I grew a 'tree tomato' in a huge pot in a light atrium at the centre of my house until, this year, it finally had to go outside. It is now too large to come back in, and I hope will set seeds (as it did in Berkshire for me) before the winter. This one was grown from my own seed. It is now standing in a sunny, very sheltered corner. I used to grow it in New Zealand, where it withstood the odd frost, but how will it do here? Should I protect the root with bubble film? – M.H., Edinburgh

A The tree tomato, *Cyphomandra betacea*, is a small soft-wooded evergreen tree, with large leaves and narrow, 3in long, red edible fruits which can be produced in the second year from seed. Indoors it can get very leggy, and requires plenty of nipping and pruning to keep it shapely.

It prefers winter temperatures above 50°F (10°C), but can withstand a little frost which causes it to die back to the main stems and sprout out again.

By all means protect the roots, above as well as around the sides of the pot, with as many layers as you can bear of bubble film, fern fronds, or old carpet. This should ensure the roots survive to next year. But air temperatures of much below 28°F (-2°C) may cut it to the ground. In Edinburgh, smaller young plants grown from seed, which can be brought indoors, will be a better bet.

Q My grandchildren put a mango seed in a pot this summer, left it behind the garden shed, and to our surprise it sprouted. How do we keep it going now? What does it need? – A.H., Somerset

A It needs a tall, warm greenhouse, if the idea is to produce fruit. In the wild it is a 60ft tree. But you can grow it as a pot plant for a few years, just like an avocado. Bring it indoors at once for warmth, and give it a light position so it can keep growing and develop some strength. Keep it on the dry side through the winter, and water freely in summer. Pinch it well to keep it bushy. The flowers, which you are unlikely to see, come in great pinkish panicles at the ends of the shoots, and are fragrant.

Q This summer a friend brought me some Joshua tree seeds from a holiday in the south-western United States and the Mojave desert. They have germinated and are now 4 inches tall in pots. Can you advise me on care and particularly watering? – M.B., Lancashire

A The Joshua tree, *Yucca brevifolia*, is one of the larger species of yucca and can grow to a dramatic 30ft or more in its native habitat. For all its size, the spiny sword shaped leaves are only a foot long, whereas the shrubby *Yucca gloriosa* we grow here has leaves twice that length. The creamy flowers have an unpleasant odour.

The tree can stand extremes of heat and cold, but not the combined cold and wet of a Lancashire winter. For us it must effectively be an indoor plant. It will require all the light it can possibly get; a heated greenhouse would be best. A gritty, soil-based compost will be needed, kept decidedly dry in winter and watered from below when necessary. In summer the plant could be lifted outdoors while it is still a manageable size.

Q Last spring a root of ginger in my pantry sprouted, and it is now a 2ft high ginger plant with three stems. I potted it in good compost and keep it damp in a west window, but the leaf tips tend to discolour. How do I care for this plant? – R.E.C.R., Surrey

A Culinary ginger, *Zingiber officinale*, looks rather like a very narrow-leaved canna, but has spikes of flower a foot long in muddy purples and yellows. It grows 3ft tall and dies down to its rhizome in winter, like a bearded iris. The rhizome should sit on the surface of the soil, and the compost be kept almost dry in winter at about 55°F(13°C). In summer it likes moist warm conditions but not direct sunlight. A north-facing bathroom is suitable. Dry air and direct sun are probably the cause of your damaged leaf tips.

When necessary, divide the rhizomes in spring, and water very sparingly until growth has properly commenced. A liquid tomato food can be applied during the growing season.

Starting ginger into growth the first time is not always easy, as it can go mouldy before it begins to root. Find the freshest ginger root you can. Chinese supermarkets have the fastest turnover and ought to be best. Press a rhizome 2–4in long into the top of a potful of just moist compost, and leave it in a warm airy room to show willing. Polythene coverings too quickly lead to rot when the rhizome is completely rootless. If you have any fungicide mixed, a quick dunk and dry off before planting may be beneficial.

Q We have two loquat trees which my daughter grew from seed eight years ago. They are now 5ft tall in pots, and enjoy being

outdoors in summer. Will they survive if we plant them outdoors and stake them well? We need the space indoors. – M.M., Oxfordshire

A Loquats (*Eriobotrya japonica*) make quite attractive evergreen wall shrubs in very favoured gardens, looking rather like woolly leaved rhododendrons. In Oxfordshire they should survive, but expect winter damage to the young shoots. They may turn out to be more decrepit than picturesque, but you can have a go. Regard them as summer foliage plants, to add a touch of the exotic.

In a good position in Cornwall or Devon, loquats may even fruit in a good year. Plenty of water suits them well. They are not fond of very alkaline soil, which may perhaps be your problem.

Kiwi fruits

Q Last year I raised four Kiwi fruit plants from seed and brought them on in the greenhouse where they have grown very energetically. How do I continue to grow them, as I can find no literature on them? – K.W.B., Cardiff

A The Kiwi fruit or Chinese gooseberry (*Actinidia chinensis*), is a rampant climber. You could grow it out of doors as an ornamental for its large, furry leaves, but for fruiting it needs to be under glass, with a vigorous pruning system similar to that used for grape vines. They can just about be grown in a large pot. If you want good fruit, it is advisable to buy a reliable named variety. For further information, consult *Fruit*, (an extract from the Royal Horticultural Society's encyclopaedia), ISBN 1-85732-905-8, price £8.99.

Q I have a six-year-old avocado in my garden, grown from a stone. The main stem and side branches are all strong and

healthy. **Is it possible to graft a cutting from a fruit tree such as a Victoria plum on to the avocado stock? – W.C., Swansea**

$\boxed{\text{A}}$ I am regularly surprised at how mild so much of the Welsh coast is. Long may your avocado thrive! But no – you cannot grow a plum on it. It is related to the bay tree and cinnamon, but not to the rose family to which plums and apples belong. It is possible to graft one species on to another close relative, such as rowan on to thorn, or pear on to quince, but the two species need to have similar growth habits, especially of trunk size and woodiness, if the graft is to succeed.

$\boxed{\text{Q}}$ **Several years ago I had considerable success growing my own tobacco. I am now keen to repeat the project. However I no longer have a source of seed or plants of *Nicotiana tabacum*. Can you help? – P.G., Dyfed**

$\boxed{\text{A}}$ *The Plant Finder* only lists one mail-order supplier of tobacco. This is Hardy Exotics, Gilly Lane, Whitecross, Penzance, Cornwall TR20 8BZ. There are others, but you would have to collect the plants in person. For seed only, write to Chiltern Seeds, Bortree Stile, Ulverston, Cumbria LA12 7PB, and watch those great paddle leaves rising up to 5ft.

$\boxed{\text{Q}}$ **We would like to plant a fruiting olive tree in our garden, in memory of my gentle, kind mother-in-law who died last month. Any ideas or suggestions? – A.J.B., Hampshire**

$\boxed{\text{A}}$ In this country olives are really conservatory plants. In very mild conditions they will survive outdoors, and there is an old tree in the Chelsea Physic Garden in London, protected by city warmth and old father Thames, which in hot years even produces a few fruit. You could grow an olive in a tub, and bring it under glass for the winter. The little yellow flowers in spring are sweet smelling, and the grey evergreen foliage is always good. That wonderful nursery, Read's (the citrus specialists), of Hales Hall, Loddon, Norfolk NR14 6QW, sells several clones of dessert olives, including 'Pyramidalis' which they regard as being the hardiest. If a garden plant it must be, and you can't grow olives, why not plant *Phillyrea latifolia*, a dark green, small evergreen tree in the olive family. What style it has: neat, glossy, evergreen foliage beautifully held, and craggy ridged bark in old age which is nearly as good as an olive's. It a worthy memorial tree.

Q I have a hibiscus I brought back from holiday several years ago, but it will not flower. I have cut it back several times, but not fed it very hard. How do I get it to flower, and should I put it out in the garden? – L.H.K., London

A The large-flowered *Hibiscus rosa-sinensis* is not hardy and cannot be planted out, although in a good summer it can be stood outdoors in full sun. (The hardy hibiscus is the species *H. syriacus*, which has much smaller flowers.) Your hibiscus is in need of more food and especially more light. Keep it on the dry side for the winter. Next spring, start a fortnightly programme of liquid feeding, and give it as much light as possible, in a conservatory if you have one, or greenhouse. It should not go below 56°F (13°C) at any time of year. Try to pinch it back to keep it bushy, rather than cutting hard back every couple of years.

Q Could you tell me where I can find a coffee plant to grow indoors? – S.M., Yorkshire

A Coffee (*Coffea arabica*), makes an attractive evergreen plant for a warm greenhouse, or suitable condition indoors. 65–70°F (18–21°C) is ideal, and higher temperatures do not suit it. It is a small tree in the wild, and needs pruning or making into a multi-stemmed bush to keep it manageable indoors. Fleeting but fragrant flowers start to appear after 3–4 years. It is not available by mail order, according to *The Plant Finder*, but seeds are available from Chiltern Seeds, Bortree Stile, Ulverston, Cumbria LA12 7PB; tel. 01229 581137.

10

Lawns

Q Every year my lawn seems to get more and more lichen in it. Last year I hired a scarifier and scratched it out, but now it is as bad as ever. What should I do?

A Lichen is really more a symptom of weak, badly aerated turf than a problem in itself. Treat the real problem and it should go away. Sulphate of iron at 2oz per square yard will (temporarily) kill the lichen. Then aerate the lawn, top-dress and feed it , to put some heart into the grass. I suspect you may be cutting the grass very short. Try letting it grow a little longer – an inch or so – to get its strength up, and if possible use a rotary machine with a grass box rather than a heavy cylinder mower.

Q My large lawn is rapidly being taken over by what I am told are ragwort, speedwell and groundsel. They are impervious to normal weedkillers. There are too many to pull out by hand. How can I control them? – J.A.C., Northumberland

A I suspect you are misinformed. Ragwort is a tall weed of rough meadows, and does not long survive a regime of close mowing.

Perhaps you weed is cat's ear, which looks rather like a cross between a dandelion and a coltsfoot. Groundsel is a weed of cultivated ground which finds it almost impossible to gain a foothold in turf, and I would not expect to find it in an undisturbed lawn. It might well appear in newly seeded areas. Speedwell is a genuine lawn weed, and it requires several applications of selective weedkiller to put paid to it. (On a large informal lawn I rather like speedwell.)

Use a weedkiller containing mecoprop or dicamba to combat speedwell. Lawn weeds vary in their susceptibility to selective weedkillers, and it is usual to have to make several applications if you want a perfect, text-book lawn. Selectives all work best when plants are growing hard, which means late spring and early summer. They are less effective in a drought. Once the ground is moist again, a light summer application of lawn fertiliser may help you have a better campaign against the weeds.

Q A tiny sedge-like plant with tufty brown flowers is invading my lawn. I believe it is field woodrush (*Luzula campestris*). Help! – J.D.F., Shropshire

A This is a lawn weed, particularly of acid soils. Test the soil, and if it is very acidic, dress lightly with lime. This is a pleasant enough little weed, which looks attractive in longer turf. But in a close mown lawn it is conspicuously coarse and tufty. The chemical control for woodrush is mecoprop. If you wish to remove the woodrush, I would work at killing it before a colony becomes too established, since its crowns become tough and fibrous. The raking out of a killed patch of woodrush will leave quite a hole in the surface of the lawn.

Q We have pet guinea pigs which graze the lawn in a movable enclosure. However the lawn itself is in desperate need of a

feed/weed and is full of moss. Are there any products which are harmless to grazing animals? – M.J.M., Kent

A Let us deal first with the weed control. I would suggest that if you are happy to have the marks from a movable enclosure on the lawn, then you should not worry too much about low-growing lawn weeds such as daisies and speedwell. If there are the likes of dandelions and thistles, you have three options. You can dig them by hand. You can apply a tiny dab of Roundup or Tumbleweed to the centre of the weed rosettes beyond the animals' cage, as the active ingredient glyphosate is relatively very safe. (This would be my preference.) Or, if your lawn is large enough to allow the animals to move around on one half only for three months, I would consider treating one half with a selective weedkiller (a much less pleasant group of chemicals) in early May, keeping the animals off that half altogether for those three months. Then in August you could move them over and treat the other half of the lawn. Take the animals off the lawn altogether for a few hours during and after spraying.

I suspect that, if you are getting very many weeds seeding themselves in, you may be leaving the cage in one place for too long until the grass is thin and the soil almost a bare seed-bed. Keep the cage moving often, and you may find the problem is much diminished.

By generally improving the lawn, through aeration and feeding (granular lawn fertilisers are harmless once they are washed in and completely dissolved), you will find the turf is much stronger and moss will be less of a problem. Moss killers can be toxic and are better avoided. Test the pH of the soil; it may be that constant grazing from animals has soured the soil and made it relatively acidic. A light dressing of lime (well away from your animals) will help to neutralise the soil.

Toadstools

$\boxed{\text{Q}}$ I have a toadstool problem in my lawn. What can I do to get rid of them? – J.S.R., Kent

$\boxed{\text{A}}$ Toadstools are just as varied in their habits as the higher plants, and you need first to determine what fungus you may be dealing with. Quite often fungi in a garden which has been newly made or re-landscaped are a sign that there is a chunk of dead wood under the surface of the lawn. It may be an old root, or even something left over from the construction of the house. Dig out the wood – which is the fungi's food source – and the problem will go away.

Other fungi, such as fairy rings, live on the turf itself, spreading outwards in an ever increasing circle. There is a fairy ring big enough to park a couple of cars in on one of my lawns, and I am informed by a mycologist friend that it is probably 90–100 years old. It is one of those rings which makes itself known simply by producing a ring of extra-bright green turf, and because of its age I am reluctant to destroy it. I find that in winter, when the grass is weakest, it shows more, but I can tolerate that. In summer, if the lawn is kept well fed to be sufficiently emerald itself, then the ring goes virtually unnoticed. It could be controlled (6oz iron sulphate dissolved in half a gallon of water per square yard, applied to a well soaked lawn) but I feel the use of chemicals is not really necessary. I quite like my ring. There is many a birch or cherry much younger than that with a tree preservation order on it.

Some other kinds of fairy rings leave a wake of dead turf to mark their emerald passage, and this kind looks unattractive in a lawn. It is no easy job to remove a fairy ring, so you need to consider carefully what you are taking on. The turf will have to be removed to at least a foot either side of the green and brown rings, and the soil below sterilised chemically. It takes time and looks a mess. The bare soil will later need topping up with fresh soil and reseeding or returfing. The old turf must be burnt or taken to the local tip; as long as it stays around it can spread infection.

Remember, finally, that small brown patches surrounded by bright green grass are made when a bitch relieves herself on the lawn. For this the usual verbal controls apply.

Q I am sure a number of people would be glad to know of a lawn sand dispenser which stops dispensing when you come to a halt. There used to be a wooden circular one which did just that. – G.T.C.W., Surrey

A Rotary 'cyclone' fertiliser/lawnsand spreaders do have the nasty habit of starting and stopping with an overdose. As you push the machine forward the wheels connect to a distributor under a hopper which spins round. The knack is to start and stop gently and gradually, so that by the time the forward motion stops and the distributor ceases to spin it is virtually empty. On small lawns it is never a bad idea to cover the lawn twice at half rate, so as to ensure an even cover. Large lawns are faster done in one go, marching at the double. Although many garden centres will lend you a spreader if you buy several bags of fertiliser, for a small lawn it is hardly necessary. It is surprising how evenly you can spread by hand in still weather with a little practice. Scott's (part of Miracle Garden Care) produce a hand spreader called the Handygreen II, which I find is accurately controllable, although it does allow dust to drift in the air, and I would be reluctant to use it for spreading lawn fertilisers which contain selective weedkillers, except on the stillest of days. On the other hand it's cheap, takes up very little room in the shed, and would also be fine for spreading grass seed.

Q I am rather pleased with my lawns as they contain all kinds of wild flowers. I know they are weeds really, but I enjoy seeing things flower in the turf. However, my lawns are always slow to become a good green in spring. Should I add more species of grass to the turf to compete with the flowers, or just fertilise it? – J.S., Leicestershire

A If you like your flower-rich turf, the last thing to do is to fertilise it. Lawns with low nutritional levels naturally provide a greater opportunity for 'flowering' plants, because the grass is weak enough to give them a real chance. I would leave well alone and add nothing. It ain't really broke. And if your neighbour's lawn is emerald green in March and April – well, so is a field of winter wheat, but how boring it is later.

Q I have a lawn surrounded by beds whose level has risen above the lawn over the years with the addition of compost. The lawn contains bluebells. I would like to raise the lawn level by laying turf over the present grass, and to add a specimen tree. Will this work? – C.S., Humberside

A By all means lay turf over your present lawn in the autumn. But will 2in of extra height be worth the cost? It will have no effect on the bluebells. The new tree might give you shade in which some of the bluebells might be allowed to prosper in longer grass and look happy. But the best way to be rid of those in the lawn is just to go on mowing for a few years. Digging them out is barely worth the disturbance unless they are in distinct clumps. There is no selective spray which would help you in this.

Getting rid of moss

Q To lessen the rampaging moss in my grass, I am wondering if lawn sand followed by a scarifier and a rotary mower to suck up all the bits, would help. Presumably I must catch the moss before the spores (or whatever mosses have) spread? – A.G., Middlesex

A The spread of moss by sexual reproduction is the least troublesome means. Far more of a problem is that every small piece broken off is capable of rooting and making a new plant. This is why you will have seen the recommendation that moss is killed with lawn sand before any attempt is made to remove it by mechanical means. Otherwise you are simply spreading it about. So go ahead with your lawn treatment. But I do agree with you about the usefulness of rotary lawn mowers for hoovering up after a lawn has been scarified. They do an excellent job. Spent bud scales in spring, evergreen oak and eucalyptus leaves in summer – all of these types of fine debris can be sucked up for disposal, and after shredding in the mower they rot much faster on a compost heap.

Q When you buy most plants or seeds, suitable soil conditions are indicated. But not with grass seed. The choice is just turf quality, from bowling-green to coarse, hard wearing grass. In my experience, finer grasses do better on sandy dry soil like mine. Is this so? – R.F.C., Essex

A You are quite right that most 'off-the-peg' grass seed mixtures do not take great account of soil conditions. They are general mixtures for average conditions. In difficult conditions it pays to look for 'bespoke' seed mixtures, which may cost more but will be worth the trouble. Instead of going to a garden centre, contact one of the specialist grass-seed suppliers, like British Seed Houses, Bewsey Industrial Estate, Pitt Street, Warrington, Cheshire WA5 5LE; or, for a mix with wildflower content, John Chambers, 15 Westleigh Road, Barton Seagrave, Kettering, Northants NN15 5AJ. It is too much of a generalisation to say that fine grass mixtures do better on dry soils, although it may be true under certain cultural conditions.

Q Over the winter I have prepared the soil in my garden to lay a lawn, and it is now ready to be turfed. My gardening books give me conflicting advice; should I lay the turf now or wait until March? The soil is dry and sandy, and I am worried about drought if I leave it too long. – J.D., Merseyside

A The reason for recommending turfing in March is that the turf is then making new roots in the spring warmth which will establish quickly. The sooner it is rooted and established, the sooner you and your family can use the lawn. But if you want to lay it sooner and can find the turf, go ahead. You will need to keep off it until it is established, but then you would not have been walking on your newly prepared soil either. At least this way the minute the roots start to grow they will be beginning to establish in situ. Avoid frosty weather for the work. If you want to lay very fine, expensive turf, the result may be better in March.

Q We live in a Georgian house close to the centre of York. To the rear is a concrete yard 5 by 15 metres, which we would like to turn to lawn. However there is no vehicular access to the yard, so removing the concrete would be difficult. Can we lay a lawn over the concrete, and if so, how? - M.L.H., Yorkshire

A It is not a good idea to lay grass over concrete. Problems with drought, or poor drainage and sour soil, would be almost inevitable. I advise you to consider living with the hard surface by putting a more attractive paving over it, or by giving it some kind of designer paint treatment. Better still, if you think the yard is light enough for grass to grow well, take up the concrete. It would have to go through the house in bags to a skip, but it is possible. The difficulty is in knowing what lies beneath. If it is another yard of rubble and clay, you will curse me. Why not make a test hole to see? If the soil is reasonable, consider cutting out some areas of concrete with a stone saw to a straight edge, to make beds for permanent planting. Or have tubs and pots. If you must have grass, lay 2in of coarse gravel first, covered by a water-permeable geotextile membrane, and followed by 6in of topsoil. Be prepared to water often.

Q My 80-year-old mother can no longer mow her 12 x 40ft lawn, and I would like to convert it into a meadow with wild flowers. The lawn has plenty of weeds and is on poor stony soil. I cannot re-dig the lawn, but could I feed it and then rake wildflower seeds into the grass? How much seed should I buy and from where?
– N.T., Lancashire

A I would dearly love to dissuade you from this, for several reasons. First, wildflower meadows close to a small house (as opposed to in the wild) look unkempt rather than natural. Second, until you make hay of the long grass in July or August you cannot walk on the thing without flattening it. And then, after cutting, it looks brown for weeks. Is this practical close to a house? Third, cutting down the hay in summer requires a scythe or a powerful mower, not just the machine you use for regular short grass. And all that hay has to be raked up and put somewhere straight away. It can be easier in the end just to cut a short lawn. Fourth, you will have all this work regardless of the quality of the wildflower content of the sward, and building up a good wildflower meadow is slow and not at all easy.

A wildflower meadow is not an option I would inflict on anyone who wants less work or fast results. But yes, I know they look wonderful in big, wild gardens. Can I suggest you simply let the grass grow this year until August, without worrying about improving the species content, and see if you can stand it practically? If not, then nothing is lost. If you like it, then start introducing plantlets of wild-flowers into the turf next spring. This works better than seed in an established lawn. Above all else, do *not* feed it. Wildflowers do better on poor soils where the coarse grasses cannot swamp them.

11

Composting and Mulching

COMPOSTING

Q I have a substantial heap of wood ash left from a winter bonfire. Can it go into my compost heap? – N.T.P., Cheshire

A It can, but it needs to be mixed in gradually as you build up the heap, with plenty of moist, green material such as grass clippings. A layer of pure ash discourages the worms to pass upwards into the upper layers of the compost, so the heap rots less efficiently.

Wood ash contains a little potash, and is therefore beneficial to plants. But beware of mixed bonfire ash where plastics have been burnt, as these can be toxic to plants.

Q The compost-maker we have been filling with garden and kitchen waste for months is now nearly full and ready for use. It is alive with slugs, snails, woodlice and other creepy crawlies which we do not wish to spread around the garden. What should we do now? – P.B.,Mid-Glamorgan

A When it really is ready for use, spread it with generosity and give the birds a banquet. There will always be slugs and woodlice in a garden, and more around a compost heap. You will only speed life up a little by spreading them out.

But what is 'ready'? Heaps of kitchen waste often have lots of sweet material which slugs and snails adore, and the open texture of the heap will encourage cave-dwelling. When it is really ready, the compost will be firm, almost solid, dark and rich, and rather too impenetrable for woodlice, snails and most slugs. The small red worms, on the other hand (which I hope you have added to the drum), will be racing up and down in it like 10-year-olds at their first disco. Give your compost a little longer if in doubt.

Q I would be pleased to know what we ought not to shred and use either as a mulch or on the compost heap. We have hedges of laurel, lonicera, leylandii and beech. – I.J., Cheshire

A On this score you may relax. By far the greater problem from unusual additions to compost heaps or mulches is mechanical rather than chemical. It is better to reserve your compost heap for relatively soft materials which will decay evenly and quickly to provide a useful product, and to add only a little woody material however fine it may be. Bits of wood and twig serve to keep the heap aerated, but they are not broken down by the microbes which break down softer materials. Softer materials decay at high temperatures, whereas wood decays by fungal, not microbial means, and the fungi are effective only at lower temperatures. If you need to store shredded woody material, keep it in a separate heap or apply it as a mulch fresh from the shredder. Only if you have space to leave your compost heaps to rot for several years is it worth mixing in hard, woody material.

Q Is it safe to put rhubarb leaves on the compost heap? I always leave it for two years before use on my vegetable plot. – R.D., Cleveland

A It is perfectly safe. The reason we eat rhubarb stems and not the leaves is that the leaves are viciously acidic. On the other hand, there are many things a worm or microbe in a compost heap might fancy at which you or I would turn up our noses. (Other worms, for a start!) If you mix rhubarb leaves into your compost heap along with plenty of other materials, there will be no problem. They will rot down and become food for worms just like anything else, even after one year. There is certainly no risk of anything unpleasant happening to humans from vegetables fed on rhubarby compost.

I have always cut off rhubarb leaves as I pull the sticks, leaving them around the parent plants as a mulch. Anything that remains in autumn is speeded in its rotting progress by a heavy dressing of manure on top.

Composting newsprint

Q Is it possible to turn newspapers into garden compost, and if so, how? – H.W., Merseyside

A Newspapers are fine for incorporating into an active compost heap, but they will not do the job on their own. To rot well they need soft green, nitrogenous matter, like lawn clippings or fresh manure, to break down the carbon-rich paper and also to overcome the inhibiting properties of the chemicals in the paper. Folded mats of paper lack air and cannot rot down easily. (Telephone directories have been known to pass through incinerators relatively unscathed.) To incorporate oxygen, screw up the individual sheets of paper first. Paper which has been through a shredder is ideal for adding to a compost heap. If you must add a thick layer of paper balls to a compost heap, sprinkle suphate of ammonia over it before adding further materials, to give extra, quickly available nitrogen. In summer you can just about get away with adding a daily paper with grass clippings and kitchen waste to a heap, but in winter papers are better taken to a recycling point.

Q I have a compost heap made up simply of grass clippings from last year. It is not very rotten in the middle. Could I use it as a mulch, or should I leave it another year? – L.D.B., Merseyside

A What you have is in effect a heap of silage, not compost. The chances are that if you use it as a mulch it will produce a spectacular crop of seedling grasses. You might use some mixed in the bottom of a planting hole for trees or shrubs, but my inclination would be to save it for next year. But do not leave it as it is. Turn it with a fork, making it into a new heap alongside the old one. This will introduce fresh air into the heap and speed up the process of decay considerably. Next year try using Biotal's Compost Maker For Grass, which speeds up the process considerably.

Q I have too much comfrey in my garden. Is there a way of turning this into good manure? I cannot recall how it is done. – I.M.B., Suffolk

A Comfrey (*Symphytum*) is a good source of potash and nitrogen. It can be used either by simply mixing the cut foliage regularly into a compost heap, or by making it into a soupy liquid feed. Simply fill a container with a tap at the bottom with comfrey leaves. Top it up with water and leave it for a month, by which time it will have rotted. The soup extracted from the tap can be used rather like liquid tomato food.

Q Can we put grass clippings which contain sycamore seeds in our compost bin without producing hundreds of seedlings when we use the compost? – A.S., Kent

A Certainly you can. A good compost heap or bin is perfectly capable of cooking the life out of sycamore seeds. The risk, perhaps, is that there are always parts of a compost heap, at the edges, which do not heat up sufficiently, and these might contain viable seeds. This is why it is important to turn compost heaps at some stage in their life, to re-oxygenate the heap and to turn the dryer, cooler outsides into the centre.

Q Our guinea-pigs produce what looks like useful manure, mixed with meadow hay bedding. Should it be composted or can it be dug into the vegetable plot? Our soil is sand over chalk, so any organic matter is helpful. – D.D.R., Kent

A If the animals were sufficiently massive or numerous, I am sure guinea-pig droppings would be useful in the vegetable patch. Hay is another matter. It will be full of weed and grass seeds and would be better composted first. The hay will break down faster in the heap if you leave the droppings in it, so my advice would be to compost the lot. I have successfully used sheep droppings to deter rabbits from grazing around young trees and shrubs, but I wonder if guinea-pig droppings would deter or attract rabbits? I know of a guinea-pig forced to share quarters with a large rabbit, whose amorous attentions had its near-cousin shaking in its boots.

MULCHING

Q I have access to a supply of wood chips which I would like to use as a mulch on garden borders. Is there a risk of introducing honey fungus? – C.C., Warwickshire

A Honey fungus is a dangerous problem, and in its more viru-lent forms can kill otherwise healthy trees and shrubs. There is always a small risk of bringing diseases into a garden with wood chips. The best wood chips are pre-composted, and the heat of composting should destroy the fungus. Equally, the spores of honey fungus are just as likely to find the chips after they have been spread in your garden. I would suggest the moisture-retaining benefits of a wood or bark mulch outweigh the risks.

More to the point, where honey fungus is already known to exist in a garden, I would hesitate to spread a thick layer of wood chip, as it could act as a ferry for the black 'boot-laces' of the fungus to travel further. I have seen a wood chip heap stored in woodland become completely riddled with honey fungus. Even heaps of leaves on a woodland floor can play host to it.

A surface mulch, in a sunny open position where honey fungus is not already present, is a safe enough bet.

Beware of using the debris from a chain saw for mulching, as it contains harmful oils from the machine which can damage roots.

Q I used to burn the trimmings from my 150ft Lawson cypress hedge, but now I have acquired a shredder. Could incorporat-ing too much of this shredded material into the soil upset its balance? – F.L.C., Devon

A I would not recommend digging the material directly into the soil, but it would make a good mulch if not applied too thickly, perhaps 3in deep. I know it is said that, to be effective, mulches must be thick enough to suppress light and seedling weeds. But very fine mulches (as shredded cypress tends to be) can make a water-excluding layer which, although conserving water below, stops it penetrating from above.

I would not mulch to that depth every year on the same border. If the old mulch is intact and weedproof, then use the next year's batch somewhere else. With time, worms and chemical action will break down the mulch, using a little of the nitrogen in the soil in the process. So some artificial nitrogen-rich fertiliser applied to a mulched border is helpful.

Continuous mulching with resinous plants can also lead to soil acidity, so unless you are growing plants which require acid conditions, such as rhododendrons, it is helpful to lime the soil lightly every few years.

Q Frequently I see leaf mould suggested as a material for mulching, top dressing beds, and mixing into compost. Where can I get it? Ingwersen's of East Grinstead used to sell it 20–25 years ago, but not now. Surely someone must sell it? – P.G., Kent

A If anyone does sell it, then it is a well kept secret among those who know. Good leaf mould is the product of much time spent raking and collecting leaves, and 2–5 years of fungal and bacterial action breaking down the leaves, plus the space for bulk storage. If it were available it ought to cost a lot; more than most people would be prepared to pay, in fact.

The best way to find leaf mould is to make your own. Turning the heap every 6–12 months will speed matters up, and if you put the leaves through a shredder initially as they go into the heap, the speed of decomposition is dramatically increased. This is especially useful with tough leaves like oak and plane, which take many years to decay. Beech and oak are thought to make the best leaf mould. They are both slow, but can be speeded up by mixing them with softer leaves like sycamore and horse chestnut.

Leaf mould is so good because it is full of bulky humus and beneficial bacteria, as well as being a gentle balanced fertiliser. Worms rise to it like trout to a fly. The next best thing for most garden purposes is old compost made with plenty of coarse, stalky material rather than green lawn clippings, and which has cooked itself at a high enough temperature to kill weed seeds. Next to this or to leaf mould, peat or coir or bark mulches are lifeless as stone. Making compost or leafmould is like making home-made wine: you have to wait for the first few years, but once the cycle is in full swing, there is plenty to go round. In the interim, or where space is short, then a bought mulch from a garden centre is the answer.

12

House Plants

Q I have grown two lemon trees from pips. They are now three years old and two feet high. I am told they will not flower and fruit because they have been grown from seed. Is there any point persevering? – H.L.T., Wiltshire

A There is every point. They will flower and fruit, but it takes longer from a pip than from a cutting – 8–10 years is quite usual. Remember this is a small tree, and most trees concentrate simply on growing for many years before getting round to reproduction. Pray that your trees may be as precocious as the 8-year-old American girl who recently gave birth to twins!

The quality of the fruit in seed-grown trees is unpredictable, and may not necessarily be as good as the parent's.

Look out for a copy of *The Pip Book*, by Keith Mossman. (Penguin ISBN 0-14-046255-4). It is a useful little book and will help you with subsequent potting-on and pruning. If you get hooked on growing citrus fruits, the place to buy good varieties is Read's Nursery, Hales Hall, Loddon, Norfolk NR14 6NS; tel. 01508 548395. *The Pip Book* is available for £4.99 from RHS Enterprises, The Royal Horticultural Society's trading arm, and books from its tremendous bi-annual list can be purchased by credit card over the telephone on 01483 211320.

Q Does double glazing affect the ultra-violet light reaching plants on window cills, and what effect does heat-reflective Pilkington 'K' glass have? – M.W., Kent

A A normal pane of glass lets through about 50 per cent of UV light, and a double glazing unit of the same glass lets through about 37 per cent. If the inner pane of double glazing is made of heat-reflective 'K' glass then only 29 per cent passes through. In certain situations, where old fabrics and paintings must be protected from the fading effects of UV light, laminated glass is used, cutting down transmission to as little as 2 per cent. Trial and error will show where different plants will thrive.

Q I have an 8ft yucca in a 15in pot, and its single willowy stem has leaves only above 5ft high. I would like to reduce the height and encourage sturdier growth. Could I cut it off at 2ft tall, and would the old stem make a cutting? – A.M.G., West Midlands

A Yuccas have such coarse, elephant's-leg trunks, that you might expect them not to respond to hard pruning. The temptation is to let that tuft of foliage go on getting further from the carpet every year, and never to reach for the saw.

But you can indeed chop the top off your yucca, and it will sprout from the cut, or a little below, or both. Do it in spring when the plant is ready to grow, rather than in winter when it is near dormant. Keep it on the dry side until it has leaves again to use water.

Cuttings are made by potting up side shoots pulled away from the stem in spring. Always use a sandy loam compost for yuccas, not a peat-based type; it is easier to control the soil moisture that way. But you can also pot up leafless lengths of yucca trunk, 1–3ft long and 2–3in wide, with some success, so long as they are kept the right way up! They are slow to sprout and root, and plenty of warmth is required.

Old plants of the hardy outdoor species *Yucca gloriosa* can also have their trunks cut down if required. This encourages shoots from the base. So does flowering, but this occurs less in those species commonly grown indoors because of lower light levels.

Q I have a new conservatory 15 x 20ft and 14ft high, built between the house and an extension of it. It has a ceramic tiled floor and is heated. Could I grow a grape vine or bougainvillea across the roof? – H.W., Kent

A With a heated conservatory so large you could do wonders. But the first question to address is, was it built for people or plants? Will it be steamy in summer and cool in winter, or have a dry, even living temperature all year?

Vines need neither nor enjoy winter heat. They are better cold in winter, and cold helps to kill off their associated pests. They prefer greenhouse border soil to a pot. They need regular training and pruning throughout the season, and 14ft is really too high for that; traditional vine houses have low sloping roofs to make training easy. If a vine or bougainvillea or any other plant, trained to the roof, becomes infested with aphids or mealy bug, then life underneath gets a little messy. Sooty moulds descend upon the Laura Ashley. Either you spray, or you use biological controls. Hot dry atmospheres encourage red spider, and the best control for that is a moist, furniture-rotting atmosphere.

Are you discouraged? I hope not. The point is, that in a room meant for living in, it is often more easily made verdant with plants in pots (as large as you like) which enjoy a dry, Mediterranean or Australasian atmosphere. There is less need to be damping the atmosphere all the time, and if pests do appear the plant can be taken outside for treatment, as long as you have not spent the last three months carefully tying it to the roof.

Try a bougainvillea trained as a standard in a pot, or a tree of mimosa (*Acacia dealbata*), an orange tree for perfume, tree ferns perhaps (*Dicksonia antarctica*), the weeping fig *Ficus benjamina*, or a Washingtonia palm. If you want some strong colour, why not grow 8ft pelargonium or fuchsia pyramids as the Victorians did?

Q Can you suggest some plants which I could keep on the two ledges of a small, double-glazed porch. They should be able to stand bright summer sun and winter cold. – T.S., London SW12

A In such a small space there can be no room for plants which will be leafless or insignificant for half the year. So I would opt for plants which are either evergreen or succulent, but which flower well too. (Those never-changing fat cacti are to my eye dreary beyond belief when sitting on a British window ledge. See them outdoors in a climate which suits them, and you will never want to have them here again – green gnomes under a grey sky.)

In London a double-glazed porch attached to a heated house should not drop below freezing except perhaps in exceptionally cold winters. And there are plenty of sun-and-drought-loving plants which will be content with winter temperatures of 32–41°F (0-5°C).

Try some of the species pelargoniums such as *P. quercifolium*, or those with scented foliage; but keep them on a lean diet to restrict their size. Flowering will not be impaired.

Of the succulents, *Echeveria harmsii* makes a miniature succulent shrub with orange trumpet flowers, and is very easy to grow. Carpobrotus and lampranthus, which could be used to trail from the sills, have starry daisy flowers. (I have seen *Carpobrotus edulis*, the Hottentot fig, growing wild on sea cliffs on the north coast of Scotland.) *Lampranthus deltoides* is a pretty grey-leaved shrublet with triangular leaves, reddish stems and pink, almond-scented flowers. *Sedum lineare* 'Variegata' is easy to find, and has needle-like creamy leaves on weeping stems. Continuing the grey theme, try *Othonnopsis cheirifolia*, another trailer with paddle-shaped grey leaves and yellow daisy flowers. It will survive well enough outdoors, but in a cold greenhouse it is twice as attractive.

Q I have a potted poinsettia (*Euphorbia pulcherrima*) still bearing a few red leaves. Can I do anything to restore its customary glory for Christmas? – R.T., London SW19

A The coloured 'leaves' on poinsettias are really the bracts surrounding rather insignificant flowers. To get them to perform a second year, they need cutting back in spring, repotting, and gently feeding through the summer to build them up for flowering. To induce the coloured bracts, plants must be given complete darkness with no electric light for 10 hours a night over a period of 8 weeks during October and November. By Christmas they should be in full colour. A temperature of 55-65°F (13-18°C) is quite sufficient through the winter.

Q I have a healthy two-year-old bird of paradise plant, *Strelitzia reginae*, which I am told will flower in another year. The new leaves are fresh enough, but the old ones go brown and split, despite sponging three times a week. Where am I going wrong? I would love to see it flower, but I am pushing 77. – R.B., Wiltshire

A However glamorous the gaping blue-and-orange 'beak' and red crest of the strelitzia may be, the plant as a whole is never very glamorous. The leathery paddle-leaves die slowly and are not a pretty sight. It does not need a particlarly moist atmosphere, but it does like plenty of water in summer. (In winter strelitzias can stay on the dry side.) Above all, it needs light – long days and lots of sunshine – to make lots of new leaves and to induce flowering.

Keep it above 50°F (10°C) in winter in your sunniest window or conservatory, feed it and water it well in summer, turn a blind eye to the worst of its old leaves, do not worry too much about sponging, do not repot it too often, and with luck it will flower for your 80th birthday. Five years is about the usual time to get one to settle down to flowering.

Q How do I feed, and especially water, a *Begonia rex*? – A.J.D., South Wales

A *Begonia rex* is grown for its large, pointed, liverish and silver leaves, which when well grown are a fine sight. Use a soil-based compost such as John Innes No.3; in summer keep it moist but never wet, and dryer in winter. For full-sized leaves, feed it with liquid feed during active growth, but not in winter. Dappled shade suits it. The sunnier the window, the more the colouring will tend to silver rather than purple. If you like *B. rex*, try to get hold of *B. manicata*, which has green leaves with tufts of claret-coloured spikes coming off the veins on the backs of the leaves, and foot high plumes of candy-floss pink flowers in spring.

Grapefruit surprise

Q A few years ago I bought a grapefruit plant which lived in my porch until it was over 5ft high. More recently I gave it to my daughter who has more space. To my amazement it has developed thorns over an inch long down the stem. Is this a cross-breed? I took it for granted it was grown from a pip. – R.L., Cornwall

A There is nothing unusual here. Citrus trees are viciously, if sparsely, spiny and the spines can be all of 2in long. They are green at first, and therefore it is easy to miss them at first glance, but once you start to prune the trees you soon notice. Commercial orange groves use selected clones grafted onto seedling stocks, and the clones used tend to be far less spiny.

Q Last month I bought a bulb in a pot, with a flower like a red hot poker. What is it, and how do I grow it? – J.T., Kent

A This will be *Veltheimia capensis*, from South Africa. The poker is about 15in long and a distinctly 'cooling' shade of red hot, not to say muddy pink. Does that sound right? It is a tender bulb. You will need to keep it either in a cool greenhouse or as a house-plant. In summer it can rest relatively dry, and the leaves may die back, if not down completely. The bulb should sit half-in, half-out of the soil, and is almost the size of an amaryllis bulb. In autumn, water it again and feed it occasionally with tomato food until it flowers in April. It is almost worth growing for the leaves alone, which are about a foot long, 3–4in broad, and with a delightfully wavy edge. If all plants had leaves as shiny as veltheimia, the manu-facturers of leaf-shine would be out of business.

Q Twenty years ago I was given a big clump of clivia in a large pot. It produced spectacular orange flowers for 10 years and then stopped. I divided it and put the pieces into three pots, but they have not flowered since. Where did I go wrong? Have they just come to the end of their flowering cycle? – D.A., Hampshire

A Clivias like to be pot-bound, and as long as you feed then during active growth with liquid tomato food, they will flower every spring for ever until they burst their pot. Division sets them back considerably, but they flower again, usually in the next year. They are not fussy about soil. You will find them sold in peat-based composts, but I prefer to see them in the soil-based type, in clay pots. Water generously through the summer, and keep them fairly dry during the winter months. A north or east window is sufficiently light, but I find that too much warmth in winter switches off their flowering clock. A winter temperature of as little as 50°F (10°C), or even a degree or two lower, encourages flowering. They can be stood outside for the summer in a shady place, but be careful not to let the leaves scorch; each leaf lasts many years and you would have to stare at the damage for a long time. If you cut the leaves back to remove damage, they bleed like jugular veins. Feed your plants, keep them cool and dry in winter, and be patient.

Q I have four daturas in pots. Last year they bloomed profusely; this year no flowers at all. I have fed them weekly with tomato food. What am I doing wrong? – C.M.P., Essex

A Given a chance and space, brugmansias (as we now have to call the woody species of datura) make a massive, greedy, fibrous root system. They should be producing those white or golden trumpets through summer and autumn. After flowering cut them hard back, and expect this to take away all the leaves. They will then shoot away again, and as spring comes they need rich feeding to maximise early growth. Tomato food (which is a high potash, bud-producing feed) can come later in the season. You need to get your plants growing hard and strong before that. Water very generously when in full leaf. A moist atmosphere is also helpful to good growth and to keep red spider away. Remember that all parts of the plant are poisonous; they are in the potato family, along with the nightshades.

Succulents

Q I have several pots of the succulent *Crassula portulaca* and the red-flowered *Kalanchoe blossfeldiana*. They regularly produce new plants from fallen leaves or shoots. What is it about their natural environment that has allowed this characteristic to develop? – A.C., Denbighshire

A Succulent plants like these come from dry conditions where water is scarce. So they store their own in the leaves, and can survive long periods without water. Consider how much neglect a potted crassula can stand. It is safer for such a species to rely on a leaf taking root after being knocked off by a passing animal than to wait for seed and rain coinciding. Call it being economical with water storage if you like, and propagation by natural cloning for survival of the species, until such time as conditions allow seed-grown plants to make the more important genetic, evolutionary progress.

Q I have just bought a magnificent, fully leaved, Dutch-raised *Ficus benjamina* 'Starlight'. After a few days we have had leaf fall by the hundred, and some of the lower branches are bare. The plant is in a dining room at 55–65°F (13–18°C). Will it recover in the growing season, and what should we do? – J.M., Hampshire

A Keep it on the dry side – and cross your fingers. *Ficus benjamina*, the weeping fig, makes an excellent houseplant for a light position, and there are dusky green variants as well as variegated forms like 'Starlight'. Such plants receive an enormous shock when they leave the stable warmth and (probably) artificial light of the nursery. Off they go in containers, plastered in leaf-shine, through garden centres, into cars, and finally into some dry, relatively dark English winter dining-room. Assuming they have not been fatally chilled somewhere along the way, the new light and air-moisture levels alone will require adjustment. Plants often shed foliage in this process. It is a natural process. But be careful not to overwater, as this can kill quickly, starting with major leaf fall. If you are confident that light is adequate, and that you have not overwatered, go back to your supplier with it; it will have cost enough.

13

Pots and Planters

Q I always start pots and hanging baskets of petunias in the greenhouse, to give perfume on our patio later in the year. Have you any other ideas for perfumed plants in pots? – J.C., Gloucestershire

A My immediate recommendation would be regale lilies. They are overwhelmingly fragrant and add a touch of class to container gardening. If you like being overwhelmed, this is the one for you. You can lift them now from the garden (or buy them), setting them three to a 10in pot, with at least 6in of soil over the bulbs. (They will produce roots from the stem above the bulb, as well as below.) Use a rich, gritty compost, and for preference a straight-sided stable pot, as the plants may get up to 5–6ft. Bring them on in a cool greenhouse, and place them with your pots outside when bud is about to break. They will last for 3–4 weeks in bloom if the roots are not cooked by direct sun.

Q I have two oleanders and invariably they both produce flower buds which show a glimmer of colour before shrivelling and dropping off. Both are in pots and overwintered in a greenhouse. – P.W., Suffolk

A Plenty of water and plenty of heat are the keys to successful flowering. Move them to a really hot corner with plenty of reflected heat from a wall. You may find that the buds nearest the heat of the wall will open properly even when others fail.

Q I was given an oleander cutting three years ago, and it now flowers well in a pot outside. But at 5ft high it is getting too big to bring indoors in the winter. Might it survive in a warm spot outdoors? – L.J., Devon

A If your oleander is going to survive outdoors, it would stand a better chance planted out in the ground rather than in a pot where its roots can be frozen. Oleanders are best kept above 45°F (7.5°C) in winter, but they will survive lower temperatures so long as they are above freezing. I would prune your plant in spring to keep it bushy in any case, and not let it get above 4–5ft high. Then you can overwinter it in a frost-free garage, keeping it just moist. Oleanders will overwinter that way with surprisingly little light (for an evergreen), and I have even seen them overwintered in a cellar with one tiny window.

Q I have an azalea, 'Mother's Day', growing in a tub of erica-ceous compost. I bought it last year to replace a 10-year-old one which dried out while I was on holiday. It flowered well the first year, but this year had no flowers at all, while appearing otherwise quite healthy apart from a few white or mottled leaves. – J.W., Lancashire

A Commercially grown azaleas are reared in astonishingly small pots, often less than half the width of the plant's canopy. This is fine when they are watered by capillary feed from below, but in a house, in dry air, it is hard to keep them moist enough. So, after flowering, pot them on into something two thirds or more as wide as the plant. If you let them dry right out they will die.

But they do need some bright summer light (with cool, moist roots) to induce flowering growth for next year. This is why they are put outdoors for the summer months in a sunny but not hot position. I always stand them in a shallow saucer, to make drying out less easy. Some people prefer to plunge them into the soil, but they will still need watering in dry periods.

Those tiny point-of-sale pots contain almost neat peat and minimal nutrition, so that if you do not pot on in good time, the plant has to make all its new growth on starvation diet. Azaleas are not at all rich feeders, but starvation weakens them and reduces flower production. Dry starvation is even worse. Gentle feeding with tomato food as the flower buds swell is always beneficial, but do not use a high-nitrogen fertiliser.

The mottled leaves suggest mineral deficiency which a dose of Sequestrene or trace-element tonic would put right. The white leaf is a symptom of previous cold check and is not a problem.

Raising agaves

Q My small collection of agaves, including *Agave americana* 'Variegata' and *A. utahensis*, fail to thrive. They are in clay pots, in a peat and sand mixture, with crocks below. They overwinter in a cool greenhouse and spend summer on a south-facing terrace. I water and feed little. I take off the offshoots, but the plants are slow to increase in size and the lower leaves wither. How can I improve their lot, or am I expecting too much at this latitude? – J.D., Yorkshire

A Agaves are those great leathery, rosette-forming plants which clothe the slopes of the hills in Athens, and on whose grey, succulent leaves the local laddos and latter-day Byrons carve their initials. They are an American race, whose African counterparts are the aloes, another group of rosette-forming monsters.

Neither group is generally hardy in Britain, but old specimens of plain green *Agave americana* will stand a little ground frost. The best treatment is to grow them permanently under glass, or to use them as outdoor specimens in the summer. The Victorians loved to bed them out singly in ornamental urns, especially the striped and variegated forms, and at Cliveden House in the Thames valley there are even bronze artificial agaves in urns on the roofline: the ultimate labour-saving hanging basket.

They are all drought-loving plants, and I would not have an ounce of peat anywhere near them. In the wild they put down long roots to quest for what little water is available, but in a pot they can actually desicate, especially in too light a soil.

So long as they are to be under glass in winter, I would repot your plants into a good loam mixed with 25 per cent coarse gravel. Continue to take off the offsets, to concentrate the energies on the main rosette, and feed gently in summer only. Water little but regularly. Emergency soakings and sudden feedings tend to produce spurts of growth and the sloughing of old leaves, whereas only a slow, steady turnover of leaves is needed. Make sure they get all the light and air possible in the winter months especially, and apply a systemic fungicide to extend the life of the older leaves.

The people to buy agaves from are Architectural Plants, at Cooks Farm, Nuthurst, Horsham, W.Sussex RH13 6LH. Here a juvenile 18in across will cost over £30, and you may find a grand-daddy 6ft across if you have room for one.

Q I am reluctant to use the new water-retaining gels in my garden, as I do not like to use chemicals if I can avoid it. Are they safe? – T.J., Avon

A What useful things these new gels are. The tiny granules swell up to many times their size with water, keeping composts in tubs and baskets moist for plants over a long period. I have no hesitation in using them. They are a complicated polymer, like wallpaper paste, and have no harmful side effects. My worry would be that, using them in the soil rather than pots or baskets, they may linger in the soil for too long. I would not wish to make an area moist for ever, or to make life difficult for future drought-lovers. As ever, sparing use of any synthetic material is recommended.

Q Should I be able to grow a mulberry as a shrub in a tub on my balcony? I have seen them similarly used 40 floors up in New York skyscrapers, and would like to make a go of mine. – P.C., Devon

A The mulberry is a tough tree and can stand plenty of cold, so that should not be a problem. But do be sure the tub is well drained so it will not freeze in a waterlogged state. You will need to prune it back a little every year to keep it in bounds, and to repot it every year (or two), trimming back the longest roots, teasing off some of the old compost, and repotting it in fresh compost.

Tough or not, it always pays to protect the tub in winter with bubble film and sacking, and to stand the bush in a warm, sunny place throughout the summer.

Q We recently inherited several pots of agapanthus. One clump was bursting out of its pot and I split the roots. Advice in books seems to be that they should live in clay pots in well-drained compost. I am sparing with water and stand them in a sunny place in summer, but so far there have been no flowers despite healthy leaves. What should I do and where should I keep them? – M.A.G., Gloucestershire

[A] Agapanthus make splendid pot plants for a sunny terrace, with their strappy leaves and tall drum-heads of Mediterranean blue. All potted agapanthus are better brought indoors for the winter, except perhaps in mildest, seaside localities. You will read that some, such as the Headbourne hybrids, are hardy. But this really applies only to those planted in the ground. In pots the risk of loss in a cold snap is always possible.

Habits vary. Some agapanthus try to be evergreen, others deciduous; some are thin-stemmed, some fat; some have narrow leaves, others broad. Height varies from 16in to 4ft. As a rule of thumb, the more the plant tries to be evergreen, the taller and fatter its stems; and the broader its leaves, the more tender it will be.

So bring in the pots after the first light frosts, by which time their leaves may or may not have turned brown. Overwinter them almost dry, in a cold greenhouse for evergreens or a shed for deciduous varieties. Repotting is done in spring. They enjoy being truly pot-bound, but to keep them flowering generously from year to year they need liquid tomato feed through the summer. Yours sound to be in need of more food and water.

The difficulty with repotting is getting the plants out of the old pots, because the brain-like mass of fat, white roots gets so tight. Soak the roots first. *In extremis* you may need to break the pot. Forget 'teasing the roots apart'. You will need to chop the rootball in two, or perhaps four, with a sharp spade. Make sure you have left 2in of space above the soil level in the new pot, because agapanthus need a lot of water in summer, and as they become pot-bound again this space will disappear.

North-facing sites

[Q] My new flat has a north-facing flat roof outside its windows. On it are several aluminium trough-shaped cans, in which I would like to grow plants. Will any shrub tolerate growing in them, and could I fill them with garden soil? – E.M.R., Gwynedd

A Whatever you grow in them, they must be properly drained. Use a layer of coarse gravel or bricks to cover the holes. You could use garden soil in the cans, but it would be better aerated and lightened with a coarser compost or shredded bark. Those cans are going to be bitterly cold in winter, and not very sunny in summer. So the choice of plants is not great. In summer you could bed them out, of course, with shade-tolerant plants such as busy lizzies. But shrubs would have to have a cast-iron constitution to survive a bad winter. Their roots would also intermingle, making periodic repotting difficult. I would aim for permanent evergreen planting in some cans and colour from bedding in the others. Then you would at least have something to look at in winter. How about blocks of box, or sweet-scented *Sarcococca humilis*, like little runs of hedge? You could then move them against the wall for protection in winter, and use them to set out a variable *parterre* in summer. Taller shrubs always run the risk of blowing over, but you might grow plants which can be cut down each spring to give colourful winter twigs, like the dogwood *Cornus alba* 'Elegantissima' (variegated white in summer) and some of the blue or orange-stemmed willows. The more I think about it, the more I think it could be fun combined with the box hedges.

Q For years I have been trying to grow *Acer palmatum* 'Dissectum Atropurpureum' in pots on my north-westerly terrace. I protect the pots carefully from frost with straw. They come into leaf well enough, then in late May the leaves start drying up and further buds fail to develop. I have bought plants from local and specialist nurseries, but the same happens. The compost contains plenty of peat and is occasionally treated with Sequestrene. – E.W., Surrey

A The cut-leaved Japanese maples all have very delicate foliage, more so than ever while it is still unfolding. The soft threads gradually uncurl and expand, like the feet of fledgling birds. A cool root run is required, and shelter from hot sun. The leaves, once expanded, can stand more sun, but while they are developing they can scorch easily. On a north-westerly terrace sun should be no problem. They do not like wet or stagnant roots, and positively prefer dryness to that. Yet anything in a pot must be watered generously to keep them moist between times. I think warm, wet, peaty soil is your problem. I would repot next March, loosening out the roots to remove much of the old compost, and replanting in 60 per cent soil-based John Innes No.3 compost, 20 per cent peat-based compost, and 20 per cent coarse grit. If your plants were bought with large, densely-rooted, peaty root balls, it may be impossible to relieve them, short of pulling them to pieces.

Q I have been given a large terracotta pot 17in high with a diameter of 14in. It should be able to support something substantial. Please could you suggest something fruitful or flowerful I could plant in it? We have south-facing French windows with a full view of whatever we plant. – G.S.H., Somerset

A You do not say whether you want permanent or seasonal planting. My feeling is that, even if the clay is reasonably frost-proof, permanent plantings never look quite comfortable in terracotta. So, a summer planting, perhaps. If you want substance, try the yellow *Argyanthemum* 'Jamaica Primrose', which makes a really woody trunk during the season, and if well fed will make a bush 3ft each way and covered in flowers from June to October. Turn the pot periodically so you are not always looking at the north, least floriferous side of the bush.

Mending terracotta pots

Q Can you recommend an adhesive or some other means for repairing terracotta pots? – R.T., Cornwall

A There are so many good pots about today that I would hesitate to repair old ones. They are never reliable again. However, there are means of saving pots. Traditionally they are wired together, twisting the wires to hold the pieces firmly against each other, and drilling the pot if necessary to ensure pressure at the right places. The best adhesives are those of the epoxy resin type, such as are used for repairing china. There are slow setting ones for domestic use, and almost instant ones for use on cars. Neither will last forever since the pot is porous and water or salts will eventually succeed in loosening the grip. But it should last a few years. A combination of adhesive and wires will guard against sudden disintegration and further breakage.

Q I wish to coat an enamel sink with hypertufa before using it as a small herb garden. Where can I buy this? – M.M.P., Hertfordshire

A Hypertufa is a fancy name for cement with roughage in it, – usually peat. The standard recipe is 1 part cement, 2 parts sand and 2 parts peat. Or if you do not want to buy a bag of cement, buy a bag of dry-mixed mortar and add peat to that. Coir is probably just as good as peat. Mix it like porridge, and plaster it onto the sink, moulding it with your hands (in gloves: cement is caustic) until it looks like a stone sink. The trick for good long-term adhesion is to roughen up the sink first. If you think you can do it without breaking the sink, use a chisel. Otherwise scar it with an electric stone-cutting wheel. Then cover it with a rough coat of an epoxy resin mixture, to leave a surface on to which the hypertufa can get a grip. Let the hypertufa dry slowly in a shady place out of the wind, to reduce cracking.

Several readers have written to tell me their preferred materials for repairing pots. M.F. of Kent, swears by Plastic Padding Chemical

Metal, made by Loctite UK Ltd, Watchmead, Welwyn Garden City
AL7 1JB; tel. 01707 821000. Peter King, editor of *Good Gardens
Guide*, uses Milliput (The Milliput Co, Unit 5, The Marian,
Dolgellau, LL40 1UU; tel. 01341 422562) because it comes in
different colours, including terracotta. A.L. of Hampshire prefers
normal (not quick-set) Araldite, available from most hardware
shops, but feels it is important to sit the glued pots over a light bulb
on his garage floor, so the heat cures the glue properly before the
pot is moved.

Q I did not appreciate that a bucket-sized terracotta pot I bought
was not frost-proof. I planted it with tulips, but it was
**damaged by frost in November. Is there any way I can improve the
appearance? It is now discoloured with a powdery surface. –**
M.S., Hampshire

A The real hazard of frost to pots is either bursting altogether,
from pressure of frozen soil, or of the surface crumbling as a
result of absorbed water being frozen. A powdery and discoloured
surface suggests just salts in your water or compost crystallising on
the pot. Limy water does this especially badly. A good scrub down
with soapy water may solve the problem. In limy areas, the use of
glazed (and expensive) Chinese pots solves this problem. On the
other hand, in some circumstances there is attraction in bloomy,
licheny old pots. Not surprisingly, those very old pots of coarser
clay tend to grow lichen less well than the finer modern clays.

Seaside problems

Q I have moved recently from a most productive garden to a flat
overlooking the sea with a 50ft long walled balcony. I am
shocked to find how little will survive the salt wind scorch.

Geraniums and begonias survive but evergreens get scorched. –
J.S., Hampshire

A Wild and salty it may be (what a recipe for retirement), but it will also be relatively mild so close to the sea. I would use hebes and olearias, and all those strappy-leaved plants you see lashing about in newsreels of hurricanes such as phormium, yucca, and cordyline. I would also make the most of succulents, such as tubs full of the elephantine *Agave americana* and baskets of trailing lampranthus and carpobrotus. Make the most of geraniums as you do now.

Q *Bidens aurea*: **where can I buy seeds please, and can I take them from this year's plants?** – W.H.R., Surrey

A Suttons list *Bidens aurea*, and all the major seed companies sell *B. ferulifolia*, which is I suspect the same thing from our practical point of view, even if they should be botanically distinguishable. Bidens seeded itself in my gravel path in Northumberland the year after I had grown it in pots nearby. So, yes, save your own seed. It is an easy member of the daisy family. It can be overwintered as cuttings taken in autumn and kept under glass if you prefer. But as it is the darling of the hanging basket industry just now, for its sprawly habit and endless yellow stars, you should find small plants easy to buy again next year.

Q **A few weeks ago you showed a picture of a succulent with several stems growing in a pot in Mr Serge Charles's garden. Could you tell me what this is, and how to grow it?** – M.O'T., Eire

A The plant was an aeonium, and a good specimen does indeed look like a bunch of large houseleeks with woody stalks.

Aeonium arboreum is not frost-hardy, but can stay outdoors down to freezing. If you bring the plant in for the winter, keep it very dry, and as light as possible.

There is a wonderful, black-leaved form called 'Arnold Schwarzkopff' which sells on sight, and a species called *A. tabuliforme* in which, table-like, the overlapping leaves look as if they have been pressed absolutely flat into great discs the size of plates.

Q How can I raise large numbers of the foliage plant *Helichrysum* 'Silver Bush'? I would like to add two to each of my 50 hanging baskets, which would cost me £100 to buy them as plantlets in April. I have a heated greenhouse and sodium lighting. – E.C.T., Devon

A Helichrysums make excellent grey foils for more colourful planting in pots and baskets. But you must always plan for large numbers of anything. If you really want your plants this year, try buying 20 plants in April, grow them hard and fast under glass, and plunder them for tip cuttings in May. Both parent plants and cuttings will be ready to go outside in June. Alternatively, if you can wait until next year, buy just a few plantlets, grow them on, and take all your cuttings in late summer, keeping them cool enough to stand still through the winter under glass.

Q Separating a paved area at the back of my house from the garden is a new low wall. The wall is broken by two entrances with steps, leading up to the garden, and on either side of the steps are planting holes in the wall top, about the size of a 2-litre ice-cream box. What could I grow in them? I would like something colourful and fragrant, such as ground-cover roses. – E.M.W., Cumbria

A These are very small holes for permanent planting, and you will have to water them like mad. I take it they have drainage holes at the bottom? I would go for regular seasonal planting, and treat them like small hanging baskets. You might even like to make liners for them, which could be slotted in with the planting already established. Roses would not enjoy having their roots cooked in little raised planters, and nor would many small shrubs. But you could plant primroses and helianthemums for spring, and verbena and petunias for summer.

14

Pruning

Q My garden is bounded in part by the side of my neighbour's brick garage. Many years ago I planted a *Cotoneaster horizontalis* to hide it, and it has succeeded. But it is now becoming too large and unmanageable. If I cut it back to its main branches, is it likely to produce enough foliage to cover the wall again soon, or should I dig it out and start again with a new plant? – R.S.B., Cambridgeshire

A It is well worth trying to cut it back (next March), especially as the task of digging out the root would be a heavy job. But cotoneasters sprout rather unpredictably from cuts into old wood. They usually do it, but not necessarily where you want them to. They appear at silly angles in the wrong place. Evenness is not quickly regained. You may find some branches will die back in the next few years. Nevertheless it is worth trying, as a new plant will take several years to cover the wall again. If it does not respond willingly to cutting in the first year, do not wait any longer: dig it out and start again.

Q I have a courtyard garden, planted with a few evergreens and a few raised beds for summer colour. In one corner the

prostrate juniper, *Juniperus x media* 'Pfitzeriana' is outgrowing its position and narrowing the path. When should it be pruned? – P.B.M., London SW6

A The honest answer is, a few years ago. This 19th century hybrid may not develop into a tree, but it is far from prostrate. The branches arch upwards at 45 degrees, and droop over at the tips. In 20 years it can make a pile five yards across and three high. To keep it small and attractive, pruning needs to be little and often, nibbling away a few inches off the leaders a couple of times a year on sides where it cannot be allowed to spread.

Pruning an old plant hard is never satisfactory. Old limbs the thickness of your wrist or more, when cut hard back, frequently fail to shoot again, or if they do, weak branches are thrown which cross back into the bush. A heavily pruned plant rarely looks attractive again.

If your plant can be nibbled into shape, then keep it. If not, I would start again with something new.

Q Can you please tell me if it is safe to prune off about 2ft all over an 8-year-old 11ft lilac, *Syringa* 'Madame Lemoine' (double white), without loss of subsequent years' blooms? The base is now bare to 3ft and I have planted a clematis to hide it and give colour later in the year. I dead-head the lilac every year, and it flowers well, but I am nervous of more severe pruning. – J.M.B., Anglesey

A If you take off 2ft all over now – in August – there will be no flowers the next year, as the new shoots produced subsequently will not have time to ripen flower buds. In the common lilac the new shoots naturally grow at the same time as the flowers, and have a long season to mature. To stabilise the flowering height of your bush, you can take back perhaps a third of all the branches by 2ft every year, leaving the remainder to flower. But to make the bush better furnished at the base will require more severe pruning. Cut all the trunks down in winter to 4–5 ft, taking the outside ones down to 3ft. Lilacs respond to this well, but need a year or two to return to generous flowering. Once the ideal height is regained, you can prune as for stabilising above. An armful or two cut for the house should do the trick.

I wonder if your clematis will thrive in the lilac? There are few plants with more greedy surface roots than lilac, so I hope the clematis, itself a hungry plant, is planted well to the side of its roots, and its stems trained across.

Rose pruning

Q A lengthy stay in hospital has kept me from pruning my roses this winter. Is it too late now?

A It is almost never too late. Now, at the end of March, I would not hesitate to prune hybrid tea and floribunda roses. If you do not prune now, the bushes will not be stimulated into making good new growth low down this year. By next year the bushes may be beginning to look rather top-heavy. You can of course prune harder next year, but it may then delay flowering a little.

Pruning roses in April may seem very cruel. You will be cutting off strong young shoots which have arisen from the wood to be removed. And, yes, it will weaken the bushes and waste their energy. But I would still prune rather than not. Only be a little gentler about it. Take less out, and leave some of those shoots which have already begun to move. And make sure the bushes are properly fed to compensate for their wasted effort. There is nothing like old manure for roses, but a granulated rose feed will do the trick, too, preferably topped off with some garden compost.

Q I have a large specimen of *Magnolia soulangiana* beside the door into my garden. It must be very old because its trunk is a foot across at the base. I need to prune it back as the path along the house is becoming impassable. When should I do it, and how? – F.S., Sussex

A Rather than take off any large limbs, it will be better to nibble it back, little by little for a couple of years. If you can achieve what you need by cutting into stems no thicker than your thumb, then I would go ahead with some pruning, in April, cutting back not to a bald stump, but to a living sideshoot. You should be able to get it back to 4–5ft thick in time. It is most important to prune all the way up the tree. If you allow an overhang to develop at the top, it will shade out the lower growths and you will not achieve a dense structure at the bottom. Take back some branches this year, top and bottom, and then some more next year, until you have it in hand. But if possible avoid the removal of heavy limbs and serious shocks to the plant. Major limbs, if they must be removed, are a winter job.

Q A Judas tree grows in the north-west corner of my small garden. It is about 20ft high and had a bonanza flowering this year. A limb has torn off taking wood with it. The tree appears top heavy and I want to prune it. How shall I proceed? – B.C., Somerset

A *Cercis silquastrum*, the Judas tree, is a plant for hot, thin soils, and is good on chalk. Softer growing conditions – rich soil and abundant moisture – exacerbate the tree's natural tendency to produce forked stems which are prone to gale or snow damage. (It is not a strong tree; if Judas really hanged himself on a cercis I reckon it was just a cry for help, not a serious attempt!) The tree can be pruned, but the response is unpredictable, new shoots not always coming where you would wish them to be. It is therefore better to thin the tree if necessary, rather than carve it back, to reduce weight and assist longevity. The curious thing about the Judas tree is that it produces flowers directly out of the bark of older wood. In the southern Mediterranean I have seen hard pruned trees producing massive patches of pink flowers on leafless limbs all of 5in in diameter. It is an extraordinary sight.

Q Will my *Fatsia japonica* grow again if I cut it back to about 12in, and when should I do this? It is now 6ft tall and growing happily, but I need its dramatic effect much lower down. If I cut it, will the pieces root? – R.C.H., Gloucestershire

A By all means cut down your castor-oil plant in spring. If it has a single stem only, you have no choice about where to cut, but multi-stem shrubs are better cut down over two years (half one year, half the next) since the bush is weakened less by this. You will get even better, bigger, glossy-fingered leaves on the new shoots. Seed is the easier method of propagation, and I would not try rooting the prunings. Is your plant indoors or planted outside? Results are usually better from heavy pruning when the plant has a full root system in the garden. Once it is growing again, feed it well.

Trimming lithospermum

Q My lithospermum has been planted about three years and is getting straggly. Should I cut it back? How much, and when? – P.M., Hampshire

A *Lithospermum diffusum*, or *Lithodora diffusa* as it is now called, is a most attractive plant but not easy to keep compact. It looks wonderful as a first-year plant in a small pot and covered in those intense, deep blue tubular flowers. In my nursery days we could never have enough of it to sell when it was in flower in the garden. Once planted, its wiry stems spread out spider-like, but you would be hard pressed to call the result a mat. Doily might be a better word, for it covers the ground most inefficiently. It serves best when grown into and amongst other low plants such as heathers and dwarf rhododendrons. (Like them, it is a lime-hater.) To encourage neatness and density of foliage it pays to nip out the tips of the leading shoots regularly, forcing it to branch out side-ways. Planted on its own, it almost always becomes bald at the centre in 2–3 years. Look out for the well-tried clones, 'Heavenly Blue' and 'Grace Ward'. More compact and lime-tolerant is the species *Lithodora oleifolia*, which has silvery leaves in an evergreen hummock. Its flowers are a fine sky blue but lack that captivating lustre of the commoner species.

Q Bearing in mind that we may have another dry summer, should shrubs have been pruned back more fiercely than usual in order to reduce moisture loss, or would this ultimatly cause more damage to the plants? – N.J., London

A There are two issues here. First, whether to prune or not. I would never hold back on pruning plants like *Buddleia davidii* or red-stemmed dogwoods in case of a forthcoming drought. If only the weather was more predictable! Better to have shrubs properly pruned, in long-term health, and flowering well, than getting old and woody just in case there is a drought. Second, how hard to prune. As a general rule plants coast through times of trial better if they are left alone. Hard pruning produces the stimulus to yet more vigorous growth, which, once underway, makes yet greater demands on the plant for water and nutrition. On the other hand, if the drought comes early in the summer (these are the real killers) before plants have had time to make new growth, then growth will be minimal, and they will be starved of energy by having so little leaf. Early summer droughts take their toll in longer-term weakness. Late summer droughts, after growth is made, can more easily be coasted through. If a shrub is only going to grow well with artificial watering, then it is in the wrong place. So my answer is, don't hard prune during a drought, but don't hold back on the off-chance of one coming along.

Q I have several *Skimmia japonica* 'Nymans' and 'Rubella' which are 11 years old and doing well. In fact they are getting too large – about 40in high and 48in across. The gardening books say no pruning is needed. But can I reduce them, and if so how and when? The last thing I want to do is dig them up and start again. – R.R., Middlesex

A If you cut down a 48in holly at the stocking tops it will be two feet high again by the next summer. Not so a skimmia. Yes, they are a tough, evergreen berrying bush, but they are slow-growing and easily shocked. They do not sprout so easily from old wood. If you can, I would nibble back and thin back your bushes to the required size, cutting in spring just before growth starts. If you have to be more drastic, do it in stages, taking down a third of the branches each year, so that the bushes are never leafless for long and thus seriously weakened.

Q I have inherited a *Callistemon rigidus*, and am not sure how to prune it. This is its third year, and the 'cones' left behind by the flowers go further and further along the stem. How far back do I cut it, and if I cut back to the cones, will it flower again beyond? – H.L., Somerset and M.B., Berkshire **also asks how to propagate callistemons.**

A Callistemons, or Australian bottle-brushes, do not require much pruning. Given bright light, hot sun and wind, they make a loose, eventually arching shrub, rather in the manner of the common broom in Britain. However, in our climate they need help to keep them suitably dense. The sheltered positions we give them because they are tender tend to make them leggy. Pinching out the leading shoots in the early years is most important. If a plant has become leggy and bald, you can cut back some of the longer shoots in spring, preferably to an existing side shoot. Stumps do not respond well. Cut below the cones if you wish. Unfortunately, the flowers are produced along the longest, strongest stems, so some loss of flower will result. The flowers do not really produce cones but woody receptacles, packed like corn on the cob along the twigs. Seed as fine as dust is released from within, and you may find the soil under pot-grown callistemons covered in minute seedlings. Cuttings should be taken semi-ripe in summer.

Q The heathers and heaths in my garden are becoming over-grown. I want to cut the areas back so that they occupy their allocated spaces. What is the best time of the year to do this? – R.F., Cheshire

A With the firm exception of the tree heath *Erica arborea*, most heaths and heathers do not respond to being cut back hard. Yes, you can reduce the area they cover by cutting back sideways in March, but do not expect old wood to sprout new shoots or old plants to look young again. It is far better to have the lot out and start again with fresh young plants. The life span of heathers varies. Some look good for 5–6 years, others for 30 if you keep them well pinched back in their youth and middle age. Replant in September/October or March/April. *E. arborea* can grow up to 10ft or more, with real trunks. These can be cut down low in spring and they sprout away well. It can live for 100 years or more.

Cutting back hollies

Q We have a 20ft holly in our garden. It berries well and was planted by the previous owners. But the top third of the tree has become rather bald and short of leaf. Can we safely cut the trunk off where it starts to get thin, or is there a way of making the top thicken up again? – C.W., Oxfordshire

A Hollies are long-lived trees, and can reach as much as 40ft in 150 years. As they start to die of old age, limbs at the top will become thin and then die back. It is perfectly possible to cut back old hollies very hard indeed. But it is always more successful to cut them off at ground level, in the winter. Growth will be back up to 6ft in a couple of years, and bushy with it. Cutting back to standing trunks always leads to further die-back later, and it is much safer to cut at ground level. Your holly is too young to be senescent. The cause of the problem may be either damage to the trunk at high level, caused by a torn branch, or perhaps squirrels, in which case cut off the trunk just below the damage and let it regrow. Or it may be the result of a root problem such as waterlogging, which must be rectified by mechanical means. Hollies in deep shade can become very thin and short of leaf, but once in the sun again they will fill out and thicken.

15

Weeds

Q For 26 years I have been trying to eradicate Japanese knotweed from my own and neighbouring gardens. Apart from the ability to break through concrete, it resists all types of weedkiller, including glyphosate which only spots the leaves. Any suggestions please? – J.L.R., Essex

A You know how hard this thing is to kill. All I can add is that any plant regularly defoliated is weakened, so never let it develop proper stems. I wonder too if you have tried putting the weedkiller down into the stems? So often plants difficult to kill survive because it is so hard to get the chemicals into their system through the leaves. Why not try cutting the stems off at 6in and putting ammonium sulphamate (Root Out) into the hollowed stems? If it helps, do let me know.

Q We have a gravel drive running alongside a border containing Japanese knotweed, and in spring knotweed shoots always appear in the gravel. Each year we snip them off at ground level, and this effectively contains the knotweed in its designated area. Could a more permanent remedy be suggested, such as sinking a vertical membrane to contain the knotweed? – J.K., Surrey

A Japanese knotweed (*Fallopia japonica*, previously called *Polygonum cuspidatum*) has a nasty habit of always getting where it wants to be in the end. It has fat, questing rhizomes that provide a tough support for those 8ft. stems. However, a strong vertical barrier will restrain it, so long as it goes down deep enough, to 3–4 ft. or more. Old corrugated iron will do, preferably set with the corrugations vertical to drive the shoots downwards rather than sideways. Set the top of the barrier out of sight, just under the surface of the soil. With this in place, and if there are no tree roots in the drive, you might try putting a little total weedkiller, such as sodium chlorate, on to the drive at this point, if the knotweed resurfaces.

It is good practice to plant new hedges at the back of a garden border behind such a vertical corrugated membrane, so that the main roots are driven downwards during the early years, thus reducing the amount of surface root in the border, and also reducing the amount of damage you will do to important hedge roots during cultivation.

Q I have a red 'Max Graf' rose which has of course turned into a monster. There are nettles growing in the middle which I cannot get at to dig out. Can you recommend a spray which will kill the nettles without harming the rose? – R.F.H., Suffolk

A 'Max Graf' is a hybrid of *Rosa wichuraiana*, and produces sprawling shoots yards long. It is sold as a ground-cover rose, whereas in fact it might better be described as what Christopher

Lloyd calls a 'ground un-cover rose'. It is low, I grant you, but it is far from weed-proof, and vicious to the hands.

To kill the nettles, apply a herbicide containing glyphosate (Roundup, Tumbleweed, etc) using a rubber glove as applicator, and keeping splashes off the rose foliage. One or two moist caresses will do the trick.

In winter apply a granular residual herbicide such as Casoron G4 to the area under the rose stems, to keep it clean through next season; and wriggle a heavy mulch through the stems, to make weeds arriving as seeds from above easier to fish out roots-and-all with just a tug.

So-called ground-cover roses are often better used over tree stumps or trailing down over walls, where the vexed question of how to weed underneath them is not a problem.

Q I have had Cape figwort, *Phygelius capensis*, in my garden for 20 years, Much as I like it, it always reappears when I have cleared a patch of it for replanting with something else. The roots run very deep. Is there any way of containing it? I hesitate to use SBK on it in case it damages surrounding plants and bulbs which it smothers. – P.S., Devon

A Brushwood killers like SBK are probably going to be your answer here. Dig out what you can first, then apply the chemical to the fresh regrowth with a heavy-duty rubber glove, rather than a spray. Your other plants below will be unharmed so long as no drips fall on them. Several treatments will be necessary, and you may do better to try more than one chemical, to see how it responds. Do not give it any respite; treat the shoots as soon as they are growing strongly, so that the plant cannot renew its strength from the sunlight.

The sister species *Phygelius aequalis* also spreads hard, but it makes more of a solid clump too, and is therefore more useful in the garden. It is not actually possible to grow very much under *P. aequalis*. The hybrid 'African Queen' is orangy red with a yellow throat. 'Moonraker' is a pale lemon yellow. All phygelius can be planted in a submerged ring of deep corrugated iron if it is felt they are a threat, but this seems extreme for a plant which is less than fully hardy.

Brambles

Q I am trying to tame 10 acres of French woodland and meadow near the Spanish frontier. Nettles and brambles are the main problems, the latter in vast impenetrable masses 10ft high and 30ft across. The local recommendation is to use a total weed-killer such as sodium chlorate. But is there a weed-killer which would allow us to grass over the affected areas straight away? Similarly, how do we get rid of brambles with minimum harm to the woodland floor? Friends in the UK could send us the necessary chemicals. – D.S., south-west France

A A weed-killer containing glyphosate will solve your nettle problem and allow you to sow grass almost immediately. But do find your chemicals in France, to be legally correct. Try a local agricultural merchant for advice. Each country has its own stringent rules on such matters, and in Germany this particular chemical is not licensed for use, despite the fact that we in Britain regard it as one of the safer weed-killers.

I would tackle the brambles first mechanically, using a brush-cutter (a metal rotating disk, like a strimmer) and a big bonfire as the first means of attack. Spraying huge clumps is dangerous and difficult, but with the plants thus reduced and weakened, you could spray the young regrowth with a chemical brushwood-killer. Expect to have to spray a couple of times for an effective kill. I find with old-established brambles that once the tops are cut off it is almost as easy to dig out the roots as to wait for them to succumb to sprays. Patience and a good spade can work wonders.

Q How can I get rid of horsetail, which has completely overrun my rock garden? I imagine it will need fairly drastic measures and may mean restructuring the whole thing from scratch. – B.L., Warwickshire

A Plainly you know how hard it is to get rid of horsetail (*Equisetum*). Digging it out helps, but it is not the perfect solution: there isn't one. To get the better of horsetail, whether by digging or chemical means, you really need to be prepared to settle for a scorched earth policy for a few years. Remove your cultivated plants to another part of the garden, taking care to bring no horse-tail root with them. Then you can start.

Option one is to use a total weedkiller such as sodium chlorate over the whole area, for a couple of years running. (You can only use this where there are no tree roots or other plants which can suffer from taking up the poison.)

Option two is to dig out as much root as you can, then spray the regrowth with glyphosate. On a rockery this means removing all the stone, which is simply not worth while. Here it is better to try the third option, which is just to spray.

Horsetail has hard shiny foliage which repels sprays. The only useful way to get the spray into the plant is to bruise the foliage first, with a broom handle. The glyphosate solution (sold to dilute as Tumbleweed or Roundup) should be further diluted, by three parts solution to one part paraffin, which also helps to get the chemical into the foliage. Several applications will be necessary.

Rampant campanulas

Q **My mother gave me a campanula many years ago. It is a lovely blue, upright and super for flower arranging – and lethal. It has spread over most of my third of an acre, and from front garden to back. The roots are deep, and impossible to dig out. Pathclear doesn't touch it, but Tumbleweed [glyphosate] yellows the leaves. However it has taken refuge among other plants where I cannot spray it. What is it and how can I get rid of it? – I.E.D., Bedfordshire**

A This must be *Campanula rapunculoides*. It is indeed lovely, and I shall grow on the plantlet you sent me to confirm identification. I may however then feel constrained to put it into a local charity plant sale.

It grows to about 30in, with pointed, heart-shaped lower leaves, and stalkless leaves attaching to the stem. It flowers from June to September. For a history of man's longstanding enmity with *C. rapunculoides*, see *Campanulas* by Lewis and Lynch, 1989, from Christopher Helm. Glyphosate does indeed kill it, but only those crowns it touches. So spray open areas, and touch those stems which have grown through other plants with the same chemical on a brush or rubber glove. Never let it seed. If you are prepared to use chemicals, then digging is certainly not worth the effort with this plant.

Q Our new house has crocuses established in grass beneath apple trees. Unfortunately there is also a tremendous number of dandelions. Is there a safe way of ridding the area of dandelions without damaging the crocuses? – G.M.McC., Devon

A This is easily solved. Crocuses, like grasses, are unaffected by the normal selective hormone weedkillers used to remove broad-leaved weeds from turf. So your options are a) spray the whole area of grass with selective turf weedkiller, b) carefully spot treat the individual dandelion crowns with 4–5 drops only of the less dangerous weedkiller, glyphosate, c) kill the dandelions by putting a small pinch of salt into the centre of each crown, or d) if they are few enough, dig them out. If the numbers are huge, the best approach might be to use a selective first, but rather than following up with the inevitable second or third treatment for stubborn crowns, follow up with spot treatment of glyphosate.

Are the dandelions so terrible in rough grass? I met some Sri Lankan tourists last year who were as reverential of our dandelion-filled hedgerows as we are of their orchids.

Q I have been in my new garden for 12 months. Having removed ancient roses and shrubs, dug the soil over for 6 months and imported loads of manure last September, I now have a problem. There are celandines everywhere. How do I rid the beds of this weed? – R.K., Kent

A Did they arrive with the manure, I wonder? Probably not; it is too soon for seed to have flowered, and unlikely that there were tubers in the manure. Beware the celandine, all ye who covet those promising heaps of molehill soil on pasture land. So often they can be riddled with celandines.

And once celandines are in the garden, they are difficult to remove. If a bed is empty, chemical sterilisation under polythene is the best option. Simply covering the beds with black polythene is not effective over one season only. Smaller infestations may be dug out and burned, taking care that none of that cluster of little white tubers falls back into the soil, for every one will make a new clump. They are susceptible to spraying with glyphosate, but you need to keep hard at them.

In shrubberies there are worse weeds than celandines, and a virtue can be made of necessity. They are attractive in flower, look wonderfully sunny and fresh with blue *Scilla sardensis* under shrubs, and disappear below ground by midsummer. The only drawbacks are that they die down rather shabbily, and that they tend to get absolutely and ineradicably everywhere else. Perfectionists will keep them to the wild garden only. Others will say, 'Ah yes, but imagine underplanting big hostas with the bronze-leaved, form "Brazen Hussy", or putting it with yellow crocuses, or Bowles' golden grass. . . .'

Q Can you help me to rid my garden of that pernicious small weed, oxalis? Is there a weedkiller which will do the job? – G.K.B., Cambridgeshire

A Weeds were never so attractive! There are several small garden species of oxalis, with shamrock leaves and tubular flowers, and while some are well-behaved, others are insidious weeds. They have a double means of increase, by fine translucent roots, and by tiny bulblets produced above and below ground. Heads they win, tails we lose.

The two troublesome species are *Oxalis corymbosa* (pinkish purple) and *O. corniculata* (yellow, sometimes with bronzed leaves). Dig out all you can, taking care not to lose any bulblets back into the soil. Burn them or bin them, but do not put them anywhere near a compost heap. Then treat what reappears (and it will, no question of it) with a weedkiller containing glyphosate. The leaves are shiny, and the addition of some washing-up liquid will help the chemical to adhere to them. Stick at it, digging and spraying regularly, until all is clear. Of course, if it has infiltrated the crowns of other plants, you may end by removing them too.

Bindweed problems

Q I have quite a lot of bindweed in my garden. I dig out what I can, but the majority is deep rooted, and breaks off to grow again. It even runs into the lawns. Is there anything which will kill it? – O.H., Isle of Wight

A With regular application, glyphosate (Roundup and Tumbleweed) will kill bindweed. It will also kill the plants in your border if it gets on the leaves. So insert tall canes into the infested borders and pull the trails of bindweed across to them so they can climb up. When the canes are well covered, mix up some glyphosate in a bucket, and using a rubber glove, dip your hand in the solution, shake off the drops, and rub your hand up and down the bindweed leaves on the canes. In 2–3 weeks the stems will die back, and more will appear. The operation needs repeating for a year or two to overcome it. It is not a pretty sight!

Really bad infestations may well be worth emptying the border for first, so you can dig every scrap out before starting with weedkillers. In that situation you might want to use the total weedkiller, sodium chlorate, if there are no trees or shrubs there to be poisoned.

Never let bindweed flower in the garden, even if it flowers in all the hedgerows around you.

Q If one weeds the lazy way, by just pulling off the emergent leaves, there should be an ideal time to do it. Too early, and there is still energy left in the root to make more leaves. Too late, and the new leaves are making energy to feed the roots. I am

thinking especially of bindweed. When should I decapitate it? –
J.S., Hampshire

As a rule of thumb, allow a plant to make all the growth it can short of making a useful area of leaf. Bracken, for instance, is cut when it has put all its energy into making that tall stalk but before the leaves unscroll from it. Repeating this treatment over three or more years will often kill it. Ground elder is best given no quarter at all, since it spreads leaf so quickly. Pull it off as soon as you can get hold of it. If you have it lurking under shrubs, slide the hover mower under there as you pass. Leave no enclave unsmitten.

Bindweed is harder than either of these to defeat by constant defoliation. Nipping off finger-length wisps has to be done with appalling regularity, and always there will be those stems which have sidled into some other plant and hope to pass unnoticed in a crowd. It is effort better spent to wait until the bindweed stems are a foot or so long, and then pull them off, hopefully with the top of the white root attached. Burn these or bin them. Leave them lying around and you will find the blackbirds flinging the white roots around the bed, disappointed they are not worms. (They do the same with the perennial scarlet nasturtium, *Tropaeolum speciosum*, whose roots are disturbingly similar.) You can of course train bindweed on to canes, and then rub the leaves with a weedkiller containing glyphosate. It kills it – eventually.

How can I get rid of ground elder? It is rampant in my garden. Last year I dug down 3ft to remove it but it still comes back. What else – what poison – what horrible treatment can I try next? – J.B., North Yorkshire

The greatest allies of anyone battling against ground elder are tenacity and glyphosate.

Glyphosate, the active ingredient in Roundup and Tumbleweed, is relatively benign as weed-killers go. But it is wonderfully efficient. It works by killing back into the roots from contact with the leaves.

To kill something as tough as ground elder takes at least one application. The first will slowly discolour the leaves until they collapse and kill most of the running white root. But invariably some will survive to show its face again, perhaps months later, perhaps a year later. Cleaning ground of tough weeds like this is always a slow business, I am afraid, and you must be patient. The real headache with ground elder is that it threads its roots into other plants where it is hard to get at. Clumps of perennials get infested with it and so do the roots of shrubs, lawn edges, and wall bottoms. Here it is much harder to treat with glyphosate, as the chemical must not be allowed to get on to the leaves of garden plants or they will die too.

Ideally you should empty the area to be cleaned of all plants, splitting perennials finely enough to see that there is no ground elder root left in the crowns. The pieces must be planted in clean ground elsewhere, until their real home is finally free of the weed.

Above all, do not give the weed any quarter. Where you cannot spray, defoliate it constantly to weaken it, and never let it flower and seed in the garden. I know someone who claims to have eradicated a smallish outbreak of ground elder over a few years simply by constant and repeated defoliation; so stick at it.

Q I have a tryffid in my new garden – a 10ft climber, with a big, white, fleshy taproot like a parsnip, palmate leaves, springy tentacles like a hop, and yellow-green flowers where the leaves join the stem. It died down in the winter, but is on the march again, with several seedlings also appearing. What is it, please? – W.R., North Yorkshire

A This is white bryony, or *Bryonia dioica*, to be found in wild-flower books rather than gardening books. Its favourite location is old hedges or low scrub. The flowers may not amount to much, but the swags of red berries on female plants in autumn are delightful. It looks as if it ought to be one of the nightshades and a member of the solanum family. In fact it is in the melon and cucumber family, but nevertheless it is seriously poisonous, particularly in root and berry.

Hogweed hazards

Q Can you tell me how to get rid of hogweed? There is a toddler who is liable to be walking into it at regular intervals, and I do not wish to risk skin burns. – M.C.C., Tyne and Wear

A Giant hogweed *Heracleum mantegazzianum*, is an extraordinarily statuesque and beautiful plant. Unfortunately it is also capable of causing serious skin blisters by contact with its leaves, or more especially its sap. Some people are more sensitive to its attack than others. Blisters appear a day or so after contact, and the reaction is photosensitive, so wash and cover up any knowingly affected skin.

Hogweed, like all cow-parsley relatives, has a hollow stem. (Imagine my surprise to have met a didgeridoo player, who had made his own instrument out of dried hogweed with a waxed mouthpiece!) If you cut off the tops carefully, wearing fully protective clothing, you can then kill the root by putting a teaspoonful of salt into the hollow stump. This is much safer and more effective than trying to spray plants 8ft tall, and the leaves and stem can be composted. But, like cow-parsley, it also produces many seeds and seedlings. These may continue to appear for a few years. If you recognise them at the seedling stage, hoe them off; if they are slightly larger, a touch of glyphosate on the leaves will see them off.

It makes sense not to have this plant when small children are regularly present. If you like it sufficiently, it will be easy enough to reintroduce from seed when the children are older. I saw a whole border of it last year, under the wall of a Norfolk flint manor house, and it was fabulous. It can be purchased from John Carter, the Polygonum specialist, at Rowden Gardens, Brentnor, Tavistock, Devon EX16 7EW.

Remember that some people are to a lesser extent affected by the other common member of the genus, *Heracleum sphondylium*, the cow-parsnip. Blistering from both plants leaves a brown stain which can last for months.

Q I have been told that the bracken I have in my garden (one frond) can cause cancer. Is this so? – J.H., Sussex

A There is some evidence that the spores of bracken are carcinogenic, and if bracken has appeared in your garden, then there must be more around nearby. Remove your frond if it worries you, but what about the rest, pumping out spores by the billion every summer? What is a reasonable risk? The Japanese cook and eat young bracken shoots, and it is suggested that this may have a bearing on the high incidence of stomach cancer in Japan. Life is full of choices. I would be more worried about the bracken smothering my precious plants.

Q I have a shrub border 25 x 6ft which is overrrun with periwinkle. I am digging out the perwinkle as it is choking some of the choicer shrubs. What weedkiller should I use to kill those roots which are inaccessible?

A I wonder which periwinkle it is? Both *Vinca major* and *V. minor* have attractive blue flowers; both are quite capable of choking small shrubs and are extremely greedy surface rooters. Digging out seems to deal well enough with the smaller species, but

V. major, will hang on to the very end. Lift the low branches of your shrubs and cut off the perwinkle at ground level. Then when regrowth begins, massage a strong solution of Roundup (glyphosate) into the new growth with a rubber glove. Several applications may be necessary. Spraying will be ineffectual as the shiny leaves repel water.

Q Three years ago we made a pebble garden on the south side of our house. It is very successful and everything grows profusely, including *Houttuynia cordata* 'Chameleon', with its pretty green and red leaves and white flowers. I did not know it was invasive, and there was no warning of this on the label. It now covers an area 10ft across. How can I eradicate it? I have painted the leaves with neat Roundup to no avail. – M.M.S., Nottinghamshire

A The first time I saw houttuynia it was growing in rough grass, and the fishy stench of its bruised leaves was pointed out to me. I tried to grow the double-flowered form for a few years in poor dry soil and almost lost it. Moisture is what it likes. You can even grow it in shallow water for the summer months. The coloured foliage form 'Chameleon' needs sun to show its best colours, and it was the darling of Chelsea Flower Show pots and planters for a year or two after its introduction. The root will run undergound when it is happy, which makes getting it out of other perennials difficult. In order to make the Roundup (glyphosate) effective you need to bruise the foliage before application, so it can gain direct entry to the plant's tissues. Or you can massage it into the leaves with a rubber glove.

16

Pests, Diseases and Vicious Beasts

Q My garden is overrun with rabbits. It is so disheartening. Could you give me the names of some herbaceous plants which rabbits do not like? – G.C., Sussex

A Rabbits are nosy and daft. There is nothing so attractive to them as something newly planted, even if they hate the taste of it. Perhaps it is the young inexperienced ones which do this. If so, we can always blame the parents. The plants to try – those which will in time will cease to be objects of curiosity and will be left alone to grow – include red hot pokers, ferns, irises, day-lilies, the hairier-leaved geraniums, pulmonarias, alchemilla, peonies, butcher's broom, honesty, foxgloves, ajugas, most persicarias, aconitums, Solomon's seal, and lily-of-the-valley. If there is a rule, it is that they avoid the notoriously poisonous and dislike a coarse, hairy leaf.

Rabbits and Potentillas

Adding to the list of rabbit-proof plants, M.G. of Hampshire writes to say that, gardening in Scotland, where potentillas do so well, these shrubs are left alone by rabbits. It was my experience in the Yorkshire dales, too, except for the mindless nibbling of brand new young plants. Would anyone care to pass an opinion on the rabbit-proof qualities of the herbaceous potentillas like 'Gibson's Scarlet'? 'Nasty, straggly things', M.G. calls them, and quite right too on her poor sandy soil. But give them a cooler climate and a gutsy soil, and, like their shrubby brothers, they come into their own.

Q Rabbits are such a problem in my garden now, coming in from woods beyond, that I am having to erect a chicken wire fence all the way round. How high should it be to stop them getting over? – F.C.L., Gloucestershire

A All but the most determined (or the most terrified) rabbits are stopped by chicken wire 36in high, so long as they cannot get a leg up from nearby planting. But you also need to dig the wire into the ground at the bottom edge too, for 9in or so. If the fence is across grass, lift out a line of sods on a hinge, let in the wire, and flip them back. Once the turf has knitted in again, spray out a 6in strip along the line of the wire to save you weeding grass out of the wire later. It will also save you the temptation of going too close with a strimmer and cutting the wire. Nylon cord is quite capable of cutting chicken wire, especially as it gets older. 1–2in mesh is small enough to exclude rabbits. Larger holes will let though the very young ones.

Moles: assorted remedies

Q Moles are running riot in a shrubbery of rhododendrons, magnolias and camellias, and are now making excursions into the lawn alongside. I have been pouring Renardine into the runs to

control them, but have been advised that diesel oil is equally effective. Will this harm the shrubs? – A.S., Sussex

A Diesel will certainly harm your shrubs, and fuel oils should not be poured anywhere near plants. On the other hand, Renardine is not cheap, and all it does is make the runs smell foxy to frighten the moles away. Do you find it successful? You could safely try the effect of diesel by putting a little on to pieces of rag or cotton wool, and putting them into the runs. Such a small amount would be harmless to your shrubs.

Following a reader's query about the effectiveness of a little diesel oil on a rag being used to repel moles in their runs, the Pesticides Safety Directorate has written to me. Its advice is that the reader should continue to use the approved repellant chemical Renardine72/2, since diesel may be harmful to other wildlife or pets. What sort of pet, I wonder, and what sort of hedgehog, goes around digging up and eating diesely-smelling rags? It may seem like madness, but it is illegal, and contravenes the Control of Pesticides Regulations 1986, to use a few drops of diesel for a purpose for which it is not intended, namely to repel moles. It is apparently acceptable to cause pollution by burning diesel in a lorry which delivers Renardine in unrecyclable plastic bottles to the centrally-heated garden store where you will drive to purchase your Renardine. Of course, no one should use dangerous chemicals for purposes for which they are not approved and intended. But surely nature conservation on a domestic scale ought be a matter of responsible common sense? It is industry, and commercial agriculture and horticulture, where legislation needs to be tightest.

I.M., writes from Oxfordshire with the delightful tale of her vicar who rid his garden of moles by putting the mechanism from a musical birthday card in a plastic bag buried in the ground. The moles have kept away ever since! A case of *post hoc sed non propter hoc*, perhaps. But I can vouch for the longevity of the mechanism.

Having once had one which jammed in 'play' mode, and having stamped on it vigorously to no avail, it spent two days playing non-stop in the wheelie bin, before going off in the dustbin lorry still playing away. How potent cheap music is, as Noël Coward observed.

The saga of how to rid a garden of moles continues. After musical deterrents were mentioned, B.Y. of Sussex writes to recommend pushing castor-oil plant seeds into the runs, having tried most other methods including (in Johannesburg) a revolver. Apparently the moles may dislike either the smell or blundering into the sharp spikes on the seeds. I cannot help wondering if, on the contrary, they like the smell and eat them. They are after all extremely poisonous. Anyone wishing to try this, with due care, will find that in the south at least it is possible to produce flower and seed on *Ricinus communis*, the castor-oil plant, and it is used widely as a bedding plant. It is in fact a tender shrub and is naturalised in many Mediterranean countries and the tropics.

Q Earlier this year I had a new lawn laid at great expense in my front garden. You can imagine my horror when soon after this the first mole hills appeared. I have tried everything from mole smokes to ultrasound mole chasers but all to no avail. Can you help? – H.H., Buckinghamshire

A I expect you have tried planting *Euphorbia lathyrus* and found that does not work either? All these methods achieve is to drive the moles elsewhere nearby. If you cannot live with them, the most efficient method of ridding a garden of moles is to trap them. Tunnel traps do not stick up above the ground like the traditional cross-over traps, and are therefore safer where children and pets are around. They can be purchased by mail order from L.B.S. Polythene, Cottontree, Colne, Lancs BB8 7BW. Tunnel traps are placed in the run between the holes, not under the hills themselves, and they must be set with dirty, unhuman smelling hands, and the soil firmed hard around either side of the trap, and all light excluded from above. One mole hill usually means there are several moles around. November is the time they are busy near the surface, when the soil is moist and the worms are busy pulling down leaves into the soil. The most effective method of control, in practised hands, is still trapping. However, on agricultural land only, those with an appropriate licence may use strychnine poison in the runs.

Discouraging deer

Q I am having trouble with roe deer coming into the garden in the early morning. They seem to love chewing off the new shoots of even the thorniest roses. Is there anything I can do short of erecting tall fences?

A There is a cheaper answer than fencing, although it may sound like an old wives' tale. Try hanging up small net bags of human hair – a small handful will do – at deer's nose height where you know they enter the garden. The smell sets their alarm bells ringing like garlic to a vampire. Open-plan gardens suffer worst from deer. Total fencing is outrageously expensive and ugly. But if you can establish boundary hedges of crude, sacrificial vegetation, using smaller fences, and narrow down entry to certain strategic points, then deterrents become a possibility. If your garden is very open, with no obvious entry routes, then some degree of fencing may be the answer.

Some weeks ago I recommended the hanging of nets of human hair in the garden where deer are known to enter, as a means of deterring them. Many readers wrote to agree that it works, however much like an old wives' tale it sounds. Some had found it unsuccessful. It would appear that it is only successful where deer enter through a narrow corridor of some kind; in open situations they just find a new way in. One reader recommends nylon stockings as more discreet than fruit nets, and proof against small birds taking the hair as nesting material. Another recommends lion dung, as available from the West Midlands Safari Park, to repel deer, while another says it does not work. The answer, it would seem, is to experiment to see what will work in your particular situation. It may be, if it does not work, that lions do not figure in the collective unconscious of your particular deer. They may just be very brave! Another reader swears by rings of moth balls hung at snout height where the deer enter. (Some people claim that moth balls will evict moles from a favourite run; but of course it cannot kill them, as is claimed for balls of pre-chewed Wrigley's Juicy Fruit gum.) One reader recommends putting old unwashed clothes, fresh off one's back, in the garden to redirect badgers. Ripe tennis socks are apparently second only in effectiveness to an electric fence.

Q How do I stop badgers digging up my lawn? I know about electric fences and foul smelling chemicals, but can you recommend a way of getting rid of whatever it is they find so delicious to eat under the turf? – J.P., Wiltshire

A Badgers will dig on lawns, looking for worms, beetles and leatherjackets, using their noses as a pig does, and making a serious mess. You might try better drainage to reduce leatherjackets, and one of the proprietary chemical controls for worms in lawns. But then your garden would have fewer worms and the badgers would (initially) be eating poisoned worms. The best answer with badgers is to try to exclude them from the garden with a strong chicken wire or pig-netting fence, or if that is impractical, to contain their passage through it to one corridor by the same means. Badgers just passing through are rarely a problem. Gardens close to a sett may find that badgers choose to burrow under a fence anyway.

Q Two years ago I planted two new apple trees in my garden, which fruited well. But each year squirrels have eaten the entire crop, even biting through plastic netting to get to them. What can I do to stop them? – R.H., West Midlands

A Nothing short of a fine metal cage will physically stop a determined grey squirrel. But not all squirrels are partial to apples. It may be that the next generation will leave them alone, or other foods become preferable. Control on a garden-by-garden basis is impossible, but a group of gardens together can make effort to have them culled by shooting, then numbers can be reduced to a level which causes only acceptable damage to trees, gardens, and local woodlands. (Red squirrels are of course a protected species and are not a problem.) Fruit trees planted close to houses and people, or in the open away from taller woodland trees, are less favoured by squirrels.

Q If I add bonemeal to the soil when planting, as is widely recommended, the local foxes immediately dig up the plants. Can you suggest an alternative fertiliser? – R.A.B., Kent

A The only limitation here is cost. Bonemeal is cheap, but there are plenty of alternatives. You might add Growmore to the soil. It is a cheap, gentle, balanced fertiliser but will not go on working as long as bonemeal. You could use one of the more expensive slow-release encapsulated fertilisers, such as Ficote or Osmocote, which come in tiny water-permeable pellets, releasing their nutrients over a specified number of weeks. Or you might try EnMag, another slow-release granular fertiliser containing trace elements.

Bird problems

Q My garden is rather colourless until the roses begin, and I would like to plant annuals. But I have bantams and a

peacock. Can you recommend plants which they will leave alone? Geraniums and pansies are fine, but everything else gets gobbled up. – P.A., Buckinghamshire

A My experience of peacocks is that they need about 90 seconds to devour a spring cabbage. A good deterrent is to put plenty of fine twigs vertically amongst newly planted annuals and other soft plants, as they hate getting one in the eye. Vegetables are better caged when there are peacocks, hens or bantams about. Hens are the most appalling scratchers, and love to dive into bare ground for a session scratching and shimmying around on their hunkers. So do hard-feather bantams, but the silkies seem to be kinder and are a safer bet amongst plants. They look quite sweet bumbling about in a the back of shrubberies like inflated wrens. But be sure to keep bare soil to a minimum as they love a dust bath. Perennials rather than annuals solve this problem better, therefore. Like pheasants, silkies do a helpful job ripping moss out of the lawn – in search of leatherjackets, I assume.

Q I have an amelanchier tree in my garden which colours well in the autumn but hardly flowers at all. Is there anything I can do to remedy this? – I.W., Bedfordshire

A *Amelanchier lamarckii*, once known as *A. canadensis*, is a lovely spring flowering tree the size of a plum or apple. Its autumn colours can be spectacularly warm, and it produces white, starry flowers in April. It needs plenty of sun to flower properly. In shade it is far less willing. But birds can take the flower buds in some areas, just as they do those of fruit trees. Watch for finches stripping the trees in early spring. If they are in evidence, there is little you can do short of netting the tree.

Q This year I planted 500 crocuses to brighten up the spring garden. Five weeks later I found that mice had eaten the lot, leaving only the tunic of the corms behind as evidence. Do you think a good dusting of flowers of sulphur at planting would deter them? I live in the country and could not hope to eliminate mice by trapping, as E.A.Bowles suggested in his book *Crocus and Colchicum*. – J.M.H., Wiltshire

A By all means try sulphur. Bowles also cited a Flemish text of 1614 showing mice eating crocuses, so the problem is as old and widespread as they come. Rubbing the corms in paraffin-soaked sand before planting works in some cases. Crocuses in turf can be protected by setting very fine wire mesh over the corms and under the turf, but this is only practical in small areas. A good cat or two helps, of course.

Slugs and snails

Q Our large London garden produces hundreds of snails but hardly ever a slug. Why? We have few enough thrushes these days, and the same goes for blackbirds. The soil is fairly acid leaf mould under beech and cherry trees. – D.M.L., London SE22

A You should be so lucky. Maybe things will suddenly change one day. The answer is probably due to a combination of local soil type and predation. Snails prefer a limy soil since they need it for shell building. And thrushes love them to death. Slugs like a soil with plenty of moisture and plenty of decaying organic matter. Perhaps the garden is too dry under the trees for slugs to thrive? Leaf mould does not necessarily mean acid soil, and the best beech trees grow on chalk soils. You might test your soil to see what *p*H it reads.

Q Nine months ago I moved into a house with a neglected garden with walls 12ft high. It is infested with slugs and snails, which I catch and throw over the walls. Do they have a homing instinct and climb back over? There are just as many now as when I started. – P.G., Wiltshire

A Who lives next door, I wonder? Do they throw them back? The trouble with slugs and snails is that they lay lots and lots of eggs and are most efficient reproducers. They are also quite capable of slithering back over, from hunger or wanderlust, but not from a homing instinct. It takes time to reduce slug and snail populations seriously. When it happens it will be the result more of your regime of cultivation and hygiene and ease of predation by birds, than by enforced aeronautics.

Q I would appreciate an opinion on the use of the new biological control for slugs, which works by means of a microscopic worm introducing fatal bacteria in the slug. Surely there could be dangers in upsetting nature's balance, by releasing vast numbers of predators into the air and soil. Does this worm also kill snails? Both are important in the food chain and a terrible problem to gardeners. – J.M.R., County Durham

A I share your concern, J.M.R. But to be hard-headed, consider the following. The microscopic worm (nematode) in question was originally found in British soil, as was the nematode used as a biological control for vine-weevils. So it is unlikely that a population explosion will be produced in the wild. Gardens are in themselves a tipping of nature's balance, and it might be argued that we do wrong in creating artificial conditions in which particular organisms – our 'pests' – can increase so markedly. Given that we shall go on gardening and growing crops to eat, it seems a best option to control the problems we have made with a naturally existing indigenous predator. In the case of slugs, most of those affected by the nematode burrow underground to die, unlike slugs dying on the surface as a result of slug pellet poisoning. Moreover the nematode cannot live in warm-blooded creatures: it is specific to molluscs. A much greater risk to the food chain are slug pellets consumed by higher animals and birds. Snails are little affected by the nematode, since they do not burrow in the soil where infection lies.

More of a worry is the introduction of organisms from abroad, such as the New Zealand flatworm, which is currently destroying our earthworms in Scotland and heading south. But I suspect we are wrong to expect the world to remain the same, just as we know it now. Life on earth is a melting pot in which organisms come and go. A balance of nature does not mean stasis, but movement around a point of balance. Man is not the only cause of shuffling the pack – climatic change and continental shift both play their part – but Man certainly is a fast dealer, and sometimes too fast for his own good.

Biological controls for slugs and vine weevils (Nemaslug and Nemasys H) are available from Defenders Ltd, Occupation Road, Wye, Ashford, Kent TN25 5AH; tel. 01233 813121.

Weevils

Q What specific controls do you recommend against vine weevils? I slaughter over a hundred every winter from my begonia tubers – and still they come. – J.L.T., Hertfordshire

A The most effective chemicals for use against vine weevils are available only to commercial growers. It is ironic that the more hazardous a chemical, the greater the likelihood that it will be made available only to commercial horticulture, which will use large quantities carefully, instead of the amateur who would use small quantities, and I hope carefully. Ah, well. A good biological control for amateurs is Nemasys H, available from Defenders Ltd, Occupation Road, Wye, Ashford, Kent TN25 5AH; tel. 01233 813121. Nemasys H is properly effective when the soil temperature is above 12°C.

Q What is eating holes in my honeysuckle leaves? It has virtually destroyed the plant and is attacking other bushes nearby. The local nursery thought it could be vine weevil, and we have sprayed all summer but to no effect. What should I do? No creature is visible on the plant day or night. – J.A., Cambridgeshire

A These long holes and loops coming in from the edge of the leaves are typical of vine weevil damage. Leaf-cutter bees also eat in from the edge but in a tidy little semicircle. Now it's autumn, damage will be ended outdoors for this year. Fork over the soil, and find and destroy as many of the white grubs as you can find, now and in spring.

Biological control

Q Whitefly thrive in my frost-free greenhouse, despite various sprays and smokes. Is the parasitic wasp a practical answer in a small greenhouse? Could I introduce it now, as the whitefly are still active? – L.A.B., Gloucestershire

A This biological control for whitefly is certainly effective, in any size of greenhouse or conservatory, when correctly managed. The tiny wasp, *Encarsia formosa*, lays its eggs in the whitefly larvae, destroying them in the process. But for the wasp to thrive and breed temperatures must be above 64°F (18°C). It is therefore not recommended to introduce them into an unheated greenhouse before May or early June. The parasites are available from Defenders Ltd, Occupation Road, Wye, Ashford, Kent, TN25 5BR; tel. 01233 813121. A list of compatible chemicals is sent out with the parasites, so you may continue to spray for other glasshouse pests if necessary.

Q For the past three years my mature pear tree has been affected by maggots. To minimise the spread I have picked from the tree about 1500 deformed fruitlets and collected more from the soil. There are now only two or three dozen left unaffected on the tree. What should I do to prevent repetition? Prior to this the tree was laden with excellent fruits. – L.C., Middlesex

A Your problem is a gall midge specific to pears, which lays its eggs in the flowers during March or April. Dozens of minute white larvae develop in the distorted fruitlets, which blacken and fall, usually in May or June. When the fruits fall, the mature larvae crawl into the soil where they remain until emerging as adult midges the following spring. Treatment is to collect and burn quickly all affected fruits. Cultivate the soil lightly beneath the tree and treat it with an insecticidal dust such as lindane in spring. The spraying of a large tree with an insecticide such as pirimphos-methyl or fenitrothion, just as the buds are about to burst, is possible but not easy. Early or late flowering pears manage better to evade the midge's attentions.

Aphids and others

Q Please remind me how to deal with aphids on the powder-puff bush, *Viburnum opulus*. It gets so spoiled by them. – J.S., Hampshire

A All forms of *Viburnum opulus*, the guelder rose, are prone to black-bean aphid attack just as the leaves emerge. Philadelphus is susceptible too. It can distort the shoots badly and lead to stunted growth, completely spoiling the effect of the flowers, which are flat and white like cow parsley. (The form *Viburnum opulus* 'Sterile' is the powder-puff bush, with globular heads.) Spray with pirimcarb or malathion, or if the bush is small, water onto the roots the systemic insecticide dimethoate. Look out for the same pest on broad beans, poppies and nasturtiums.

Q I have some young pines and Douglas firs along the boundary of my garden, planted three years ago as a shelter belt. They have all grown well, but now they appear to be covered in little white tufts at the base of the needles. What is this, and will it harm the trees? – B.M., Lancashire

A This sounds like an attack of adelgids, small sap-sucking insects which look rather like woolly aphids or mealy bug. Conifers are particularly prone to them, and while not fatal, they do stunt the growth if the attack is severe. The problem is often worse in shady or sheltered situations. Spray infected trees with malathion or pirimphos methyl in April, and again three weeks later.

Q Last week I found caterpillars eating holes on Solomon's seal in my garden. The next day there was not a leaf left. Is this common? I have never known anything eat Solomon's seal. – J.P., Cumbria

A If you find sawfly caterpillars on Solomon's seal, in late June or early July, you have three choices. You can do nothing and watch it be quickly defoliated. Or you can pick them off by the score, from under the leaves, and squash them (you will never get them all). Or you can spray generously and at once with an insect-icide containing permethrin or malathion, making sure you get under all the leaves. I spray, because I think this is a high-value plant, and I grow it in relatively important positions. I would not want a hole in the border for three months, or to lose that wonder-ful butter-yellow autumn colour. In a woodland garden you might wish to leave the caterpillars to get on with it, rather than resort to chemicals. Certainly the plant is tough as they come, and seems to be little weakened by the loss in the subsequent season. I found that having sprayed for three years, I had a run of several years without any sign of sawfly; but this year a few pounced again and got short shrift.

Q Lupins are one of my favourite flowers, but every year they get covered in horrible aphids. I do not like to use sprays in my garden. Is there anything I can do to get rid of the aphids? I am tempted to give up lupins altogether. – J.G., Lancashire

A The lupin has its very own aphis, which has become wide-spread in Britain since 1981. Lupins used to be so easy 20 years ago, and a reliable, satisfying plant to let children grow from seed; but not now. The lupin aphis is a fat, greyish monster, and it loves to colonise the bud spike thick as a coat of paint. The buds are often sucked dry before they even begin to open.

Where attacks are serious, a regular use of insecticides from early in the season is required to allow the plant a clear run at flowering. If you do not want to spray – with pyrethrum, dimethoate, pirimcarb, or malathion – then perhaps you should give up lupins. You will be joining many others if you do. Hand control of these aphids is rather a losing battle, and an explosively slimy business.

Can I suggest you try thermopsis instead of lupins? The species to try is *Thermopsis villosa* (*T. caroliniana* in some catalogues). It forms a self-supporting clump of pea-like leaves over which rise soft yellow spikes to around 3 ft. You might think it was a yellow lupin, and it flowers at much the same time. Unlike a lupin it is thoroughly perennial (lupins are best grown as biennials), and after flowering, when the lupin collapses in a mildewy heap, the thermopsis remains substantial to the end of the season. Avoid the brighter yellow *Thermopsis montana* except in wild gardens, as it does not make clumps but runs like a fox in a hen house.

Q I am losing a four-year battle against woodlice. Help! – P.L.B-L., Norfolk

A The way to beat woodlice is by cleanliness – the Jean Brodie technique. Clear your greenhouse of all dead or decaying leaves, old boxes, stacked pots and seed trays until no hiding place remains. Lift up plants in pots and deal with any woodlice you find lurking underneath or in the drainage holes. If there is a concrete or paved floor, pour dilute bleach down the cracks when you clean out the greenhouse after the winter. (Keep it well away from roots, of course.) Woodlice live largely on decaying vegetable matter, and usually trouble live plants only as seedlings. They are normally only a problem in greenhouses or in vegetable gardens. If damage is great, and you are sure woodlice are the source of the damage (they only feed at night, so take a torch and look), then you can destroy them by dusting their day-time hideaways with insecticide dusts containing pyrethrum or lindane. You may need to do this again after a week or so.

Q How should we treat our 'Mermaid' rose which this year was attacked by leaf-cutter bees? – G.M., Sussex

A Leaf-cutter bees remove conspicuous semi-circles from the edges of leaves in summer. Their favourite plants include roses, lilacs, laburnum and even rhododendron. The recommended treatment is to spray or dust with lindane when activity is first noticed, but in most cases damage is not severe enough to warrant the use of insecticides. In the case of a tall climbing rose like 'Mermaid', spraying would not be easy anyway. Leaf-cutter bees are solitary creatures and do not dwell in communal hives as do honey bees. If there are signs of damage it does not mean that there are thousands of other leaf-cutters all waiting to pounce, and you may find that there is no problem at all in subsequent years. Just grin and bear them if you can.

Q I have a large and handsome sycamore tree at the bottom of my new garden. In the spring a sticky material descends from it together with what appear to be whitefly. The material lies on the surface of the leaves of shrubs below. What is this and how do I deal with it? – J.A., East Yorkshire

A Sycamores play host in spring to aphids, which drop their excreta onto plants below, where they become mouldy. The polite name for this shower is honeydew, though I cannot imagine why. There is little you can do to treat aphids on a large sycamore, but you can hose the shrubs below regularly, to stop the moulds becoming unsightly. Smoother leaves are improved more easily than rough-textured ones.

It is unlikely you have whitefly on the tops of leaves. They prefer the underside, and fly off in clouds when disturbed. Your white patches will be moulds. The same problem occurs with many trees including oaks, birch, and limes. The cute and disarming pink-leaved sycamore, *Acer pseudoplatanus* 'Brilliantissimum' is just as bad once it has grown to a significant size.

Scale insects

Q I am losing the battle against scale insect in my conservatory. Half the plants on the floor are now infected, although plants on window ledges have remained clean. I spray with malathion but it does not seem to have much effect, and I have to wipe the leaves of honeydew deposits all the time. – V.C., Nottinghamshire

A Scale insects are messy creatures and bad news in a conservatory. The adults, which remain for their lives largely in one place, are scaly enough to resist sprays, although they may be wiped off tough-leaved plants with a soapy sponge. The time to kill them is at the juvenile stage, just after the eggs have hatched, when they crawl off to find a feeding place, perhaps onto the next plant, but not as far as a window ledge. At this stage they have little scale to cover them and are susceptible to malathion or pyrethrum based sprays. The trouble is they can hatch at almost any time of year under glass, so you need to inspect very closely and often, perhaps with a lens, to see when the crawlers are around. Then spray at once, and repeat the operation a couple of weeks later. You can also use systemic insecticides such as dimethoate to kill the static females before they lay eggs, but do read the labels carefully, as systemics can be harmful to some ornamentals. When temperatures under glass reach at least 70°F (22°C), scale insects may be reduced by biological control, in the form of a minute parasitic wasp, *Metaphycus helvolus*. It is supplied by Defenders Ltd, Occupation Road, Wye, Ashford, Kent, TN25 5AH; tel. 01233 813121.

M.B. of Sussex and J.E.B. of Norfolk write to say how bad woolly aphid has been on apple trees this year, and ask how to treat it.

Woolly aphid is a small sap-sucking insect which attacks, in particular apples, hawthorn, cotoneaster and sorbus. It has been noticeably bad on pyracantha, too. The insect protects itself with a white woolly covering, and can cause cankering and distortion of branches in severe infestations. Badly cankered branches are better cut out. The young insects overwinter in cracks in the bark, and tar oil wash where appropriate will help reduce them at this stage. The insect is more of a problem in hotter continental climates. Smaller forms of apple trees can be painted locally with malathion, or even methylated spirits, early in the season when the insect first becomes apparent. On larger trees this is impractical, and spraying is also difficult. Alternatively you can use a systemic insecticide such as dimethoate.

Better than these is the biological control, a parasite called *Aphelinus mali*, which was introduced to southern England in the 1920s and is still around, working away. It is not commercially available in the UK, according to the biological-control supplier, Defenders. So before rushing to spray, look hard to see if there are any blackened, parasitised insects on your trees, and if so then spare the insecticides to encourage the parasite. Try looking for some on someone else's tree, scrape some off and introduce the parasite to your trees. Unfortunately the parasite is not a certain cure, as it is not as fast a mover as the aphid, and colonies of aphids can be found thriving on one tree, while the parasite is in evidence on its neighbour.

Q I have lilies in tubs on my patio which are being eaten by black, slimy maggots. I have also seen a bright red beetle on the plants occasionally. I have sprayed with an organic insecticide, which seemed to control it pretty well, but by that time the damage was done. – A.B., London SE9

A The lily beetle is a relatively new pest, but is now not uncommon in southern England. It is under half an inch long and conspicuously red. The larvae will eat lily leaves, and the beetles eat leaves, flowers, stem and all. The minute you spot any signs of nibbling on lilies, check for larvae or beetles and destroy them by hand at once. Spraying with bifenthrin or pirimphos-methyl is reasonably effective.

Fungi

Q We have honey fungus in our garden, killing trees and shrubs. There have been toadstools of it on ash and plum trees. We recycle leaves and grass cuttings into compost. Are we spreading the fungus with the compost? – D.W., Buckinghamshire

A Honey fungus in its more virulent forms will attack apparently healthy trees mid-season and in full bloom. It spreads by long wiry rhizomorphs undergound, which pierce living as well as dead tissue, and go on to attack and sometimes kill the whole plant. It can spread enormous distances by this means, and a meal of a good stump will give it strength to shoot off in search of pastures new. Moreover, where there is a toadstool there are also spores. Millions of them. And they are far more efficient than your compost in spreading the fungus. Carry on composting, try not to put twigs or wood in the compost, and above all dig out and burn old stumps, infected or not. Hygiene is the best control once honey fungus arrives in a garden. Ironically, in old woodlands, it is kept at bay by the activities of other fungi, and is not such a serious problem. It is a serious disease only in the artificially clean and clinical world of gardens.

Q During the summer a large bracket fungus has grown at the base of our hundred-plus-year-old oak tree. I believe it is *Inonotus dryadeus*, and according to our fungus book it is parasitic. Is it likely to harm the oak, and what action should be taken? – D.B., Oxfordshire

A There is bad news and good news. This fungus eats away at heart wood destroying the core of the tree. If it were on a beech tree, I would be more worried, since they, having been eaten alive, tend to fall over quite soon. Oaks are a different matter. They survive such rots into old age, shedding limbs and branches, but continuing to live with a hollow trunk. So for safety's sake it would be wise to have a tree surgeon inspect the tree, to see if it is structurally sound or likely to shed limbs in unfortunate places, such as on you or a house. He may say leave well alone, and look at it again in a few years. You have options. All is not lost. But you cannot cure the tree.

Diseases

Q **In autumn hundreds of sycamore leaves, covered in black spots blow across my lawn. My roses also suffer from blackspot. Is this the same disease, and should I be clearing them up and burning them?** – A.G.W., Carmarthen

A Rose blackspot and tar spot seen on sycamores are two completely separate diseases. The former can do serious damage to roses, by causing defoliation, but the latter simply makes the sycamore leaves look disturbingly spotty. Just compost the sycamore leaves as usual.

Q **Our garden is plagued by a dreadful rust attacking rhododendrons, viburnums and a stewartia. It has killed one rhododendron, and I have had to cut other plants hard back. We spray with fungicide and pesticide but it makes no difference. What to do?** – M.O., London SW6

A Rusts are specific to their hosts, and so one type would not attack this range of species. It is more likely to be a cultural problem or a disease in the ground. Plants dying out wholly or patchily may be a symptom of honey fungus. Root diseases can arise as a result of drought, waterlogging or even gas leaks. Your problem plants are all tough enough species, so I would cease spraying and look for a more basic problem underground.

Q I grow the large-flowered tuberous begonias in a wood-framed conservatory. They are usually covered in flowers, strong, and almost like shrubs. Last year one got mildew, and this year they are all covered with it. I treat the dry tubers with flowers of sulphur in winter and have sprayed the mildew this year but to no effect. – J.M., Leicestershire

A Spraying against mildew once it has got a real hold in some-thing as soft as a begonia is usually ineffectual. Next year try spraying earlier in the year, before the infection strikes, to clean up your stock again. Do not grow them too hot and dry. Because they are so top-heavy in pots it is easier to grow them under glass, I agree, but you must give plenty of ventilation to avoid the greatest heat. If it is any consolation, my *Begonia sutherlandii,* which grew cleanly for 10 years in the north, this year succumbed to mildew in the south, even outdoors. I had assumed it to be immune.

Q My morello cherry is 18 years old, and suddenly this year a great proportion of the flowering shoots have died and withered, so there are no cherries. What is my problem? – V.E.D., East Sussex

A This looks like fungal die-back, caused by a canker bacterium. It is a serious problem which is very much on the increase. The offical answer is to prune back to 3ft below the damage, but that sounds like cutting off most of your tree. Spray with a copper-based fungicide during leaf fall, and see what happens next year.

Q I have a 12ft oak tree which grows happily enough but is always covered in black, sooty moulds. The black effect stays on the bark and twigs through the winter. – L.B., North Yorkshire

A Oaks may be good trees under which to garden because of the lack of surface root, but they can sometimes be very dirty trees. Aphis infestations drop their excretions onto lower leaves which then become covered in black moulds such as you describe. There is also a creature similar to an aphis known as the oak phylloxerid. This, too, colonises the leaves, and, while it can do an established tree little harm, it also produces moulds. Phylloxerids can weaken young trees, but as your tree is growing well there seems no cause for concern except on aesthetic grounds. If you feel the need to treat the problem, the tree is probably still small enough to treat with a systemic insecticide containing dimethoate. If the tree is growing under or near mature oaks, however, they will be part of the problem, too, and there will be no point in trying to use pesticides.

Q I have been having trouble with browning and premature leaf fall on hypericum bushes in the last few years. Could this be a rust of some kind? – N.R., Yorkshire

A It could indeed. Orange-brown pustules appear on the older, lower leaves first, causing a very shabby appearance by late summer. But hypericums are generally tough: I have not known them to be killed by rust. The problem is always worst on dry soils in hot years, and I would imagine that in 1993 you were little troubled by it. To control it, clear away and burn the old leaves of deciduous species in autumn, and spray fortnightly through the summer with mancozeb or another suitable fungicide (check the label for suitability).

Q This year our fuchsias under glass have suffered from what we believe is botrytis. We realise part of the problem is ventilation – we have a solar dome – and this we can solve. But what is the best treatment for botrytis? Must we destroy all the infected plants? – T.G., Yorkshire

A You should find with proper ventilation that the extremely soft, disease-prone growth is no longer a problem. Often mould and mildews of fuchsias are a symptom of a minor infestation by aphids, and next year you should also check that plants are completely free of such pests. There is no need to destroy the plants. If they are still in leaf under glass, spray them with any suitable fungicide and water some on to the compost. Then dry them off slowly for the winter, cut back the tops, remove any remaining dead leaves, and rest them leafless in a cold but not frosty place until you repot them and start them into growth again in the spring.

Q Every year my *Clematis* 'Jackmanii Superba' gets mildew and the flowers are spoiled. This year I mean to make an effort to defeat it. Which fungicide should I use? – M.T., Sussex

A Choose a fungicide containing carbendazim or mancozeb. Start at the beginning of the season if you wish to defeat it, even though signs of mildew may not yet be apparent. With fungicides, a programme of prophylactic spraying is more effective than fire-fighting after the disease has struck. If you can keep the plant clean for a year, it may well stay that way.

Q For two years my rhododendrons have suffered 'black bud' – the terminal buds blacken and dry through the winter, but remain on the plant. One plant is 50 per cent affected, while another has only one or two buds damaged. Is this insect damage from inside the bud? – G.V.A., West Sussex

A This is a fungal problem known as bud blast. Infection becomes apparent in autumn, and the bud dies through the winter. By spring it is dry, blackish or brown, and covered in minute prickle-like structures, by which means the fungus is spread. To control the problem remove and burn all affected buds as soon as you are sure they are dying. Spraying with bordeaux mixture or a fungicide containing mancozeb, just before flowering, will help; but for a plant which has lost half its buds you will need to continue spraying every few weeks. It is possible (but unproven) that bud blast is associated with infestations of the otherwise harmless rhododendron leaf-hopper, seen in late summer and notable for the red bands on its wing cases. If you are sure leaf-hoppers are present, and find after a season or two that direct control of the fungus is not working, then you might try spraying with an insecticide containing malathion, during the period from June to September. Personally I would need to see the association between bud blast and leaf-hoppers proven before I began to use a pesticide so widely and regularly in the garden.

Q In my small garden I have a 'Beurre Hardy' pear tree. I have noticed black spots on the leaves. What are these? – S.K., Oxfordshire

A From the leaves you sent me I see the tree has scab. To a greater or lesser extent this will debilitate the tree and reduce cropping. Burn the fallen leaves this year. Next year buy a proprietary fungicide from your garden centre, and spray regularly from bud burst until July. Look out for those containing mancozeb or carbendazim.

Q Our gooseberry bushes are looking decidedly poorly, with small brownish spots on the leaves. Can you help? – A.G.C., Gloucestershire

A Your bushes have currant leaf spot, which affects black and red currants too. Clear up and burn all affected fallen leaves. Spraying with carbendazim or mancozeb can be done now, and again through next season, pausing a month before the fruit is ripe, and continuing again after picking.

Q My willow tree is exhibiting signs of infection with curling leaves falling off and the stems cankered. The traditional treatment is with bordeaux mixture but my garden centre insists that this is no longer available. Can you suggest an alternative? – G.T.R., Cornwall

A Bordeaux mixture is available in the Vitax range of garden products, at £2.12 for 175gm. The fungal disease you are fighting is willow anthracnose, which is especially prevalent on weeping willows in wet seasons. Control on large trees is simply not practical, but the trees will survive all but the worst attacks. If your tree is small enough to spray, do so at 21-day intervals from before bud burst next year until July.

Q For some years I have been plagued by outbreaks of mildew on my greenhouse vine. I understand sulphur is one of the best treatments. Where can I find it? – F.B., Devon

A Powdery mildew and the grey mould botrytis are the bane of vines under glass, attacking both leaves and fruit. Botrytis especially is found in association with aphid attack, growing on their excreted honeydew. These fungal diseases will be solved not just by using fungicides (systemic or sulphur), but firstly by improving ventilation. Vines need heat, not least to ripen the fruit, but they also need maximum fresh air to combat disease. So ventilate religiously, making sure you open up early enough and close up late enough in spring and autumn. Think of those Victorian kitchen gardeners getting up at the crack of dawn. Sulphur is available in small packs from the manufacturer Vitax.

Q I have an 11-year-old flowering cherry tree which produces lots of fruit. Unfortunately the bark is split in various places on the trunk, and the leaves bear dark spots. It is obviously diseased, but I would hate to cut it down. – E.M.S., Surrey

A Your tree is affected by bacterial canker, which can cause limbs to die back in severe infections. It is not easy to control on large trees. The disease makes spots on the leaves in summer, and then transfers to the bark via wounds and leaf scars in autumn and winter. Control, in so far as it is effective, is by spraying the leaves with bordeaux mixture in spring to control spotting, and again in August and October. If your tree is as badly affected as it sounds, removal may be simpler than control.

Q We have a beautiful old oak tree in our garden, but it has fungus growing at ground level on three sides of the trunk. I

am concerned that it will weaken the tree, and I assume that the first thing I should do is to remove the fungus. Do I also need to apply a fungicide, and is there a way of injecting this into the tree? – J.A.N., Sussex

A If only you could remove the fungus! This looks like one of the root- and butt-rotting fungi, probably the beef-steak fungus *Fistulina hepatica*, and there is no cure. Removing the fungus brackets from the trunk will have no effect. These are merely the fruiting bodies of a fungus which is inside the tree, slowly devouring the roots and heartwood. It is more common to see just one colony of bracket fungus on a tree. The fact that you have them on three sides suggests that the disease is widespread. There are only two things you can usefully do now. First, don't panic. Such diseases take many years to run their course before the host dies, and, as yours seems to be showing no sign even of crown loss yet, it may well be early days. Second, get a qualified tree surgeon to inspect the tree and make sample bore holes to determine the extent of the rot. The greatest risk with all root- and butt-rotting fungi is total or partial collapse of the tree, and it may be wise to remove some weight from the crown for safety's sake. But oaks will put up with beef-steak fungus for many years, and rarely fall right over. So keep a close eye on its general health. Have it professionally inspected every few years. And settle for the fact that its glory days are soon to be over. Plant some more.

Q Eighteen months ago I moved into a new property in the New Forest where there is a Scots pine tree 40 years old. At the end of last summer I noticed it had a red/orange fungus at its base and asked a tree surgeon to inspect it. He reported that the fungus was *Fomes annosus*, which attacks the roots, and that the tree should be felled. Is there any alternative to felling, and is it safe to replant another large containerised Scots pine? – V.B., Hampshire

A *Fomes annosus*, or *Heterobasidion annosum* as it is now known, is a common killer of Scots pines. It is a fungus which can pass from root to root, or enter through stem damage above ground. It is not curable, nor is it easy to tell how far the infection has spread underground. What can safely be said is that, as with all root rots of substantial trees, at some time the tree will fall or blow over. Better to bite the bullet and have it felled with minimal damage, than to wait until it flattens half the garden or damages buildings. It would make sense to have the stump ground out professionally, and to replace it with a fresh pit of soil before replanting. Only rarely does this pathogen of conifers attack deciduous trees, so I would replace your pine with an appropriate deciduous tree. If you really want a Scots pine, plant a few little ones for a few pence each, and see what happens, rather than spending large sums on heavy containerised stock. The risk is not worthwhile, and small pines grow so fast anyway.

Q My nectarine is suffering from severe leaf-curl problems again this year, despite spraying in October and again in early March with copper fungicide. Is there anything else I can do? – S.M., London NW1

A Peach-leaf curl is a fungal disease which reddens and blisters the leaves of peaches, almonds and nectarines. It is common on all three out of doors, but less so under glass. It will not kill the tree, but it will weaken it, and make it look sickly. Spray through the winter months with a copper fungicide. If only a few leaves are affected, pick them off to stop the fungus spreading. On larger trees you may just wish to live with the problem.

Q I have a path lined with 20-year-old conifers 10ft high and 3ft apart. This year four in a row have gone brown all over and died. I have not removed them as it will spoil the feel of a hedged alley. – A.G., Essex

A The problem could just be drought, as life (and old age) in a hedge is fearsomely competitive. It might be the fungus *Phytophthora*. It might also be honey fungus (*Armillaria*) which will often run through a hedge, killing as it goes. If so, there is no need to panic, for modern research suggests that there are forms of honey fungus which are only really a problem for old, stressed plants and will not run around the garden killing strong healthy plants as the most virulent forms will. (There are milder forms still which can live on plants for years and never do any harm.) Conifers which have gone completely brown will not recover, so you must re-think your alley now. If disease is the problem, the trees are better removed and burnt, which may mean it is hardly worth leaving the remaining trees in the row. Certainly, if disease is present it would not be wise to try to replant more conifers into the gap. I should take the whole row out, roots and all. The soil will be thoroughly exhausted so double-dig the area and incorporate lots of manure and old compost and bonemeal. Grow tall, non-woody plants to edge your alley for a few years, such as delphiniums, the grass *Miscanthus sacchariflorus*, or nasturtiums on a trellis. After that, if the opposite hedge is still healthy, try replanting the missing side with conifers.

Lichen

Q We noticed lichen on our azaleas two or three years ago, and now it is spreading to other trees and shrubs. How serious a problem is this, and is there any way of dealing with it? – B.M., Hampshire

A In a moist climate where the air is relatively free of pollution, lichen will often try to grow on trees and shrubs. The south west of Ireland grows some remarkably spectacular encrustations. Lichen is not in itself a serious problem. It will, however, play host to a population of insects and fungi which, on fruit bushes, for instance, or trees with ornamental bark, can be a problem. A winter spray with tar-oil wash will solve the problem, but is not the pleasantest of substances to handle, and you may wish just to live with the lichen.

Q I have a patio laid in rose-pink paving slabs, but it becomes very slippery owing to bird droppings falling from an overhanging sloe. Please would you advise me on what I should use to clean the paving. – J.A.O., Pembrokeshire

A There are several choices, both mechanical and chemical. You could hire a high-pressure hose, or even a steam hose (from *Yellow Pages* tool-hire shops) which do an excellent job. Or you can scrub away with a yard broom and a bucket of hot water and Flash, which is reasonably harmless to plants. If the run-off is not going to reach plants, you can scrub it clean, then spray on a mild solution of bleach; but be careful not to walk it on to carpets. Rinse off the next day. Vitax make a Path and Patio Cleaner, available from garden centres at £3.35 for 1 litre, which can be used to remove stains from concrete, stone and asphalt, as well as general cleaning. If you want to do a more thorough and long lasting job with chemicals, you may wish to consider using a masonry biocide, available from builders' merchants. But these are only as good as the mechanical aftercare; you cannot beat regular brushing.

Q An old friend has recently moved into a flat whose garden had unfortunately been treated with a heavy dose of weedkiller drift, possibly from a railway track. Is there any remedy? – B.R., Kent

A This depends on what chemical was used. Glyphosate is one of the better chemicals in terms of its eco-friendliness, and so is used a good deal commercially. But a little goes a long way when it comes to killing plants, especially soft herbaceous ones. Selective weedkillers, on the other hand, are more easily resisted by plants, although they are nastier chemicals. The leaves may curl, and some distortion may occur, but many plants eventually shrug them off, and grow away normally again the next year. Remember how some lawn weeds seem infuriatingly immune to selective weedkillers? So the answer for your friend is to be patient and see what survives. If she can establish a case against her trigger-happy neighbour, she should make a noise.

Q My mature 6ft forsythia bush has developed carbuncle-like growths on various parts and is dying back in these areas. Is there anything I can do to save the rest of the bush as it casts the only shade in my south-facing garden. – M.J., Middlesex

A Your forsythia probably has crown gall, a bacterial infection with the splendid name of *Agrobacterium radiobacter* var. *tumefaciens*. It is not readily treatable, but nor it is usually fatal. Prune out galled branches and burn them. The bacterium lingers in the soil for many years, and it can attack a wide range of fruit and ornamentals.

Q Why do some gardeners recommend adding detergent to chemical sprays, and what effect is it supposed to have? – C.L., Oxfordshire

A Soap is an old-fashioned insecticide, but detergent serves another purpose. It reduces the surface tension in the water droplets and helps sprays to stick to plants with shiny leaves, instead of running off uselessly. When using weedkillers for spot treatment on shiny leaved plants, it also helps to massage the chemical into the leaf with a rubber glove, to ensure adequate absorption. Glyphosate on ground elder is a case in point. Insufficient absorption can persuade you to think the chemical is ineffective, whereas it may never have had the opportunity to work because it ran off.

Q I have two established, productive bush apple trees ('Bramley' and 'Newton Wonder') both affected with bitter pit. I am told to spray while in leaf with a calcium compound. What is this, and where do I get it? – J.W.McC., Shropshire

A Bitter pit is a problem of the fruit only, and appears as small brown sunken areas of skin and more small brown marks throughout the flesh. To minimise the problem, first make sure the trees never lack for water, perhaps by giving them a mulch as well as water in dry periods. Second spray with hydrated calcium nitrate to increase calcium levels in the shoots and fruit. Lack of calcium is thought to be a contributory cause of bitter pit. Calcium nitrate is available from Garden Direct, Geddings Road, Hoddesdon, Herts EN11 0LR; tel. 01992 441888.

Fasciation

Q Could you please tell me why a clump of daisies in my lawn has had deformed flowers for the past two years? It produces flat stems, and there were seven heads on the widest stalk. – J.H., Berkshire

A This abnormality is known as fasciation, after the Latin *fasces*, the bundles of rods with an axe in the middle ceremonially carried by Roman lictors. Fasciation occurs in both woody and soft plants. I have seen it prominent on stonecrops (*Sedum* species) and on *Euphorbia characias*. There is a willow, *Salix udensis* 'Sekka', which is grown specifically for its flattened, fan-shaped twigs, and is much valued by flower arrangers. The effect of fasciation can be rather repulsive. Like giving birth to a child with six heads, it shrieks of the unnatural. It is caused by a chemical confusion in the plant's branching mechanism, causing several stems to grow in parallel, like pan pipes, where only one should be. The result is often poor, distorted flowers which may fail to open and usually fail to set seed. It is most common in the flowering stems of plants, and therefore it is not in a position to affect too seriously the woody structure. In herbaceous plants it can be ignored as a curiosity. Plants which have fasciated stems can also still produce normal stems. The tendency to fasciation lasts for the life of the plant. Cutting away the fasciated stems does not usually stop further fasciation then or in future years. Sometimes fasciated stems fail to bring their flowers to opening and shrivel first. Others, including my *E. characias*, manage to flower, The result is macabre – a three foot woody stem, topped by a woody, ridged fan the size of a man's hand, crested with a row of terminal grey leaves and small flower clusters. Cut and dried, they are the next best thing to driftwood for arty-crafty flower arrangers. What causes the mutation in the first place is unknown. Post Chernobyl, maybe, but not propter Chernobyl; fasciation, like other forms of mutant cell division, has been with us for ever.

Q My garden pond is covered in duckweed. I have tried skimming it off but there is always some left behind in waterside plants. Soon it is covered over again, and I can't see my fish. How can I get rid of duckweed?

A Duckweed (*Lemna minor*) is a floating, surface weed with tiny bright green leaves. It rapidly makes a sheet of foliage which will fill a pond completely. Skimming is as good a treatment as any, using a coarse net or a wire rake. Set the water stirring in a circular motion, so that the weed comes to meet you from the far side. It can all be safely composted.

Q Last summer, for the first time, our long-established garden pond (4,000 gallons) became infested with blanket weed. Other ponds in the neighbourhood were also affected. I have tried two or three proprietary remedies without success. Can you suggest a solution? – R.D.W., Surrey

A Blanket weed is an accumulation in the water of algae, which can in sufficient concentration become harmful to fish and mammals. The cause of this proliferation of algae can be attributed to increased levels of nitrates and phosphates in the water, plus high temperatures and low rainfall and rate of flow. This is a problem which in recent years has been vexing the owners of large ornamental waters everywhere. The currently favoured control, if not eradication, is the use of barley straw. Submerged barley straw gives off a chemical as it decays which inhibits the growth of algae. The chemical begins to be produced after a month in the water. One to three rectangular, old-fashioned bales will treat an acre of water, so you can scale the ratio down to suit your pond. The straw must be loosened out – it's no good put in as a compressed bale, – and put into a chicken-wire cage or boom. In a garden pond a small cage can be anchored almost invisibly at the inlet side. The deterrent effect lasts for about six months. It is a cheap remedy and it really works.

17

Tricky Situations

Q Is it possible to sterilise soil in a microwave oven? –
C.G.J., Devon

A This sounds to me an eminently sensible idea, so long as you
do not wish to sterilise half the garden. I am informed that it
does indeed work, but I cannot say I have tried it. Cooking time of
course will depend on the amount of soil you put in, and the power
and evenness of the oven. A good stir half way through the cooking
time never comes amiss to ensure even cooking and distribution of
heat. By putting the soil in quite moist it would be possible to steam
the soil for a few minutes, without turning it to charred powder.
Think with satisfaction of all those dying bacteria and exploding
slugs' eggs!

A microwave could be very useful for sterilising small amounts
of soil or compost into which seed is to be sown. Fern spores are
traditionally sown in pots of peat on to which boiling water has
been poured, so that the spores get a clean and exclusive start. A
microwave would make a good substitute for boiling water. At boiling point of course most plastic pots melt, so you would need to use
clay pots. But I suspect that the quality of most clay pots is insufficient to withstand a microwave. I can imagine impurities in the clay

expanding faster than the bulk of the pot and bursting out to the surface. An oven-glass bowl or jar may be the answer. There is some experimenting required here, and I should love to hear the results.

Terra Al Dente
Several readers have replied to me with their favourite recipe for sterilising soil in a microwave. The following method seems to be the blueprint:

Fill a 4-litre ice cream box with sieved, lightly compressed, evenly moistened loam or leaf litter. Cook for 7–10 minutes in a 650 watt oven, to achieve 176°F (80°C). Cool at once, spreading out the soil in a thin layer.

Season to taste, with blood, fish and bone meal.

Q I bought several plants from a gardening club sale last autumn, and planted them around the garden with their labels. Five months later there is not a word to be seen on the labels. Can you recommend a genuinely permanent marker for plastic plant labels?

A Experience tells me that even the best spirit-based markers fade in time, and it can be enraging to find things muddled up because of this. The greater the exposure to sunlight, the faster the marking fades, so try to push the labels well into the soil. If you do use a felt pen for labels, make sure it is spirit-based, not water-based. When it begins to get dry – usually after an unreasonably small number of labels – throw the pen away.

I have despaired of spirit markers and always use an HB pencil. It may not be so easy to read; there is less contrast, and you need to keep it well sharpened. But it will still be legible after several years, which is what it is all about. Even then, birds and small people rearrange labels or remove them altogether. The final answer, if you need to be sure of a name, is to keep a notebook.

Q I am developing a large garden, with many unusual shrubs and perennials. I have tried all manner of plastic and copper labels but, because of my handwriting none looks up to much. I would like some labels which will last and complement the planting. Please could you recommmend something? – B.D., Dordogne, France

A To my eye, the laminated plastic labels used by botanic gardens look too utilitarian for garden use. They are clear but grimly plastic. With the passing years, even they get brittle. I prefer anodised aluminium labels of the stick-in or tie-on variety, which are punched with a set of dies and a hammer. They are sold by Alitag Plant Labels, Unit 1, 35 Bourne Lane, Much Hadham, Herts SG10 6ER; tel. 01279 842685. Similar but harder zinc labels, marked by an engraving pen, are produced by Wartnaby Gardens, Melton Mowbray, Leics LE14 3HY; tel. 01664 822549. Pen and pencil can be used on both aluminium and zinc.

Q Can you recommend some scented winter-flowering shrubs to plant by our back door, which faces west? The soil is heavy but well drained.

A This sounds a perfect place to plant *Sarcococca humilis*, the sweet box; and, indeed, like box it will make a neat evergreen bun 2ft high, covered in the sweetest smelling white tufts of flowers. One on either side perhaps? You could also use *Daphne odora*

'Aureomarginata', a sprawling little evergreen with yellow margins to the leaf and the most pervasive and seductive of perfumes. On the wall I would plant *Azara microphylla*, a delicate airy evergreen shrub or small tree. It would make a good support for summer clematis, but in late winter its little yellow flowers give off great warm-smelling wafts of vanilla. What could be better at a bedroom window!

Q I am struggling to find a stockist of really large water butts. None of my local garden centres sell them, although I have seen them at the *Gardener's World* Live show at Birmingham. Can you help? – D.G., Humberside

A Big water butts take up a lot of retail space and sell only in small numbers, so you do not see them in garden centres. I suggest you try a local agricultural merchant or builders' merchant. So often they can supply you with these larger items which garden centres do not readily stock. And often you will pay a much smaller price.

Why do not the water companies offer to sell us all large, water-saving butts at an economical, bulk-buy price? It would be a great coup for their public relations. We should all write to request it.

Dry spots

Q I have three old tamarisk bushes 15 ft high. Honesty and Japanese anemones thrive below them in the sandy soil, and spring bulbs, but annual bedding is drawn forward to the light and looks poor. What could I grow under them for summer colour? – R.H., Essex

A This is going to be a naturally dry and difficult spot in summer, and, as you are already finding, spring and autumn colour may be easier to achieve. Dry shade is always the worst shade in which to garden. However, there *are* plants you could try. There is the bold yellow and cream foliage of *Symphytum* x *uplandicum* 'Variegatum', foxgloves, Solomon's seal, acanthus, and the creeping yellow *Waldsteinia ternata*.

If it were me, I would cut the tamarisks back hard to let in more light and moisture. If they are a necessary screen, you might do one a year for three years, gradually getting them down to a smaller scale, and then keeping them to 6–8 ft by regular pruning.

Q I have an old oak tree at the roadside, protected by a preservation order, which exudes stickiness and dirt onto the shrubs below. The tree absorbs most of the moisture from the ground and this year, despite liberal watering, it seems many shrubs will have to be replaced. I am sure little can be done about the sticky deposits, but perhaps you could suggest suitable replacement shrubs? Perhaps some form of ground cover might be better in this location?
– H.J.N., Kent

A Oaks are reckoned to be one of the better trees under which to garden because they are not shallow rooted. However, if you are troubled with honeydew from aphids in the tree as well as drought, then you have a real problem. I should be inclined to encourage the lower branches to grow downwards to screen the road, and to concentrate on ground-cover plants. Deciduous ones will endure the honeydew better, but you might try the evergreens *Iris foetidissima* var. *citrina*, *Epimedium rubrum* and *E.* 'Sulphureum' and the hart's tongue fern *Asplenium scolopendrium*. Perhaps a simple planting of a couple of these in large groups could be combined with snowdrops, aconites, scillas and anemones. Try growing a carpet of *Claytonia siberica*, a small purslane only a few inches in height, which seeds generously about and in cool conditions can flower from May to October. It is usually pink but there is a white form too.

Q Are there any publications which give information about gardens open to the public in France and Italy? – B.G., West Sussex

A 1994 saw the long awaited publication of *French Gardens: A Guide*, by Barbara Abbs. It is a neat little paperback which just fits in the car's glove compartment. I have seen it in the bigger bookshops, but you can also get it from the publisher Quiller Press, 46 Lillie Road, London SW6 1TN.

France is not of course riddled with gardens open to the public in the way Britain is, and the book looks very slim compared even to our National Gardens Scheme's 'yellow book'; but it is a good pointer to the principal gardens of all sizes. It only remains for someone to do the same service for the gardens of Italy. The publisher, Mitchell Beazley, is in fact due to launch a series of guides to the gardens of western European countries in spring 1998.

Barbara Abbs is otherwise known to the gardening world for setting up her Horticultural Speakers' Register, now run by the Royal Horticultural Society. Produced on an annual basis, it is a godsend to local horticultural society secretaries across the land.

Q Can you recommend a prostrate conifer to fill a 6ft space in my rockery? It must be not more than 15–18in high. I could go to a nursery and buy anything, but it must be the best. – J.F., Essex

A There are not many prostrate conifers which, when they eventually reach a width of 6ft, are still only 18in tall. Nor will they fill the space quickly because they will be (relatively) dwarf forms, used to growing slowly in harsh natural conditions. Forms of *Juniperus horizontalis* are very flat indeed ('Glauca' and 'Bar Harbor' are of the blue tint), and forms of *Juniperus* x *media* arch up above 18in. *Juniperus sabina* 'Tamariscifolia' or *Microbiota* *decussata* would fit the bill and they are relatively fast, but in the end will still only make a green slab of foliage.

If I could, I would persuade you to plant something other than a conifer, something which would at least offer you some flowers. You might try a group of three *Halimiocistus sahucii*, a low-growing evergreen which covers itself in white 'rock rose' flowers in May – June, and will happily stay under your height restriction. They will also fill the space much faster.

Clay soil problems

Q I have a number of fast-growing conifers which I wish to remove and replace with evergreen shrubs limited to about 8ft. tall. There are drains running through the ground nearby, and the soil is clay. What species should I plant? – G.R.J., Essex

A On clay you will have to avoid those shrubs which belong to the heather family (Ericaceae), such as rhododendron and pieris, but apart from that the choice is wide.

There are all the different laurels, which are tough and would not baulk at going into ground impoverished by conifers. If you enrich the soil well, which surely must be worthwhile, then you could plant less crude evergreens like sweetly-scented *Osmanthus delavayi*, *O.* x *burkwoodii*, and *O. decorus*. *Mahonia* 'Charity' and *M. lomariifolia* combine scented flowers with architectural foliage, and offer a fountain shape to contrast with the more usual rounded shapes. If you are prepared for spines, there are good evergreen berberis such as *B. julianae* and *B. sargentiana*, the latter making a splendid fountain of stems which might be mistaken for a bamboo at a distance. Non-invasive bamboos such as *Fargesia* (*Arundinaria*) *murieliae* or *Phyllostachys nigra* are another possibility, as are all the berry-bearing skimmias and hollies, green or variegated.

Of all these, I would suggest the most likely to make a bee-line for your drains are the laurels. For the rest, take a chance; they will be no worse than your conifers.

Poisonous Clematis

Following the praises I sang for *Clematis armandii,* H.J. of Yorkshire has written to warn of its poisonous quality. Now it is not uncommon for some people to produce blisters from the sap of buttercups, which are in the same family (Ranunculaceae) as clematis. H.J's puppy ate prunings of the evergreen *C. armandii* and only just escaped with her life. Serious blistering extended from her mouth and throat as far as her stomach, and the poisonous nature of the plant was subsequently confirmed by plant scientists at the Royal Botanic Garden, Kew. So *C. armandii* is another plant which gardeners should be aware of as potentially dangerous. This is no reason not to grow it. There are dozens of poisonous plants in our gardens, from hellebores to foxgloves to oleanders, which can kill. The fact that so few people die from this cause is tribute to the common sense of generations of parents in warning their children of the dangers at an early age.

Beware the Forget-me-not!

Q L.P. of north London, writes to warn people susceptible to plant allergies of her recent experience with forget-me-nots. Having cleared a lot from the garden, she developed simple nettle rash followed by a full-blown allergic reaction requiring steroid treatment.

A Forget-me-nots are in the family Boraginaceae, and if, like L.P., you are allergic to borage, then beware also the forget-me-not, or scorpion grass as it is sometimes known. Other members include alkanet, viper's bugloss, comfrey and lungwort, and all have that hairy, rasping leaf which to other creatures perhaps acts as a warning. Certainly, in my experience these plants are left well alone by rabbits.

Comfrey contains alkaloids which when consumed in sufficient quantity can be seriously poisonous to humans and animals. They are present in the new leaves especially, but persist even in dry foliage. Conversely, comfrey is an excellent source of plant food, much used by organic gardeners. The leaves contain large amounts of minerals relative to their fibre content, and can be soaked in water to make a nutritious high-potash 'soup' suitable even for feeding tomatoes. Allow a couple of pounds of comfrey foliage to ferment in a covered 3 gallon bucket for a month, strain – and away you go.

Q I am about to go to Greece to stay with friends and would like to take seeds as a present. They are busy restoring a property and have no time for gardening. I would like to sow something pretty for them that will stand heat, drought, and neglect. – S.R., Hertfordshire

A Take some spider flowers (*Cleome*). In hot climates they grow so much better that you wonder why we bother with them here. They will be bushy and a yard across, like pink clumps of *Euphorbia characias*. Take that, too; it will self-seed for them in future years.

Against white-painted walls as you find everywhere in Greece, the red tassels of love-lies-bleeding (*Amaranthus caudatus*) make a fabulous, stark display. The tall double opium poppies will do well, as will Californian poppies (*Eschscholzia*) and prickly poppies (*Argemone*). Look for the giant fennel, *Ferula communis*, which will make a mound of feathery foliage and in future years send up a barge pole of green flowers.

Q My small back garden has walls 5ft 6in tall, mainly north-facing, topped with some shaky trellis. I am fed up with all my

plants hot-footing it over the wall and giving my neighbours a lovely display while I end up with bare stems. I intend to start again, and do not mind removing the trellis. Can you suggest some plants, perhaps evergreens, which would prefer to stay at home? – M.J., Lancashire

A A classic case of north-wall syndrome. The plants are being drawn up to the sunlight and then make most of their sun-ripened flowering wood at the top, facing into your neighbour's garden. The best solution would be to replant a mixed border of species which actually enjoy shade or at least cool roots, and will not be drawn to the light. You could grow herbaceous rodgersias, hostas, cimicifugas, aconitums and ferns, with rhododendrons and Japanese maple.

It would not be an easy option to stay with colourful climbers such as roses, but it could be done. Choose varieties recommended for a north wall ('Gloire de Dijon', 'Aloha', 'Mme. Alfred Carriere', etc) and be prepared to tie the whole plant in afresh each winter, to really pull the growth down on your side of the wall. These are vigorous roses and they will still do their best to grow over the top. Evergreens to train on the wall include garrya for its tassels and pyracantha for its berries. Plant choisya for its aromatic foliage and *Azara microphylla* for its warm, vanilla scented flowers.

North-wall syndrome applies to bedding and heathers, too; it pays not to plant them sloping away south from you, or you will miss the best of the colour and the faces of the flowers. Plant them to run north from you, so that you look at the more colourful, sunny side of the plants.

Worm troubles

Q I put down gravel paths around my garden a couple of years ago, but worm casts are ruining the surface. How can I get rid of the worms without using chemicals? – J.M., Lincolnshire

A I suspect your paths may have thick gravel laid directly on to the soil? To lay a gravel path properly, a 4in deep hardcore base is needed under the path, with a top surface only of your chosen colour of gravel. But even then, worms may work their way in from the sides. A solid edging strip of wood, brick or tiles is invaluable for keeping gravel paths clean of soil and the worms which will follow it.

It is important to have no organic matter in the paths to tempt worms. Rake up leaves in good time, before the worms can pull them down, and keep a good surface of loose, scrunchy gravel. Compressed surfaces of fine gravel make happier going for worms.

The cleanest gravel paths are made by digging out the soil to leave a slightly convex soil bed. This is covered with heavy-duty polythene, and the rolled hardcore and gravel laid over that.

Q C.W. of Hampshire asks: My garden has only 9in of soil over limestone bedrock. In spite of generous manuring twice a year and occasional and expensive doses of Sequestrene, even climbing roses turn yellow and chlorotic. What should I do, and when, to counter this extreme alkalinity?

A If you are a very keen gardener, you should sell up and move. Do it in winter when the garden will be leafless anyway. If you are a gardener of normal, healthy enthusiasms, then you should stay put and make the best of it. You must swim with the tide, and grow things which will withstand the extremes of drought and lime.

Make the most of raised beds, or terraced beds, which can be filled with imported soil. A good depth of humus-rich soil will at least solve some of the drought problems. Continue the good work of manuring and composting with whatever you can get hold of.

I would not try to fight the alkalinity. Sequestrene is expensive and only of short-term benefit. It works by supplying plants with iron which has been made unavailable to them by the lime. (The iron in Sequestrene is in a form which cannot be locked up by the lime.)

No doubt you have found books in your local library on gardening over chalk, which will provide a palette of lime-loving plants. But I would also recommend you make an exploratory visit to Highdown garden, made in a chalk pit by Sir Frederick Stern at Goring-by-Sea in West Sussex. It now belongs to Worthing Corporation. April is the best time to go. To see what will withstand dry conditions, look at Beth Chatto's gravel garden – an ex-carpark – at Elmstead Market, east of Colchester, Essex.

Q For the last couple of years I have been trying to rescue a badly neglected herbaceous border. I would now like to convert at least part of it to a formally tailored shrubbery. The soil is poor and limy, and rhododendrons do not grow here. The border is backed by a dry stone wall through which grow ivy and nettles. Could you please advise me as to the most suitable plants? – M.L., Oxfordshire

A I like the sound of a 'formally tailored shrubbery'. It makes me think of those wonderful Victorian shrubberies, of rolling mounds of contrasting evergreenery. Such simplicity of planting would contrast well with the colour of the remaining herbaceous border.

I would plant hollies, with perhaps a variegated one or two for contrast. You could grow the Strawberry tree, *Arbutus unedo*, which flowers and fruits concurrently in late autumn, and is happy on limy soils despite being a member of the heather and rhododendron family. *Phillyrea latifolia*, in the olive family, is a small evergreen tree of great distinction, which I would not be without. There are any number of cypress-like trees to use at the back, and you could choose according to the speed required.

I would plant box towards the front, and for its low arching habit, the laurel *Prunus cerasifera* 'Otto Luyken'. I would grow flamboyantly spotted laurel *Aucuba japonica* 'Crotonifolia' (male) and the all-green form 'Longifolia' (female) for their broad, glossy foliage and berries. Broad-leaved evergreens such as these are invaluable in a garden, and so much fewer in number than the small-leaved or cypress-type evergreens.

For perfume I would plant any of the mahonias, especially *M.* 'Charity' and *M.* 'Undulata', and *Osmanthus* x *burkwoodii* and *O. decorus*.

Wildflower gardening

Q **Having seen a documentary of the Prince of Wales's garden at Highgrove, I decided that I too would have a wildflower garden under the trees in my little wood. Last summer I sprayed the ground elder and have subsequently dug the wood twice and applied tons of compost. Where may I purchase wildflower seed for a woodland planting? – T.P., Surrey**

A I wish I had your faith that the ground elder was beaten after one season. I bet that compost will kick-start all the lingering pieces into life, and I would be prepared to spray again before planting or sowing. (If it cannot stray into nearby closely-managed gardens, then perhaps you can afford to ignore what is left and proceed.)

Grass seed can be bought with wildflowers included, or you can buy the flower seed separately. Most wildflower/grass seed mixes are intended for relatively open situations, and vary more according to soil type than suitability for light and shade. I would choose a seed mix from one of the main seed suppliers. Try British Seed Houses Limited, Bewsey Industrial Estate, Pitt Street, Warrington, Cheshire WA5 5LE; tel. 01925 654411. Other species could be added to the mix to suit your purposes, or plantlets introduced into the sward in future seasons.

Many garden centres now sell wildflower seed of individual species, and the seed list of the Hardy Plant Society (available to members only*) is an invaluable source of suitable exotic woodlanders. Seed of the commoner plants such as bluebells, foxgloves and Queen Anne's lace are easily collected from hedgerows without seriously depredating stocks there.

Remember that seed-sown wildflowers take several years before the perennials included in the mixture begin to flower. Good flowering meadows take years of proper maintenance and plant introduction to become impressive.

* Apply to: Hardy Plant Society, The Administrator, Mrs Pam Adams, Little Orchard, Great Comberton, Pershore, Worcs, WR10 3DP.

Q Can you suggest some ground-cover plants which would survive in a bed under some straggly box trees and a yew? It is not fully shady, but dry. I do not wish to rely on watering. – M.D-B.

A There are perhaps three options. First, you could simply not plant at all beneath your trees, but clean up their straggly trunks to make them tree-like, bring the grass up to the trees, and enjoy the coarse grey corrugation of the box bark and flaking brownish red of the yew. One so rarely sees a sizeable box tree these days (it can grow to 15ft), and it seems a shame not to take advantage of its good character. Second, you might drastically cut back the trees in March, so that they become fully clothed to ground level, and the problem of planting beneath would disappear. Third, if you opt for ground cover, you need to build up a layer of soil on the surface, with compost, imported soil or leafmould, into which you can then plant. Box and yew make a great deal of hungry, white, surface roots, which will come running for whatever compost you offer. The plants to choose, therefore, are those which also run on the surface and can take quick advantage of an annual top-dressing of 2in of compost and a handful of general fertiliser. Try *Euphorbia amygdaloides* var. *robbiae*, which is evergreen and will light up the shadiest, driest corner with lime green. At only 2in high *Waldsteinia ternata* makes a mat of running surface stems covered in yellow strawberry flowers. Where there is sun to open the flowers, pale purple *Crocus tommasinianus* will naturalise amongst other plants. The evergreen *Iris foetidissima* will bring some semblance of lushness with its strappy leaves and red berries, as will the evergreen hart's tongue fern, (*Asplenium scolopendrium*), which is available in all manner of fancy crimped forms. Lily-of-the-valley should grow if given a good start in some decent soil. Where root competition is fiercest, try a carpet of the large, glossy-leaved Persian ivy, *Hedera colchica*, which in sun at least can be used in its variegated forms, 'Sulphur Heart' (yellow) and 'Dentata Variegata' (creamy white).

Q Could you please recommend a replacement for ivy on a west-facing garage wall. I would like something more attractive, easily manageable, possibly flowering, and not a hazard for young children. – J.W., Derbyshire

A Why not try the purple-leaved grape vine, *Vitis vinifera* 'Purpurea', which has even richer autumn colours. Through it you might grow a couple of clematis, – the large-flowered 'Mme. Edouard André (rich crimson) for May to July, and the smaller-flowered 'Minuet' (white banded pale purple) for July to September. On a garage wall there would be no more volume of prunings than from ivy.

Q I have just returned from a holiday in Madeira which has made me very disappointed with my garden. Can you suggest

some strong, colourful plants to keep a large border at the centre of my garden flowering into the autumn? – K.J.F., Cambridgeshire

A There are plenty of good plants to flower late. Amongst the best is *Aconitum carmichaelii*, rather like an October-flowering royal blue delphinium but totally self-supporting. If you want strong colours, try *Aster* 'Violet Queen' (18in) or *A.* 'Alma Potschke' (36in), a thoroughly shocking blue-pink. There are good late pokers too. The Victorian variety *Kniphofia uvaria* 'Nobilis' is a vibrant fiery orange of fully 6ft. 'Percy's Pride' is a limy-yellow three footer, which I find is often at its best in November if the weather is at all kind.

I am especially fond of joe-pye weed *Eupatorium maculatum* 'Atropurpureum'. Its season starts rather late in May when wine-black stems begin to rise steadily to 6ft from the soil and furnish themselves with strong, beautifully poised foliage. They require no support whatever. In autumn fluffy heads of dusky pink a foot across top each stem. One sunny day in September, I began counting red admirals on my clump of eupatorium and gave up at three dozen.

Remember there are bright autumn bulbs too, like *Colchicum* 'Lilac Wonder' and *Nerine bowdenii* and *N. undulata*.

In a different vein, September and October are the best months for 'summer-flowering' heathers such as calluna and daboecia. If you have an alkaline soil you will of course be able to grow only the spring heathers (*Erica carnea, E. darleyensis*, and their cultivars) unless you relish the business of raised beds of acid soil.

Ground clearance

Q We have cleared some ground on the edge of woodland and wish to plant a yew hedge. First we need to poison all the old weeds, including virulent ivy, which covered the ground and trees and everything in sight. We turned over the earth with a bulldozer.

What would you recommend to clean this very dirty ground? –
A.L.D., East Lothian

A It may be a slow process requiring several treatments, but spraying with glyphosate will kill ivy. Safely away from the roots of trees and other plants, I would have suggested you use sodium chlorate on ground like this, waiting a year until this total weedkiller had leached away before you begin to plant. As it is, if you have bulldozed all the ivy into the soil, it will continue to reappear for at least a year, during which time you can spray what emerges.

When clearing an ivy-infested area for planting, it is better first to pull up and burn all you can. Alternatively, if you are prepared to spray, then this is your best opportunity; the ivy will never again have so much leaf through which to absorb a chemical. Once it has died back, still burn it off, either pulled up into a bonfire or where it lies, with a paraffin or gas-flame gun. During cultivation, dig or pull out all the root you can find, so that only the minimum is left to be killed as it struggles to re-emerge. It's a cruel business.

Never hurry to install a permanent planting on weed-infested ground. It pays to wait and to have the ground thoroughly clean before you begin.

Q Can you recommend a variegated evergreen, preferably a conifer, to grow under a window in semi-shade? It must be no more than 3–4 ft high. – J.F., Essex

A Unfortunately shade and variegation do not go together. Most unusual foliages, whether they be golden, purple or variegated, become weak in shade, and frequently return to plain green.

Conifers fare worse than broad-leaved plants in shade, and begin to look moth-eaten. You would fare much better in half shade with a broad-leaved evergreen.

The spotted laurel *Aucuba japonica*, is an excellent, easy foliage shrub, and still shows its colours well in shade. I would go for a really good form, such as 'Crotonifolia'. This is male, and for fruit a female form will also be needed. You might try skimmias also, which would berry well, or perhaps the dwarf holly *Ilex crenata*, which has a yellow form, 'Golden Gem'. There is a golden box too, *Buxus microphylla* var. *japonica* 'Aurea', at its best in sun, but acceptable in some shade. If you have acid soil, you might try a rather wonderful blueberry, *Vaccinium glaucoalbum*, which is a small suckering shrub with rounded foliage, sea green above but a startling white beneath. I love it, but it is rather slow.

Q Our Victorian terraced house has a small front garden with a lawn in the middle. The lawn is poor, attracts dandelions from other gardens, and serves no real purpose. I would like to get rid of it altogether. I would however like to keep a bit of green surface, to cheer me up in winter – perhaps just 4 or 5 square yards. A possible solution seems to be a chamomile lawn, made from the non-flowering variety 'Treneague'. Can I grow such a lawn from seed? – G.K., Lancashire

A Chamomile lawns are not easy, nor are they cheap if you make them from 'Treneague', which as a non-flowering variety has to be propagated from cuttings and bought as plants. Five square yards even at just one plant per square foot is a lot of money to throw at such an unreliable effect. Chamomile lawns work better in the imagination than reality, and need a lot of attention to make them dense, even, and attractive. Dandelions will continue to arrive and take hold but selective weedkillers would kill your chamomile too.

I would look for something much easier to maintain. If you want to look on to greenery in winter (and I agree, psychologically it can do wonders) you might consider a low (12in) pattern of clipped box with an internal space or two for summer planting. It would suit the house, make minimal work (clipped twice a year), and would cost no more than your chamomile lawn. Do try it. Unless I am much mistaken, parterres are coming back into fashion very fast in gardens large and small.

Lasting attraction

Q Outside my kitchen window are two beds, each 6 x 10ft, which separate the paved terrace from the lawn. They are open on all sides, and are planted with a mish-mash of everything, – delphiniums, roses, catmint, a peony, lilies, pinks and so on. It is a wonderful muddle in June for a week and a horrid mess for the rest of the year. Can you advise me on how to replant, so that as I wash up I can look out on to some colour, some texture, and above all some satisfactory shape. – M.D-R., Buckinghamshire

A There are many approaches to this. One would be to put a low hedge around the beds – box, perhaps, or sweet-scented *Sarcococca humilis* – and fill the centres solidly with snowdrops and the royal blue *Scilla sardensis*. These could stay in all year. Follow with tulips, early and late, and perhaps forget-me-nots; then for summer and autumn fill the whole lot with an *Argyranthemum* such as 'Jamaica Primrose', which would flower from June until October. This is a vigorous, half hardy bush, and you can plant them 30in apart in good soil. You might sneak in some annuals amongst the argyranthemums to add tones of orange and mahogany to the yellow. *Rudbeckia* 'Rustic Dwarfs' would do, or *Calendula* 'Art Shades'. Better still, use both. Sow them directly amongst the argyranthemum plants in June for a show-stopping autumn display.

Another approach would be to stay with a mixed planting of

shrubs and perennials, as you have at present, but to choose plants with a longer flowering season and which have some satisfactory form and substance for most of the year.

The acme of curved formality must surely be a bed of heathers and dwarf conifers, and there is nothing so lacklustre, so relatively unchanging, so unresponsive to sun and even the passing breeze. But you can plant to great effect in the same blocky way using mixed shrubs and perennials. If a dash of symmetry seems attractive in a winter prospect, then you might first put a substantial box ball on each corner of the beds. Then you can fill the interior with all manner of good things. Pools of helianthemum, pinks, *Alchemilla erythropoda*, and *Geranium renardii* would sit in the ground row. *Anthemis cupaniana* is a sprawling evergrey daisy, perfect for spilling out on to paving, and *Geranium* 'Russell Prichard' and *Osteospermum jucundum* will do the same, flowering from June to October.

In the centre might be mounding shapes like the woolly willow *Salix lanata*, santolinas, the dwarf lilac *Syringa meyeri* 'Palibin', and *Spiraeas* 'Goldflame' and 'Anthony Waterer'. Of evergreens I would choose *Mahonia* 'Undulata', perhaps a dwarf pine, and for its fabulous perfume *Daphne retusa*.

To leaven this you would need more upright shapes; grasses would be good, even quite tall, columnar ones like *Miscanthus sinensis* 'Silberfeder', which are self-supporting and last well into the winter. Agapanthus would bring variety with its drum-stick heads, and I would add the spikes of the smaller kniphofias, which with careful choice can these days flower anywhere between May and November.

Within this matrix of generous groups could then be interspersed all kinds of incidental plants. I would use bulbs, such as all the different drum-headed alliums, or tall, pure white galtonias for midsummer; colchicums and nerines for autumn, and camassias for spring. Then there are biennials like the steely grey sea-holly, *Eryngium giganteum*, and short-term perennials like *Euphorbia wulfenii*.

Choose nothing which is not self-supporting and nothing which has not good foliage as well as flowers, and you will be well on the way to a bed of good form and substance. Try to arrange it so that the evergreens and plants which can stand through the winter are spread evenly through the beds, to give a feeling of winter emptiness.

If none of these ideas appeals, you might grass the beds down and opt for some clever topiary, or a pair of good-quality large urns filled with a mob-cap of bedding.

Q We have a beautiful weeping ash tree, with its branches trimmed to allow cars to pass underneath. In spring there are snowdrops and all colours of crocuses under the branches. What could we grow in the bare earth for summer, and when should we feed or mulch the tree? – J.B., Cheshire

A So long as the tree is happy and healthy, there is no need to feed it. However, its roots are greedy and will be close to the surface, which will reduce competition from either weeds or plants you wish to grow there. If you want to grow much, you will need to mulch regularly with old compost, manure, and/or a general fertiliser. Drought will be your biggest problem, and this is why the most successful plants will be spring woodlanders which expect dry shade in summer. Why not take the season right through with bulbs, using bluebells, *Cyclamen hederifolium*, autumn-flowering *Crocus speciosus* and colchicums. Once you start to look at perennials, the scope widens. You could use *Iris foetidissima* (plain or variegated), *Waldsteinia ternata*, *Cardamine trifolia* and *C. pentaphyllos*, *Euphorbia robbiae*, lily-of-the-valley, male fern, Solomon's seal and the smaller dicentras. At the height of summer herbaceous colour in deep, rooty shade, is difficult to achieve, and hardly worth the effort.

Stabilising a bank

Q Close behind my house, and shaded by it, is a steep earth bank. During heavy rain, water washes the soil down the bank. What ground cover plants would stabilise the soil? – G.A.T., Somerset

A You need plants which bind under the soil as well as on the surface, so sprawling plants with only a tap root would not do. You also need plants which, if not evergreen, at least retain some cover through the winter, to prevent erosion. Grass might be the most efficient ground cover of all, mown with hover mower on a rope from the top of the bank. Otherwise, try *Geranium macror-rhizum*, pulmonarias, *Alchemilla mollis*, bergenias, lily-of-the-valley, day lilies, male ferns, hostas, *Persicaria affinis*, Solomon's seal, and *Trachystemon orientale*. In a case like this, it is better to plant more thickly than is strictly necessary to speed up the achievement of complete cover.

Q In December you recommended protecting tender perennials with bracken or fern fronds. Which perennials are deemed tender, and would bark chippings be as effective? – K.P.M., Berkshire

A It is penetrating frosts which do damage to tender perennials, and the heavier and wetter the soil, the greater the likelihood of damage. Therefore the amount of protection required depends upon how free-draining the soil is. The worst penetrating frosts are those which follow a heavy snow melt, when the soil is saturated.

I prefer to protect plants with as free-draining a material as possible, and therefore – on the string-vest principle – I prefer a covering of fern with all its air pockets, to a poultice of wet bark mulch. On the other hand bark is better than nothing, especially the coarse, open-textured, chipped bark. Perennials benefiting from protection in most parts of the country include *Salvia uligi-nosa*, francoa, gaura, some agapanthus, romneya, eucomis, *Geranium traversii*, and many others.

Q Is there a low ground-cover perennial as good as the poached-egg plant, *Limnanthes douglasii* – i.e. one that is bee-friendly, evergreen, hardy, prolific? – N.R-C., Powys

A Strictly speaking *Limnanthes douglasii* is a hardy annual, but once sown it certainly continues to maintain a presence year in year out from its own seedlings, unless you hoe them off. Its common name comes from the white, yellow-centred flowers, which appear in profusion 6in high over pale green, finely divided foliage. It comes from the western United States. The flowers are sweetly scented, and are pleasant in a pot by the door. Another favourite of bees, a low spreading, long-season if not evergreen perennial, is *Geranium dalmaticum*. It spreads by underground rhizomes to make dense patches of cover just a few inches high. The leaves are neat and shiny, and colour well in the autumn, leaving a patch of coppery foliage. The flowers come on 4–5in stalks in early summer, covering the whole clump with pale pink. (There is also a white form.) Bees loll about in it like pigs in clover.

Q A drive bisects my front lawn and is about four feet below it. The fairly steep banks were left as grass, but this has not been successful as the soil is heavy and the banks dry out easily in summer, being subjected to full sunlight. I would like to replace the grass with low ground-cover plants and would appreciate your recommendations. The house is late Georgian and I try to confine myself to plants which were available then. – P.D.H., Devon

A Something so plain as a sunken drive through a lawn does not call for complicated planting, I suspect. I would go for one plant end to end, preferably evergreen. It needs to be quick to cover, in order that the soil does not wash away, and something which – once established – will not, for the same reasons, need division every few years. Ivy would be the simplest and most stylish solution. Glossy banks of dark green *Hedera helix* 'Hibernica' or *H. colchica* would look good in winter and summer. Kill the grass with glyphosate but plant the ivy into the dead turf (to stop erosion) at 18–24in centres, and peg down the trailing arms. No planting dense enough to cover quickly will be cheap to install. Is the grass such a problem? Grass might in the end be the easiest solution, in which case, sound out a high-quality turf supplier on the best specialist turf to suit your soil and position.

Winter colour

Q I would like to plant something in my garden to flower in December, in memory of my grandson who died last December. My garden is small, and there is room for a shrub but not a tree. – S.I.C., Warwickshire

A You might plant a witch hazel for its sweet-scented yellow flowers, or the pink *Viburnum bodnantense*. But they are dreary things when not in flower. Why not plant the rose 'The Fairy'? If you give it a warm place with a little shelter, it manages to be still in flower most Christmases, as well as looking good throughout the summer. To find those delicate pink flowers, so fresh and so unlooked for, in December, might be the memorial you need.

Q We have a set of three curved brick steps leading from one lawn to another. The bricks have flaked and split over time, leaving them unsightly. What could I plant on them which would be low-growing and provide a carpet of greenery to hide the damage, and which would be sweet smelling when trodden on? Thyme or chamomile? It will be very dry, and the steps face south. – B.E., Bedfordshire

A I ought to encourage you to repair such attractive steps. But on the other hand I do like to see steps with plenty of cracks for planting too. If you want to cover the brick thoroughly I would suggest you use a small, slow growing variety of ivy. It could be clipped back tight to the riser every spring and would give you a glossy green stripe across the steps. Thyme or chamomile will not be easy to establish in lime mortar, and whatever you plant will have to be started by making a hole first, to get the roots past the mortar and into some soil. I would plant in the corners first and let the plants spread to the centre. For this reason something with a creeping root would be fastest. Would a mixtue of plants be acceptable? You could grow *Corydalis lutea*, *Campanula portenschlagiana*, ivy-leaved toadflax, and in the eastern arc the tiny fern *Asplenium trichomanes*. With a really dwarf cotoneaster you might run a minute thin 'hedge' across the face of the steps.

Q The back of my house faces south-west, and has a good York stone patio. The walls were covered in cotoneaster when we came, and I have replaced this with ceanothus, white wisteria, clematis and fremontodendron. They have all flourished, but I am concerned as to how I can feed and water them adequately through the slabbing. – C.B., Birmingham

A I assume there was space enough between the paving and the wall to make a decent planting hole and start your new plants off satisfactorily? If so then don't worry: you can liquid feed at the root when you feel it is necessary. If you had to squeeze your new plants into a small crack against the wall, it might make life easier to take up a slab beside them, so you can feed and water. But if all are flourishing I would leave well alone. The paving will keep the roots cool and moist so far as the rain shadow of the wall allows. As with any wall climber, a regular couple of cans of water in summer, perhaps containing some liquid feed periodically, will be enormously beneficial, especially in the early years.

Q Our Lake District garden slopes steeply down to an open level area which is perennially damp, and floods from a nearby beck after rain. Weeding is very difficult. What combination of flowering shrubs and plants, including ground cover, is possible under these conditions? – J.B., Cumbria

A At some distance from the house, and in difficult soil conditions, I would settle for a relatively wild style of gardening. You need broad, simple strokes applied generously. Plant the 24in yellow candelabra-type *Primula florindae*, to self sow, and a few plants of *Gunnera manicata* if you have space; its huge umbrella leaves will make shade to suppress the grass and allow the likes of primulas an easier existence. Try big blocks of *Eupatorium maculatum* 'Atropurpureum' for tall, late colour. Deciduous azaleas would grow, as would the wonderfully scented 'swamp honeysuckle', *Rhododendron viscosum*. Try pink *Kalmia latifolia* to follow on, and sorbaria and holodiscus, both of which have plumes of white flowers and blend very happily from garden out into countryside.

Moss lawns

Q I have a small lawn under some trees which is mostly moss but with some persistent grass. How do I kill the grass so that I can have a complete moss lawn? – R.T., Hampshire

A Do not disturb the 'lawn' by trying to dig out the grass. Simply spray out the grass with the right weedkillers. Mosses are largely unaffected by paraquat, and so weedkillers with that ingredient only may be used if non-persistent species of grass are present. You will need to spray perhaps only twice a year once the moss has fully colonised, in order to eradicate new seedling grasses. If persistent grasses like couch are present, then use a weedkiller containing glyphosate. This seems to discolour but does not kill most mosses, and will also clean up tap-rooted weeds like thistles and dandelions. Moss lawns can be most attractive. I have seen areas of sphagnum moss growing in wet rubble under birches in Scotland kept clean by two applications of paraquat per year. It is a most exciting effect. As a general rule, undisturbed and impoverished soils make the best moss lawns. Flat and green they may be, but of course no moss lawn stands up to wear and tear like grass. I would be fascinated to hear of readers' experiences of moss and other weedkillers.

Q We go twice a year to look after family graves in Cambridge. We would like to plant them with something, but the soil is unpleasant, heavy, chalky boulder clay. We have tried thyme, heathers, and various herbaceous plants, including irises which would not flower. Bulbs do well. What might we plant which would keep going without a great deal of maintenance? – E.H., Kent

A The trouble with anything small is that it will be overwhelmed by weeds with twice-yearly maintenance only. You need something which is tough, perennial, and can make a colony which looks comfortable with a certain amount of weed competition, or which can suppress the weeds. Why not try acanthus? A colony of this dark foliage in sun or shade is most dignified, and smothers weeds once it is established. It would be slow to settle on clay, but would accept it. You could plant snowdrops and spring snowflakes underneath.

Q Leading to our rear garden is a windy passage facing north west. A stout lattice frame is being built where the passage ends. We need your advice on the type of evergreen climber to plant to cover it, up to 10ft high, which will be fully hardy. – P.R., Leicestershire

A I would unhesitatingly use a large-leaved ivy such as *Hedera colchica* or its yellow variegated form, 'Sulphur Heart'. You need not let it get too dense, and you could grow through it one or two of the smaller, spring-flowering clematis, varieties of *Clematis alpina* and *C. macropetala*. Unless you are desperate to have ever-greenery, why not use the deciduous *Hydrangea petiolaris*? It may not be evergreen, but it it very twiggy and often keeps its seedheads through the winter on rich brown stems.

Q Last August I excavated the sediment from a large garden pond. I have spread it over an area of some 1500 square yards. It has dried out well, is friable, 2–3 ft deep in some places, and has a *p*H of between 6.5 and 7.0. It is surrounded and shaded by oaks. I would like to plant the area with rhododendrons and azaleas, but I am unsure when the sediment will be ready for planting. – F.J.P., Kent

A Sounds wonderful. I would plant in March. Rhododendrons and azaleas will love that acid or neutral soil. Dredged silt from ponds with trees nearby usually has enough leaf and twig material in it to produce quite a coarse, open-textured soil, despite the fine particles of the silt proper. And this is what rhododendrons need. By March the silt will have had ample chance to settle, and any gases from anaerobic decomposition under water will have escaped. So plant away. Inspect the plants next autumn to see if further irregular settlement has left them either too high or too low in the soil and adjust accordingly. Is the land under the silt area acidic? If not, worm action over the years will bring alkaline soil up into the silt and raise the *p*H until it becomes unsuitable for rhododendrons. But that is many years away. Enjoy them while you can.

Q We garden in south-west France on pure chalk. We have two sloping stone screes at the top of a retaining wall, in key positions. It would be nice to grow something substantial there, to look good throughout the year, but to make a high point during summer. It would have to withstand heat, drought, spring frosts, and of course lime. Does anything spring to mind? – M.H., London SE10

A Try the following two brooms. *Genista tenera*, from Madeira, makes a soft, weepy mound of slightly silver foliage 6–7ft high, with yellow flowers in June. It is so much more graceful than our common English broom. *Genista aetnensis* is taller – up to small tree sized – but it is so light and airy that it casts only a little shade. It flowers in August. You could also grow cistus, *Phlomis fruticosa*, and for foliage the evergreen *Euphorbia characias*.

Sun-seekers

Q I planted a number of shrubs in February last year, in a sunny London garden, although surrounded by trees, and they have tended to grow horizontally rather than vertically. Camellias and lavateras have been especially bad. Is there any reason for this, other than lack of attention? – W.W., London SW11

A Plants will always pull towards the light, when it can only reach a garden from on high through a gap in trees. I suspect your shrubs are just too shaded. At the foot of walls the wind also buffets plants, causing them to lean away from the wall. The result is usually stems at 45 degrees rather than horizontal, so check to see if there has been some physical damage to the upright leading shoots, causing the energy to be diverted into side branches. Could this be the family vandal, or window-cleaner syndrome? A vigorous placing of ladders can be the death of borders under walls. Fortunately your plants can be trained to hug the wall. The lavateras can be cut back in spring and this year's shoots watched more carefully. The camellias will require a cane to persuade upright a single central leader.

Q Two years ago I had my garden relaid as a scree garden with a special membrane under the stone. Since then horsetails have pushed through over a large area. I have used Roundup to kill it, but more keeps appearing. How do I eradicate the problem, as this was meant to be an 'easycare' garden and it is giving me a lot of work and expense? – L.C., Hertfordshire

A Geotextile membranes designed to let water through but discourage weeds work well, but they cannot suppress tough pernicious weeds like horsetail. Scree gardens, rockeries, or any other new plantings, with or without a membrane, should never be attempted before all pernicious weeds have been eradicated from the site first. You have no choice now but to persist with the weed-killing until the site is clean. If you knew the horsetail was present, and told your contractor so, and were advised that the membrane would suppress it, then you have a case against the contractor. Talk to him, and see what help he will offer.

Q What tree or large shrub could I grow to survive in ground saturated by the inefficient soakaway at a cesspit? The ground water will contain detergents as well as the obvious nutrients. It is in a rough paddock close to woodland. – M.P.K., Surrey

A This could be rather wonderful, and the detergents should not be a problem. I assume you are on acid soil, so if you want a splash of bright pink why not try some plants of mountain laurel, *Kalmia latifolia*? It loves good rich wet soil, and the icing-sugar pink flowers in midsummer are most attractive. As an evergreen it will draw water all year round. (I take it you will fence off anything you plant from grazing animals? Kalmia would not do animals any good.) Alternatively you could plant a deciduous conifer, such as the swamp cypress *Taxodium distichum* or dawn redwood *Metasequoia glyptostroboides*. Both have good autumn colour. Willow trees such as *Salix alba* and its forms would do well, and could be pollarded to maximise the winter bark colour. If you wanted something shrubbier, say 6–10ft, try *Salix moupinensis* or *S. fargesii*. Both have broad, glossy, un-willow-like foliage, which is very glamorous, and shining mahogany winter buds and bark.

And finally. . . .

Q I have yet to read a gardening article that even begins to imply that there is ever a day of rest. Is there? – A.D., Oxfordshire

Yes. And it is likely to occur again next year.